LADY
ON THE HILL

LADY
ON THE HILL

HOW BILTMORE ESTATE
BECAME AN AMERICAN ICON

Howard E. Covington Jr.

WILEY

John Wiley & Sons, Inc.

Published by John Wiley & Sons, Inc., Hoboken, New Jersey
Published simultaneously in Canada

For general information about our other products and services, please contact our Customer Care Department within the United States at (800) 762-2974, outside the United States at (317) 572-3993 or fax (317) 572-4002.

Wiley also publishes its books in a variety of electronic formats. Some content that appears in print may not be available in electronic books. For more information about Wiley products, visit our web site at www.wiley.com.

Library of Congress Cataloging-in-Publication Data:

Covington, Howard E.
    Lady on the Hill : How Biltmore Estate Became an American Icon / Howard E. Covington, Jr.
      p. cm.
    Includes bibliographical references (p. 307) and index.
    ISBN-13 978-0-471-75818-1 (cloth)
    ISBN-10 0-471-75818-3 (cloth)
    1. Biltmore Estate (Asheville, N.C.)—History. 2. Asheville (N.C.)—Buildings, structures, etc. 3. Cecil, William, A. V. 4. Mansions—Conservation and restoration—North Carolina—Asheville. 5. Historic buildings—Conservation and restoration—North Carolina—Asheville I. Title.
    F264.A8C687 2006
    975.6'88-dc22

                          2005017412

Printed in the United States of America

10 9 8 7 6 5

*To William A. V. Cecil, and his beloved wife, Mimi,
and others who have long labored in the vineyard
of private preservation*

Contents

Foreword
by Lord Rothschild

Biltmore is an astonishing creation. A château, set in rolling, wooded countryside with spectacular views of mountain ranges, it has its own vineyards and winery, elegant gardens, and is decorated and furnished with paintings and works of art that would not look out of place in museum collections in London, Paris, or New York. Yet Biltmore is not what it seems. It is not to be found in the Loire Valley in France, but rather in the southern Appalachian Mountains in the United States. Nor is it the product of centuries of aristocratic inheritance, but rather the vision of an extraordinary man, George Washington Vanderbilt.

In building Biltmore, it was as if Vanderbilt, perhaps unconsciously, was paying homage to another astonishing creation across the Atlantic—the house with which it has been my privilege to be associated for more than twenty years—Waddesdon Manor in Buckinghamshire, England. Waddesdon is a Rothschild house, created, as Biltmore was, to provide a refuge and respite from city life for its owner, Baron Ferdinand de Rothschild in 1874. Waddesdon was a place where he could enjoy the company of family and friends, and above all provide a showcase for his collection of spectacular treasures: English eighteenth-century portraits; French eighteenth-century furniture and porcelain, carpets and textiles (often with royal provenance), paneling, sculpture, rare books and manuscripts; and what he called his "Renaissance Museum"—goldsmiths' work, maiolica, and enamels of the sixteenth and seventeenth centuries. Like Biltmore, Waddesdon was assembled with the pleasure principle firmly to the core. Guests were to be treated with every consideration for their comfort (not one but three kinds of tea were offered in the morning, along with two kinds of milk) in the most luxurious of surroundings. A weekend at Waddesdon would entail delicious food and wine, conversation and games, exploration of the estate and gardens (including the ornamental dairy, the huge range of glasshouses that grew fruit and flowers for the house, and Ferdinand's prized aviary of exotic birds), and, of course, a chance to enjoy the matchless collection of treasures. Like Biltmore, the house was constructed to a high technical specification with the early use of electricity and elevators and under-floor central heating fired by a furnace powered by its own gas station.

Perhaps these parallels should not surprise us too much. After all, G. W. Vanderbilt was brought to Waddesdon in 1889 by his architect Richard Morris Hunt while on a tour of Europe looking for inspiration for their own project—interestingly, both Hunt and Gabriel-Hippolyte Destailleur, Ferdinand's architect, chose the famous spiral staircase from the château of Blois as focal points of their facades—and the great country houses built by the Rothschilds across Europe in the nineteenth century were already renowned. Yet the resonances do not cease with the architecture. The builders of both houses seem to have shared an innate reticence despite the magnificence of their surroundings. Just as G. W. Vanderbilt carried a passenger's luggage at Biltmore Station without demur when mistaken for a porter, Ferdinand enjoyed recounting how, at one of his famed Baron's Treats, when several hundred local children and their families were entertained with fun, games, and a splendid tea at the manor, he was told to "get off the grass and don't smoke your pipe, it ain't allowed" by one of his guests.

After the deaths of their founders, both houses were protected by powerful, charismatic women—in Biltmore's case Edith Vanderbilt, G. W.'s wife, and in Waddesdon's Miss Alice, Ferdinand's unmarried sister who inherited the estate and was fiercely protective of and the North Carolina Collection at Chapel Hill also proved useful in developing the backstory of Asheville and its recovery as a tourist destination.

Others on Director Ellen Rickman's staff of Biltmore's Museum Services were equally gracious, hospitable, and helpful. I am especially grateful for the work of staff members who during the past ten to fifteen years gathered interviews with Biltmore employees and acquaintances of the Vanderbilt and Cecil families to create the Biltmore oral history collection. These personal accounts of life and work on the estate provided insight into important personalities, such as Edith Vanderbilt Gerry and Junius G. Adams, and helped fill in many of the gaps that existed in the archival record. My thanks for the advice and assistance of the estate's landscape historian, William Alexander, who has a deep appreciation and understanding of the contribution of Olmsted and Chauncey D. Beadle to the Biltmore story.

Biltmore House Manager Rick King literally and figuratively unlocked many of the doors of the château. He led me to corners of the house that are not open to the public but which were important to my understanding of the house and its caretakers over the years.

Biltmore Company executives Richard Pressley and Steve Miller were enthusiastic champions of this book. It was they who engaged me and provided free rein in my work. They were generous with their time and responded to my questions with candor and good humor. The also offered unlimited access to materials that were invaluable in piecing together the modern story of Biltmore, much of which they began shaping in 1979 as part of William A. V. Cecil's first management team after the estate was divided between Cecil and his brother, George.

I was pleased to reunite with Asheville attorney John S. Stevens, whom I had come to know and respect some years ago when

Acknowledgments

For most of the visitors to Biltmore Estate in western North Carolina, the story of this magnificent place remains confined to the last twenty-five years of the lifetime of its creator, George Washington Vanderbilt. Occasionally, images of life on the estate beyond these early years made their way into print. But the history was largely anchored in the years from the onset of construction in 1890 through Vanderbilt's death in 1914.

Just how Biltmore survived under private ownership for more than a century was easy to overlook when there was so much immediately at hand to awe visitors. Yet, this account of private preservation is as impressive as any that can be told about America's largest private residence.

The construction of Biltmore and the development of the estate in the late nineteenth century are well documented. For those looking for that detail, I suggest John M. Bryan's *Biltmore Estate: The Most Distinguished Private Place*. Other books about the Vanderbilts, such as *The Vanderbilts and the Gilded Age* by John Foreman and Robbe Pierce Stimson and Jerry E. Patterson's *The Vanderbilts*, will help readers better understand George Vanderbilt's remarkable accomplishment.

This book, however, is the twentieth-century story of the estate—from the Roaring Twenties, through the Depression and World War II, to the rise of tourism in the southern mountains at midcentury. Much of the raw material for this story came from the Biltmore archives. I thank Biltmore's archivist, Suzanne Durham, for her patience and understanding. She retrieved boxes and files in the midst of a renovation that at times made her work all the more challenging. The clip files of Pack Memorial Library in Asheville was calculated that Biltmore contributed $350 million to the local economy in terms of employment and tourist revenue. This is the result of creative marketing, imaginative business strategies such as the opening of the winery in 1985, careful husbandry of resources, and huge investment.

At Waddesdon, we are faced with a similar equation, and a similar aim. The house, its surroundings, its contents, and what it stands for are uniquely precious. The Centenary Restoration, initiated by my cousin Dorothy and carried out under my chairmanship of the management committee, succeeded in putting the manor, from the roof to the cellars, in good order for the future, and our drive is toward sustainability. Since we reopened after this fundamental overhaul, visitor numbers have risen to close to three hundred thousand a year. The huge costs of maintaining the property, the garden, and the curatorial and conservation needs of the spectacular collection are met by a family charitable trust devoted specifically to the upkeep of Waddesdon, the National Trust, visitor income, and the profits from a growing catering, retail, wine, and corporate entertaining business. Biltmore, as an outstanding example of commercial success, has been both a model for us and a major influence on our thinking.

The future looks bright at Biltmore, now in the hands of a new generation of Cecils, William Amherst Vanderbilt Jr., and this book is a timely reminder of the efforts of the Vanderbilt family to secure it. Having watched Biltmore's developments over the recent years with great interest, I was honored to be asked to contribute the foreword, and I hope that for Biltmore, and everyone involved with this national treasure, the twenty-first century will be as impressive as the twentieth has been.

her brother's legacy. Alice did not face the prospect of opening Waddesdon to the public for the first time. That challenge fell to my cousin Dorothy, the widow of James de Rothschild who bequeathed the manor to the National Trust in 1957. That he did so was partly a tribute to his generosity, partly a response to Ferdinand's own fear expressed toward the end of his life that "the pictures and cabinets cross the Channel or the Atlantic and the melancholy cry of the night-jar sound from the deserted towers," and partly a consequence of the realities of the post–World War II world for great country houses, even those owned by Rothschilds. Biltmore, of course, has stolen a march in this respect, opening to the public in 1930 before the establishment of the Biltmore Company, welcoming an impressive 39,913 visitors in that first year. Waddesdon's doors first opened in 1959, with 27,183 visitors.

Not all of the years that followed were easy on either side of the Atlantic. At Biltmore, visitor numbers fluctuated thanks to larger economic issues like the oil crises of the 1970s. The house and its treasures were greedy of resources, and the estate had to fight off threats from road building and a proposed new airport. At Waddesdon, the problem was almost too many visitors to a house that had not been designed to accommodate them. A timed ticket system had to be introduced to regulate the flow.

The modern era at Biltmore could be said to have begun with the tenure of William Amherst Vanderbilt Cecil, who joined his elder brother, George, in managing the estate in 1963. It was his clear vision and determination that Biltmore's future should be secured through being profitable that made the company the success it is today. According to an old friend, William believed that "when you live on a big estate, the first obligation is to preserve it. The second is to improve it. The third is to leave it in better shape than you found it." Those of us who know firsthand how difficult an equation this is to balance salute his achievement. By 1985, it

I was a newspaper reporter covering the N.C. General Assembly and Stevens was in his early years of public service. Stevens's perspective was unique; he brought to the story his twenty-five years as Biltmore's outside counsel as well as an appreciation of the history and the personalities of his native Asheville.

I am especially indebted to Elizabeth Sims, Biltmore's vice president of marketing, who shepherded this book through to completion. Her unfailing assistance provided steady navigation through Biltmore's present and past.

Of course, this entire exercise would have been bootless without the full and willing cooperation of William A. V. Cecil, the members of his family, and many of his old friends and associates, both at home and abroad. Bill Cecil made himself available whenever I asked and eagerly burrowed into his files to retrieve information and details in answer to my questions. I thank him for his patience and forbearance through hours of interviews. I hope he enjoyed our time together as much as I did.

More than fifteen years ago, as Cecil was preparing the estate for its centennial celebration, I put in a call to him to talk about a book as part of that event. As it turned out, John Bryan was already at work on an architectural history of the château. He said that would do, and I thought I had lost my opportunity to write about one of North Carolina's most fascinating places.

Nearly a decade later, Hugh Morton of Grandfather Mountain—a good friend who had known Cecil for half his lifetime—urged me to again contact Cecil. Morton and Cecil shared much in common. Both were grandsons of men of singular vision, and both had dedicated their lives to preserving national treasures. There was another book at Biltmore, Morton said. Beneath the glamour of the château, the grandeur of the estate, and the rich history that enfolds it all, was a story about Cecil's determination to demonstrate that private preservation could succeed. I hope readers find themselves as grateful to Hugh for his suggestion as I am.

And to my wife, Gloria, this assignment proved more satisfying than others with which she has provided support and encouragement. Waiting for an overdue husband is far more enjoyable in the gardens of Biltmore than in the parking lot of a university library.

LADY
ON THE HILL

CHAPTER I

A Centennial Celebration

The evening was clear and cool, and the pale hues of the late September sunset hinted at the glorious display of mountain color soon to arrive. William Amherst Vanderbilt Cecil had worried about the impending weather, since rain had prevailed for days before the centennial celebration at Biltmore Estate. To his delight, the clouds moved on, and this evening on the cusp of fall in 1995 was truly magical. As the concluding fireworks burst overhead, Cecil heard a child say she now knew how the "stars are born."

On this night, Cecil was surrounded by his extended Biltmore family much as his grandfather, George Vanderbilt, had been on Christmas Day in 1895, the occasion marked as the official opening of his new home in North Carolina. It was then—as it was a hundred years later—the largest private residence in the United States.

Cecil had planned this celebration especially for current and retired Biltmore employees and their families. Some of them measured their length of service in decades, even generations, including one old hand who had been a driver for George Vanderbilt's wife,

Edith. The Vanderbilts had annually welcomed those who worked and lived on their estate to a Christmas party complete with presents all around. This gathering was considerably larger; the swarm of guests numbered more than eighteen hundred.

Following a dinner of Carolina barbecue on the South Terrace, all had settled into chairs on the front lawn for a concert by the Asheville Symphony Orchestra. Before the orchestra began its presentation of a selection of mostly twentieth-century tunes, Cecil stepped to the front of a long stage. He was beaming with excitement and pride. Wearing a burgundy blazer familiar to his Biltmore family that he accented with a tie in a lively plaid, he was a hard man to miss. As he began, it was clear his purpose was sincere.

"I only wish my grandparents could see all of you gathered here together," he said, "and see how many of us it takes to keep their dream a reality. I think they would be amazed."[1]

He spoke of the mystique of Biltmore as well as the enduring connection between its people and the house and land. "It has been thirty-five years since I first came home to Asheville and decided to rebuild what my grandfather had built with great determination in the late 1800s," Cecil said in a voice that still carried evidence of his continental schooling. "I intended to do my utmost to bring back the dignity of Biltmore House so she could once again be the grand lady on the hill.

"It has taken diligence, effort, ingenuity, and a strong stubborn streak to bring her back to her glory. Today, in our centennial year, Biltmore Estate is, I believe, as my grandfather had envisioned her to be."[2]

The orchestra's finale of Tchaikovsky's *1812 Overture*, accented by the thunder of a cannon and the boom of the star-creating fireworks, rebounded off the front of the house, rattling the windows and stirring the soul. Finally, all made their way to their cars accompanied by a tattoo from Scottish pipers.

Eighteen hundred current and retired employees and their families turned out for a centennial celebration of barbecue dinner on the South Terrace, a concert by the Asheville Symphony Orchestra, and a fireworks display that lit the sky over the esplanade.

The following night, four hundred guests—mostly family and friends from the United States and abroad—dined and danced at a party that spread throughout the first floor of the château. A midnight buffet was served in the Banquet Hall, and Biltmore wines flowed freely as Cecil's guests filled the grand rooms of the first floor, from the Winter Garden to the Tapestry Gallery, where a dance band was installed. Cecil and his wife, Mimi, circulated until the early hours, when the pipers returned for another salute. "By dawn," Cecil wrote a British friend unable to attend, "the Cinderella Ball was over and the daily shuffle of visitors was back to normal, no trace of anything out of the ordinary left."[3]

Biltmore's centennial was more than a birthday party. It was a celebration of the success of Cecil's extraordinary career. During his thirty-five years on the estate in Asheville, North Carolina, he had accomplished what everyone said could not be done. He had taken a down-at-the-heels Gilded Age mansion that was a drain on the family business and turned it into the most successful privately preserved historic site in the United States, perhaps the world. With creativity and an innate feel for promotion, reinforced by grit and determination, Cecil had seen to it that Biltmore Estate would remain for future generations to enjoy.

The estate had become a travel destination with more visitors each year than Thomas Jefferson's Monticello, George Washington's Mount Vernon, and Elvis's Graceland. With more than eight hundred thousand guests in 1995, it would soon surpass even Colonial Williamsburg in paid attendance.

Such a record was never assured. On at least four occasions—before and after Cecil came home to tend to his patrimony—the distinctive château designed by Richard Morris Hunt could have ended on the auction block. Such an end would have drawn little more than a whimper from twentieth-century preservationists whose tastes ran more toward patriotic venues, such as the home of Paul

Revere, rather than the opulence of the Gilded Age. The fate for the exquisite landscaping of Frederick Law Olmsted could have been just as severe had the land been subdivided into building lots. In the 1950s, as Cecil pondered his own future, the directors of the family-owned Biltmore Company regarded the estate as little more than a real estate holding company. Partitioning the estate's twelve thousand acres for residential housing or commercial development was a very real option.

Instead, Cecil managed to preserve as well as restore the distinctive château and about eight thousand surrounding acres. Moreover, he had confounded the preservation world—as well as members of his own family—by accomplishing his mission without the support of government aid or grants from outside foundations. Cecil had realized a dream that even his grandfather had found elusive: he had made Biltmore Estate a self-supporting, working enterprise. This achievement was all the more remarkable since Vanderbilt was not bothered by the burden of modern-day taxation. In recent years, Cecil's Biltmore Company had paid more than $10 million annually in local, state, and federal fees and taxes.

Under Cecil's hand, the estate had become one of western North Carolina's most important economic engines. A 2004 study showed that it produced about $350 million a year in benefits to vendors, hotel owners, restaurant operators, shopkeepers, and others who served the tourist industry. At the time of the centennial, more than seven hundred people worked on the estate and in its various enterprises including the vineyards and winery—a $20 million investment that Cecil had launched in the mid-1980s. He envisioned the winery carrying the company forward after the house tours eventually reached capacity.

Cecil had followed his own rules in creating the modern Biltmore. "There was no book," he often said. "We wrote it." He took his lessons from Madison Avenue and people-pleasers like Walt

Disney, not historical societies and Colonial Williamsburg. He promoted Biltmore as a tourist attraction and found his allies within the travel industry rather than academia. Every available dollar was invested in promotion. To make his money go further in the early days, he wrote his own advertising copy and took his own photographs, winning awards for his efforts along with lower ad rates.

Even after he began delegating work to assistants—who were mostly talented young people he promoted from within—he was in and about the house daily, shooting photographs, tending to tourists, entertaining visiting journalists, arranging rooms, and making decisions. He was a polymath who came up with a week's worth of ideas before he finished his Monday morning shave. He gave his departmental managers budgets and expected them to make the numbers work. Those who didn't, or couldn't, found work elsewhere. Those who remained formed a bond with Cecil and with Biltmore. "They get proprietary about it," said Cecil's wife, Mimi. "They want to make sure it is okay and it is done right. Around here, we do things right."

Cecil's flair for promotion earned Biltmore a reputation within the preservation community as being too commercial. His detractors complained that Biltmore's admission fees were too high and that visitors deserved more interpretation of the house, its contents, and the Gilded Age. They believed historic house museums should "teach" with docent-guided tours and signage explaining works of art or distinctive furnishings. Cecil did none of that. His guests wandered virtually at will among the rooms that were open for viewing. "Biltmore runs contrary to what we all thought we ought to do," said a person who came out of the upper echelons of Colonial Williamsburg management.[4]

Many in the preservation community simply didn't believe that an owner of a historic property who was committed to making a profit could be serious about preservation. Since most attempts at private operation had turned into demonstrations of sleaze and profiteering, there was no place for a for-profit venture in the world of preservation. Some critics even discounted Cecil's winery, which he installed in the estate's abandoned dairy barn, saying the addition made the property even more of a theme park. In time, Biltmore's presentations of the house and the people who once lived there would exceed standards set by the American Association of Museums. The estate failed to qualify for membership because of its corporate structure, however.

There was nothing cheap or tawdry about Biltmore; the estate didn't even have a gift shop until the late 1980s. "The lady on the hill is a pretty good disciplinarian for you," Cecil often said. "She sets a very high standard."

Indeed, Cecil invested in Biltmore to his own detriment. One of his lawyers had discouraged him in 1980 from doing anything to the property since it only increased his annual tax bill. Yet in the fifteen years after he received that advice, the Biltmore Company invested $35 million in restoration, improvements, and annual maintenance. It was profits, Cecil would say later, that allowed him to hire his first curatorial professional. "We don't preserve Biltmore to make a profit," he said. "We make a profit to preserve Biltmore."

He made no apology for Biltmore's admission price, which had been higher than every other comparable historic property. Cecil believed that Biltmore was unique, and visitors, rather than the government, should contribute to its survival. With the middle of the market crowded by so many mediocre venues, Cecil told his protégés that "there was always room at the top." And what he was asking of tourists was honest, especially when he was paying taxes on a National Historic Landmark—a designation granted the estate in 1963—and most of his government-owned or nonprofit competitors were not. "At Biltmore," Cecil said, "we believe that the visitor should be the one to help pay for the preservation of the property."

Such thinking usually left Cecil on the outside. Detractors didn't believe his numbers or they discounted his efforts. When Biltmore was losing money in the early days, the company's red ink was evidence of what others considered Cecil's bootless exercise. After Biltmore began to produce a profit, he got no credit for his creativity and was told, "Well, that's Biltmore," as if success had been a foregone conclusion.

From the day the château was first opened to the public in 1930, Biltmore was such an overwhelming experience that guests left believing they got their money's worth. Biltmore visitors experienced the Gilded Age and its lifestyle on a scale that defied common understanding. Plus, they were treated with such courtesy and hospitality that they left almost believing that George Vanderbilt himself had issued the invitation. Woe to the parking lot attendant found chewing gum or to the guard with his hands stuffed in his pockets. Indeed, visitors came to Biltmore and they kept coming back. By the 1990s, when the company began using sophisticated marketing measurements, the results of customer satisfaction reports by Biltmore visitors were comparable to those enjoyed by five-star resorts.

For years, Cecil searched for relief from an ultimate accounting of inheritance taxes that could require the dismantling of it all when his heirs settled with the government. Unfortunately for him and his heirs, U.S. tax laws weren't written to accommodate the private owner who cared for a historic property rather than leaving it to the government or sheltering it in some tax-exempt status such as a foundation. Lawmakers in Raleigh and Washington discouraged Cecil's efforts to install something simi-lar to the British system that protected owners as long as they met certain standards and opened their homes to the public. Accommodating legislation to benefit a Vanderbilt was not the stuff of reelection.

Cecil argued that private preservation not only worked but was superior. He paid taxes and served the public good. Plus, he did it better. Bureaucrats and hired administrators brought unneeded burdens to the task and shared none of the incentive or passion for success held by a private owner. Cecil even founded the Historic House Association of America in an attempt to carry the fight for tax relief to Congress and export his message of private enterprise.

Over the years, Cecil had enjoyed advantages not available to the owners of many other historic properties. He started with a structure that was fundamentally sound although a bit run-down. The foundation and infrastructure were as solid as when Vanderbilt had been in residence. Moreover, his grandfather's collection of art and furnishings was all in place. Thus, there was no need to recover family holdings that had been given away or sold over the years—a terrible expense and aggravation for others. Cecil had fifty thousand pieces in the Biltmore collection from which to choose as he opened new rooms to the public. Most beneficial of all was Biltmore's location. When Vanderbilt created the estate in the late nineteenth century, Asheville was a remote resort town deep in Appalachia. The modern-day Biltmore sat at the intersection of interstate highways that had opened the western North Carolina mountains to millions of tourists from all compass points just when family travel was becoming most affordable.

Cecil capitalized on it all, as well as inventions of his own, to return Biltmore to its glorious past. If George Vanderbilt himself had appeared in the Banquet Hall that Saturday night in September 1995, he would have felt right at home. Before the party for hundreds, he could have joined the Cecils and sixty-four special guests at a table laid to suit a wealthy scion. The menu for the sumptuous meal reflected the bounty of the estate: tenderloin of Biltmore beef, Biltmore field greens, Carolina apple turnovers, and vintages from the winery, including champagne and claret.

William A. V. Cecil and his wife, Mimi (seated center of photo), hosted a banquet for sixty-four friends, family, and close business associates in the Banquet Hall as part of the festivities of the closing night of the centennial celebration of Biltmore Estate.

Beyond, the other rooms were aglow. The guide ropes were down, the utility mats were stored away, and fresh carpets covered the floors. A chair was for sitting, not for display. The house was to enjoy. Vanderbilt's favorite furnishings, his collection of books, Karl Bitter's sculpture, and the sixteenth-century tapestries remained where George Vanderbilt and his architect had placed them a century before. For this night at least, Biltmore was not a historic house museum. It was a home.

"We were going to have a banquet. We were going to have a dance. We were going to open the house as it was in 1895, the way it would have been," Cecil told his house manager as preparations began for the celebration.

The morning after the banquet, the magic of Biltmore was as vivid as ever, although early visitors saw no evidence of the Cinderella night that had just ended. That had all disappeared with the rising of the sun. The château, the gardens, and the winery were once again open for business.

CHAPTER 2

George Vanderbilt's Dream

A sheville needed some good news in the early months of 1930. Winter had been hard on a city careful about keeping up appearances of prosperity and success. In October 1929, the release of Thomas Wolfe's *Look Homeward, Angel* had simply pole-axed Asheville, or Altamont as Wolfe called it, with local personalities he held accountable in print. If such national ridicule wasn't enough, visiting businessmen, including the state's most respected banker, warned that the smoke from homes and factories that hung over the valley threatened Asheville's reputation as a tourist resort. Moreover, the economy was wobbly and the tax coffers were empty. Schoolteachers had already been laid off because there was not enough money to pay their salaries. The *Asheville Citizen* carried eight full pages of legal notices listing real estate in jeopardy due to unpaid taxes.

Then came news that was bound to lift the sagging tourist trade. The Asheville Chamber of Commerce announced that Cornelia Vanderbilt Cecil and her husband, John, had consented to admit the public to the magnificent mansion that her father had built on Biltmore Estate south of the city. On March 15, 1930, with a Pathé movie news camera capturing the occasion, the Cecils welcomed the first paying guests to their château.

About three hundred visitors from a dozen states turned out that first day. It was chilly, with guests squinting in the bright sunshine as dignitaries marked the event. Altogether, it was a fine beginning. Cornelia's welcoming remarks were carefully scripted, brief, and delivered on the steps just outside the front entrance. Unlike her gregarious mother, George Vanderbilt's widow, Edith, Cornelia wasn't keen on public appearances or her own celebrity. She shifted uncomfortably from foot to foot but smiled generously nonetheless. John stood quietly by her side. She described Biltmore as a place that had given her much pleasure, never hinting that she would soon leave the estate and never return. She told the mayor, the chamber people, and the assorted officials gathered at the front steps that she was pleased to open the house as a gesture of goodwill to Asheville and as a memorial to her father. "After all," she said, "it was his life's work and his creation."

That much was certainly true. Biltmore was the centerpiece of an estate that had once covered upward of 120,000 acres—no one ever quantified the total with any certainty—and had all but consumed her father, George Washington Vanderbilt. He had created a home of monumental proportions on a working estate the likes of which had never been seen in the United States. But Vanderbilt discovered there was a limit to his fortune. By the time of his death in 1914, he was struggling to retain the château and a relatively small amount of the vast estate that surrounded it.

Even in the midst of his financial discomfort, George Vanderbilt probably would never have considered turning his home into a tourist attraction. Biltmore had been his retreat from social fussiness.

George Vanderbilt's daughter, Cornelia Vanderbilt Cecil, and her husband, John, welcomed the first visitors when her father's château was opened to the public on March 15, 1930.

One of the first things he did when he began assembling land for his new home was to buy out his neighbors. In later years, tourists were permitted to visit the grounds. Carriages crossed the narrow Swannanoa River that ran along the estate's northern boundary near Vanderbilt's nursery at Victoria and carried visitors along the estate's landscaped roads where they could drink in the natural beauty of the countryside. On Wednesday and Saturday afternoons only, the owner's indulgence followed in the tradition of English nobility who permitted the public to cruise the deer parks and forests of their country estates. The Biltmore excursions were carefully limited to the outlying roads, which included the first paved surfaces in western North Carolina. Carriages were forbidden to cross the esplanade when the family was in residence. Visitors only gained a view of the house if they were lucky. Perhaps with the help of a friendly member of the house staff, who was properly rewarded when the master was away, tourists might get a peek in the front door.

This public opening was different, however.

For the first time, visitors drove right to the château's massive front doors, parked their cars beside the esplanade, walked in, and presented their two-dollar tickets to guards outfitted in smart, black-serge uniforms bearing gold stripes and gold buttons stamped with a V. Paid admission guaranteed a tour of a dozen rooms on the first and second floors. That was but 5 percent of the 250 rooms that architect Richard Morris Hunt had included in the mansion. Yet the tour more than satisfied guests who saw ceremonial hangings once owned by France's Cardinal Richelieu, sixteenth-century Flemish tapestries, a chess set that had belonged to Napoleon Bonaparte, a library of academic proportions, and art and sculpture from the greatest masters of Europe and America. There was even a rumor that one of the bathrooms contained a tub once used by the Caesars. This report was totally untrue but survived as gospel for decades. Such was the allure of Biltmore. By the end of 1930, nearly thirty-nine thousand visitors had accepted the Cecils' invitation to see their home.

Visitors also enjoyed breathtaking views of the mountain range that framed the house on the horizon and found a magnificence that defied imagination. "The ordinary mortal, the tourist, the passing sightseer is overcome by the sheer bigness of the entire estate," wrote M. V. Moore from Asheville's Patton Avenue. "He goes his way . . . groping for words to describe the home and the absurdity of calling the Sphinx—big; the Colorado Canyon—pretty; the Biltmore House—beautiful. It takes a master of words to even approach picturing this most beautiful home in America. It lifts from the land of every day into the land of make believe."[1]

When the château opened for visitors, more than forty years had passed since George Vanderbilt first visited Asheville in the winter of 1888. The southern highlands had long been a haven for southerners escaping the summer heat. It all began with Charlestonians retreating to summer homes around Flat Rock, south of Asheville near the South Carolina border. It was only after the opening of the railroad in 1880 that Asheville gained wider notice, especially among northerners seeking a respite from the harsh New England winters. The new Battery Park Hotel near the center of Asheville still smelled of fresh-cut pine when George and his mother took rooms for an extended stay.

George was twenty-six, the youngest child of William H. Vanderbilt, who had inherited the bulk of the financial empire from his father, the great Commodore Cornelius Vanderbilt, who in his day had been the richest man in the United States. George was slender, of medium height, and darkly handsome with a thin mustache. His high forehead accentuated a narrow face, a deep chin, and deep-set eyes. His permanent address was the family mansion

This portrait of William Henry Vanderbilt's family was painted by Seymour Guy in 1873. George, the youngest in the family, is seated in the chair in front of his father.

at 640 Fifth Avenue in New York City, but he had traveled widely abroad, collecting art and treasures that suited his fancy. On one trip to Japan, he returned with twenty cases of carved ivory. He had recently acquired a home in Bar Harbor, Maine, where the noted landscape designer Frederick Law Olmsted was reshaping thirty acres of grounds.

Unlike many of his age and station, George was not consumed with the social swirl of the Gilded Age. He preferred outings on his yacht, the *Lucille*, and the relatively informal Bar Harbor compared to the ostentation of his tribe's favorite haunt, Newport, Rhode Island. He was quiet, studious, and, of course, rich beyond the imagination of most Americans. Although he was not as well endowed as some of his seven brothers and sisters, his inherited fortune was in the neighborhood of $13 million.[2] He had been tutored at home before he enrolled at sixteen in what later became Columbia University, where he graduated with high honors.[3] A personal library filled the walls of his suite at 640 Fifth Avenue and contained volumes in eight languages, in which George was fluent enough to converse virtually anywhere in the modern world, much of which he had seen by the time he turned twenty-one.

George filled his life with art and philosophy rather than finance. His name was noticeably absent from the *Directory of Directors*, an inventory of those running U.S. businesses. He was especially fond of architecture and passionate about opera. When the Metropolitan Opera was performing in New York, he attended four or five nights in a row.

The trip south in 1888 was both an adventure and in aid of his mother, who suffered from chronic malaria. Asheville's climate and altitude were reputed to be a healing environment for a number of ailments. The place suited her, as it did George, who was said to be "haunted" by the fear of tuberculosis.[4] While his mother came under the care of Asheville's Dr. S. Westray Battle, a prominent physician with a cultured clientele, George often rode on horseback to explore the countryside. He was especially taken with the long vistas that carried his eye to the mountain peaks on the horizon. One of the most prominent was Mount Pisgah, whose summit at more than five thousand feet capped the far ridge line about twenty miles away to the southwest.

On a return visit in the late spring of 1888, Vanderbilt was accompanied by his friend and attorney, Charles McNamee, when the two found a particularly enjoyable spot about six miles south of Asheville. The end of a small ridge offered such a commanding view of Pisgah that Vanderbilt and McNamee rode directly to the landowner's house and purchased it along with ten acres of land. McNamee moved quickly to buy the surrounding land to cleanse the landscape of unsightly cabins that were the homes of subsistence farmers happy to exchange their meager holdings for cash. Within the year, McNamee had accumulated several thousand acres for Vanderbilt.[5] Additional land was added, including the farm and shack of one stubborn neighbor who reportedly held out for $75,000 on property said to be worth no more than $200.[6]

In short order, George's vision for a comfortable country home grew beyond that of most of his siblings, who were known for their huge, elaborate mansions in Newport. Vanderbilt founded Biltmore—a name that drew upon his family's ancestral home in Bildt, Holland—with a purpose far grander than pure seasonable pleasure. With an inherited fortune produced from a railroad empire fat with profits of the Industrial Revolution, George set out to build an estate based on an old-world agrarian model of manor house and tenant farms with an accompanying village, parish church, and school. The house would be handsome, to be sure, but more importantly it was the focus of a larger investment that would be capable of producing an income and sustaining itself for years to come. Plans called for herds of sheep, a swine farm, and a poultry operation with the usual chickens as well as Mongolian and English pheasants to be released onto the land. One of the first enterprises was a nursery to supply plants for the landscaping of the estate and eventually to meet a market of gardeners around the country. There was talk of a five-hundred-acre truck farm to produce food for the house as well as for sale in local markets.

Biltmore would become known for many things, but two of the young man's early investments marked it more than others did. First was the dairy farm that Vanderbilt stocked with a herd of more than two hundred purebred Jerseys from the family farm in Long Island, New York. Second was the establishment of the first managed forests that were developed under Olmsted's plan by Vanderbilt's friend, Gifford Pinchot.

Work began in 1889 on the house designed by Richard Morris Hunt, who had traveled widely in Europe with Vanderbilt, gathering ideas and making plans. As work commenced, hundreds of laborers and craftsmen in stone and wood were drawn to jobs that offered steady wages. Vanderbilt quickly became the largest employer in western North Carolina. The volume of building materials was such that a three-mile railroad spur costing nearly $80,000 was laid to the house from the main line that ran beside the Swannanoa River. Over the next five years, the limestone mansion rose slowly on a site that offered a prospect of the French Broad River and the mountains beyond. For his design, Hunt borrowed from the style of the French Renaissance châteaux of the Loire valley, especially the Château de Blois. Even aside from its sheer size, Hunt's creation was unlike any other in the United States. Asked to compare Biltmore with his other accomplishments, he would say, "They are but pigsties in comparison, nothing but pigsties."[7] Olmsted called Biltmore "the most distinguished private place, not only in America, but of the world, forming in this period."[8]

Soaring spires and gargoyles marked the exterior of the mansion front, whose impressive silhouette was matched only by that of the distant mountains. Inside, Hunt provided for every modern convenience. Despite its hundreds of rooms, the space enjoyed an easy and logical flow. In addition, the building was fully wired for electricity, elevators carried guests and staff between floors, and three steamship boilers produced heat centrally that was carried to every room. In the summer, cool air rose through a series of airways that used the chimneys for draft. Although Vanderbilt himself could not swim, an indoor pool was provided for the pleasure of his guests, as was a bowling alley and a gymnasium.

Hunt built the house on a landscape sculpted by Olmsted. His Biltmore commission was the largest, and the last, of his career. His influence was profound. Olmsted sited the house, then set about

*In September 1900, George Vanderbilt's family came for a visit to see the
Vanderbilts' infant daughter, Cornelia, who was born the month before. From left
to right, enjoying tea on the loggia are Edith Vanderbilt; Edith's former chaperone,
Mlle. Marie Rambaud; George's sister, Lila Vanderbilt Webb; George's cousin, Effie
Caesar; an unidentified couple; and George.*

designing a winding road about three miles long that turned arrival
at the mansion gates into a breathtaking event. The farms, the forests, and, of course, the gardens, all felt his touch. His masterpiece
was to be a nine-mile arboretum drive along which he planned to
showcase varieties of trees, shrubs, and woody plants in much the
same way that Hunt's mansion presented Vanderbilt's collection of
art. A hundred years later, Hunt's mansion would leave visitors
in awe, but it was Olmsted's creative genius in the use and rehabilitation of the land that would set the estate apart. The designer

himself called it "the first great private work of our profession in the country."[9]

Indeed, Vanderbilt filled his house with treasures from abroad. Carpets, paintings, sculpture, and furnishings of all manner and size arrived at the railway station in the village that Vanderbilt constructed just outside the Lodge Gate. Finally, impatient after five years of work, Vanderbilt refused to wait for the finishing of his château and simply moved in. He officially occupied the house in October 1895, taking up residence in completed portions of the north wing while work continued on the main rooms on the first floor. In December, with nearly thirty members of his immediate family as his guests, he celebrated Christmas in his new château. Presents were handed all around to family and staff alike from under a fir tree that stood forty feet tall in the Banquet Hall. At the time, he was thirty-three years old.

Among the treasures Vanderbilt found abroad was a mistress for the manor. In 1898, two years after his mother's death, he married Edith Stuyvesant Dresser of New York, to whom he had given considerable attention the year before in London at the Jubilee Celebration for Queen Victoria. The June marriage stunned New York society. George was thought to be a confirmed bachelor after none of the repeated rumors of earlier engagements had proved to be true. The couple honeymooned in Spain, then spent the balance of the summer in Italy. In October, George and Edith returned to Biltmore, where they were welcomed by a huge floral horseshoe with the words "Good Luck" spelled out with blossoms of goldenrod. Nursery workers tossed flowers to the bride as the carriage passed by. That night there were fireworks.

Construction at the estate seemed to have no end. Barns and estate buildings, houses for farmworkers, and a large creamery were added to the working side of the farm. At the same time, work continued on the model village outside the Lodge Gate that included

The château in 1910. The Italian Gardens are on the left.

the Hunt-designed All Souls Church (consecrated in 1896), a two-story office building, a rail depot, and more than two dozen trim and neat cottages.

Then it all stopped abruptly, with entire rooms in the mansion unfinished. A scientific museum that Olmsted had planned as the centerpiece of his arboretum remained on the drawing board. Some speculated that Vanderbilt was simply exhausted with the constant interruptions of workmen and architects, more troublesome now since the arrival of Cornelia, the Vanderbilts' daughter, who was born in the house on August 23, 1900. It was also said that Vanderbilt refused—or was simply unable—to pour more cash into the estate that had consumed perhaps as much as half of his entire fortune.

There seemed to be no logic in the unfinished work. The front row of organ pipes was installed in the loft of the Banquet Hall, but the others were dummies, and there was no organ. A large room just off the entrance hall that Hunt had designated as a music room was left with a bare subfloor, brick walls, and a rough, unfinished ceramic tile ceiling. An adjacent room particularly suited for afternoon tea was left in the same condition even though it offered a fabulous vista of the mountains. Edith made do with rudimentary decorations. She draped a woolen fabric in billows from the ceiling and cast assorted cushions about the carpets that covered the rough, concrete floor. For years it was called the "tent room."[10]

Vanderbilt's deteriorating financial situation clearly was a consideration. For some time, he had ignored warnings from advisers who told him that his architects and builders were spending more than his bank account could afford. In fact, cash flowed in so many directions that a final cost of the house became virtually impossible to calculate. A grand total remained buried in boxes of bills and receipts that no one ever tallied to the penny. Losses on other investments also may have forced him into retreat. He began scaling back at Biltmore and reduced his annual maintenance at the estate from $250,000, the cost in the early years, to about $70,000.[11] By 1906, he had closed the poultry operations and announced plans to lease out his forestland as a hunting preserve.[12]

George was helped by the sale of a portion of his art collection, and he leased the Fifth Avenue mansion he inherited upon his mother's death to financier Henry Clay Frick. Things remained dark, however. In 1907, he sent word to put virtually all of his North Carolina property on the market, saving only a thousand acres around the château. A year later, he and Edith closed the house entirely. The servants were dismissed, the pleasure horses were sold, and the family sailed for Europe where they could live comfortably on less money.[13] Budget cuts continued into 1909 when Vanderbilt notified Dr. Carl A. Schenck that he would no longer underwrite the operation of the Biltmore forestry school—the nation's first—that Schenck had launched in 1898. Schenck left in a huff due to a dispute over a hunting lease he had authorized and sued for back wages.

During his years at Biltmore, Schenck had created something on Vanderbilt land that had never been attempted before in the United States—a managed forest plantation where harvests did not exceed the annual growth. Heretofore, American loggers had simply stripped the land of trees and left the denuded acres to restore themselves. Some of Vanderbilt's property was in this condition when he acquired it, but the vast tract also included large stands of virgin timber. Schenck introduced European forestry techniques that in time demonstrated that a managed forest not only produced more timber but also conserved the soil and improved the total environment.

The men at Schenck's school were not just students but disciples who wrote songs about the tough, demanding German whose large, bushy, handlebar mustache earned him the nickname of the Kaiser. Aboard his large bay mare named Punch, Schenck led them into the depths of Pisgah Forest where they set up camp and lived for weeks at a time. After Vanderbilt ended his underwriting of his school, Schenck relocated and produced four more classes before leaving the United States in 1913 for Germany and service in World War I.

With the New York newspapers watching the Vanderbilts' every move, the news reports of George and his estate provided a significant bump for Asheville, an otherwise sleepy mountain resort. Likewise, changes on the estate always sent a tremble through the countryside. Rumors in 1898 that Vanderbilt was forsaking North Carolina had proved false but carried enough credibility that the town had organized a chamber of commerce to rebut the widespread press accounts. "The estate," as it was called locally, remained the area's best employer and its richest source of local tax revenue. When Vanderbilt was late in 1909 with payment of his property taxes, local schoolteachers didn't get their pay.[14]

Even in hard times, North Carolina was never far from Vander-bilt's mind. He named his private rail car the Swannanoa. Corne-lia's nickname was Tar Heel Nell. Even after he curtailed expenses, he remained devoted to Biltmore. The family continued to live in the château about six months out of the year, even longer in 1905 when George took personal charge of operations on the estate. He spent hours walking in the mountains and pursuing an intense study of the trees, flowers, and natural beauty he found there. A frequent companion was Chauncey D. Beadle, a Canadian who had come south to work for Olmsted and stayed on to complete his plans after the great designer became incapacitated and later died. Olmsted's restored forests and the lush gardens near the château were a delight, but it was said that Buck Spring Lodge high on Mount Pisgah was the most appealing spot of all.

The lodge was an expansive Adirondack-style complex of four buildings made primarily of chestnut logs, some of them forty feet in length. The main building, whose porch was sixty feet across, had a central hall with five thousand square feet of floor space. This building was connected by a breezeway to adjacent sleeping rooms for guests and on to a kitchen and a dining hall. Hunt began designs for the lodge before he died, but it wasn't finished until 1902 under the direction of his son, Richard Howland Hunt.[15]

The lodge sat just under Pisgah's summit in the saddle of a ridge off to the southwest. The site was nearly twenty miles from the château and almost as deep into the mountains as Vanderbilt could go. Access initially was only on horseback, but an early trail was widened and improved, and the contorted route with frequent switchbacks became a showpiece of mountain road construction. From this aerie at roughly five thousand feet above sea level, the air was easily ten to twenty degrees cooler than at the château. Guests enjoyed an unparalleled view of deep, green forests with only the breeze and the birds to disturb the quiet. In the early summer, a

(above) George Vanderbilt's remote mountaintop retreat was Buck Spring Lodge on Mount Pisgah. Some of the chestnut logs in the walls were forty feet long.
(right) George and Edith Vanderbilt on the lawn at Buck Spring Lodge.

lush valley just below was transformed into a field of color. The profusion of rhododendron, laurel, and native azaleas earned it the name the pink beds. Vanderbilt spent one entire summer at Buck Spring, coming down only for a haircut at the village of Candler.

Vanderbilt's retreats to Buck Spring expanded the awe and mystery of the estate and exaggerated tales of an eccentric millionaire. His agents handled virtually all local affairs, and Vanderbilt developed few intimate acquaintances in Asheville. Once he was mistaken for a porter by a passenger alighting from a train at Biltmore and dutifully carried the man's bag without correcting the traveler's mistake.[16] Perhaps his closest friend in North Carolina and a frequent dinner companion was the Reverend Dr. Rodney Rush Swope, the rector at All Souls Church, where Vanderbilt paid all expenses, including the salary of a choir director brought to the church from New York City.

Vanderbilt sought out Swope as the rector for All Souls. The minister was nearly ten years older than his patron and in his prime when he arrived in North Carolina. His ministry in Wheeling, West Virginia, had strengthened an otherwise small church, and he had left an indelible mark with his efforts to bring adequate health care to that community. Swope was a compelling preacher— an "orator," said one longtime member of All Souls—who challenged his parishioners to not only save their own souls but tend to their fellow man as well. It was a social gospel that Vanderbilt himself embraced and underwrote with his philanthropy. "[Swope] was motivated by a divine discontent with the injustice and unfair inequalities suffered by the man," wrote one biographer. He and Vanderbilt, who was said to have considered the ministry for himself, spent hours discussing theology and the local charities that Swope supervised on Vanderbilt's behalf.[17]

Vanderbilt was reserved among strangers but demonstrated a quick wit and a depth of understanding and knowledge of a wide

George Vanderbilt's library at the château held more than twenty thousand volumes covering the arts and sciences in a variety of languages.

range of topics when he was finally engaged in conversation. He was gentle, compassionate, and generally tolerant of missteps by those who worked on the estate, even when they took advantage of his generosity. It was said that more than one employee embezzled money, but Vanderbilt never pressed for criminal prosecution. But relations with his staff didn't always go smoothly. He had one long-time employee arrested after the man threatened to kill him and burn down the château.[18] In 1906, a group of teamsters from Great Britain quit in a group, leaving Vanderbilt with no drivers for his carriages. Later, the paid members of the All Souls Choir went on strike. Critics said the replacement singers brought in for a sacred concert produced a program "below the usual standard."[19]

His neighbors could be even more troublesome and expensive. Much of the farther reaches of the estate had once belonged to the University of North Carolina. Locals had long used the land as their own, hunting and fishing without any notice of ownership until Vanderbilt marked boundaries and installed rangers to control poaching. Trespassers were brought before the local magistrates, who were clearly sympathetic with tradition and imposed minimal fines. After fires were ignited in Vanderbilt's forests, which the estate's rangers traced back to disgruntled mountaineers, Vanderbilt pledged gifts to public charities if the trespassing came to an end.[20]

In 1912, Cornelia was twelve, and the family bought a home in Washington, D.C. Vanderbilt's purchase was a house at 1612 K Street, the home of the late senator Matthew S. Quay of Pennsylvania. It accommodated the family nicely. Edith enjoyed the political and social world of Washington far more than New York. Strategically located near the diplomatic center, their home was a frequent stop for diplomats and politicians. Moreover, the city provided a suitable school for Cornelia, and Washington was within a day's train ride from Biltmore.

The family's arrival in Washington coincided with the federal government's new interest in creating national forests in the East, much as had been done in the western United States. In 1911, Congress had responded to the awakening in conservation begun under President Theodore Roosevelt, who had named George Vanderbilt's old friend Gifford Pinchot as the nation's chief forester. Congressional passage of the Weeks Act created the National Forest Reservation Commission and included an appropriation of $10 million to be spent over five years for the purchase of land in the southern Appalachians and White Mountains of New England, where virtually all accessible reaches were being cleared of marketable timber to satisfy a voracious demand for lumber. Conservationists feared that if the forests were not renewed, the scarred mountainsides would lead to dire consequences such as flooding and silting of mountain rivers and streams. Vanderbilt's Pisgah tract of nearly ninety thousand acres was considered a prime acquisition.

Vanderbilt opened discussions about the sale of his vast forest in the fall of 1912 and presented a formal offer that following spring. The tract spread across four counties, from the banks of the French Broad near Asheville to beyond Pisgah's summit. It appeared to be a one-of-a-kind opportunity for the commission's staff, which produced a detailed survey of the land that concluded with an enthusiastic recommendation. Vanderbilt's asking price of $690,000 was well within the accepted range of prices for land that had already been acquired, the report said.[21]

Government foresters were especially excited about the ease of purchasing such a huge tract unencumbered by competing title claims, a common problem in remote regions. They also emphasized the historic significance of the nation's first managed forest where smaller trees had been left to mature while older growth was removed in an orderly fashion. Moreover, Vanderbilt's offer included more than $70,000 in improvements, including ninety miles of roads. Of this distance, seventeen miles were suitable for automobiles, which was more paved mileage than in most North Carolina cities. Vanderbilt's foresters had prepared another 165 miles of graded trails. There were twenty-six houses—"after the pattern of the houses in the Black Forest of Germany"—that the estate's rangers used in mild weather. Vanderbilt's engineer estimated that the streams and creeks on the property had sufficient flow to produce 30 million kilowatt-hours of electricity. And game was plentiful. The forest was full of deer, turkey, and pheasants. The streams were home to rainbow and brook trout whose numbers had grown through annual restocking.[22]

In late May 1913, the entire commission came to inspect the Pisgah land. It was an impressive entourage that arrived in Asheville and included four members of Congress along with President Woodrow Wilson's secretaries of war, agriculture, and the interior. Chauncey Beadle, the estate superintendent, met the commissioners at the train. After lunch with local dignitaries at Asheville's Langren Hotel and a drive through the estate, the group set out by automobile for Buck Spring Lodge along one of the first improved roads to reach that deep into the mountains.[23] The commissioners spent two days on the property, then returned to Washington with acceptance of Vanderbilt's offer apparently assured. A month later, however, the commission announced it would not buy the land.

Politics may have played a part in the commission's decision. The United States had just been through a national election that saw an outpouring of support for Eugene V. Debs, the socialists' candidate for president. Perhaps 1913 wasn't the time for Washington politicians to be paying a scion of America's richest family hundreds of thousands of dollars, no matter how good a deal was on the table. In addition, Vanderbilt's asking price was equal to more than a quarter of the commission's annual appropriation. Correspondence would later reveal that the commissioners also took advantage of Vanderbilt's personal interest in the land; he was doing a fine job of reforestation, and it wasn't costing the government a dime. The commission's stated reasons for turning down Vanderbilt's offer were the asking price and complications of a timber contract that covered three-quarters of the property, although the commission's own staff called it "one of the best that has been put into effect by a private owner for safeguarding a timber tract."[24]

Vanderbilt had sold the timber on some of his Pisgah land in 1912 at about the same time he sold another twenty thousand acres near the Gloucester community in nearby Henderson County, but his offer to the government had taken account of the timber sale. His asking price for land covered by the timber contract was $5.75 an acre while the uncut remainder was priced at $12.75 per acre. Excused from the timber sale, as well as the offer to the government, was land on the east side of the French Broad in the vicinity of the house as well as five hundred acres surrounding Buck Spring Lodge.

The Vanderbilts spent the Christmas holidays in 1913 at Biltmore, much as always. Presents for the estate family—now numbering several hundred—were prepared and handed out from under a tree in the Banquet Hall. After the first of the year, the Vanderbilts returned to Washington. A few weeks later, George fell ill. His doctors diagnosed appendicitis and performed surgery. He was said to be recovering well when he died unexpectedly on March 6, apparently as the result of a pulmonary embolism. He had fainted shortly after taking lunch in his bed, with Edith, Cornelia, and nurses in the room. Edith summoned doctors, but her husband was dead by the time they arrived. He was fifty-one years old.[25]

The report of his death appeared on the front page of the *New York Times*. Nearly half of the story recounted his creation of Biltmore, which was called the "finest residence in this country."[26] Funeral services were held March 9 in Washington Cathedral. As services got under way in Washington, a memorial service was held at All Souls Church. Vanderbilt's body was interred in the family mausoleum on Staten Island. Edith said afterward she had hoped her husband would be buried at Biltmore. Among the honorary pallbearers were Gifford Pinchot and Chauncey D. Beadle from Biltmore.

George's death unsettled Asheville. Rumors resurfaced that the estate would be chopped into pieces and parceled out to buyers. Edith quickly announced through All Souls rector Dr. Swope that she considered Biltmore her home and would continue to do so.[27]

Soon after her husband's death, however, Edith reopened discussions with the government for the purchase of the Pisgah land, dropping the price for all the land to $5 an acre, or $200,000 less than the price her husband had asked for a year earlier. She wrote Secretary of Agriculture David M. Houston on May 1, 1914, saying, "I make this contribution towards the public ownership of Pisgah Forest with the earnest hope that in this way I may help to perpetuate my husband's pioneer work in forest conservation, and to insure the protection and the use and enjoyment of Pisgah Forest as a National Forest, by the American people for all times."[28]

The new offer prompted a serious second look by the commission. "It can not be said that the same amount of money can be used more advantageously," the staff foresters wrote in again recommending the purchase to the commission, "for this is undoubtedly the cheapest tract that can be presented to the commission." Furthermore, the government could no longer depend on the generous attention of a private owner. The staff warned that if the property wasn't incorporated into the national forest, then it most likely would be broken into smaller tracts and sold. "If this tract passes into private hands it will mean the loss of the first and most conspicuous example of forestry in America." Three weeks after it was presented, the commission accepted Edith's offer on May 22,

1914. The addition of the 86,700 acres was the largest single purchase made by the commission.

Once the Pisgah lands were gone, however, Edith became even more earnest than her husband in keeping the château and the gardens—the heart of the estate—embedded in the remaining property. While over time she would dispose of outlying tracts, she retained more of the land surrounding the house—about fourteen thousand acres—than the thousand acres her husband had planned to keep when his financial problems were most severe. As a result, the estate remained large enough to demonstrate in years to come the vision of George Vanderbilt, Richard Morris Hunt, and Frederick Law Olmsted.

CHAPTER 3

Edith Vanderbilt

R aleigh was under a blanket of snow on the morning of February 2, 1921, when Edith and Cornelia Vanderbilt stepped from the train that had brought them to the state capital for an extraordinary occasion. At eleven that morning, Edith was due to address a joint session of the North Carolina General Assembly. No one could recall the last time a woman had been asked to do that.

A full day was ahead. Before she continued on to Washington, D.C., that evening, Edith would deliver her first major public speech, accept the presidency of the North Carolina Agricultural Society and State Fair, attend a reception with the state's political elite, and leave the locals in a swoon. None had expected the mistress of Biltmore to be so likable and gracious as well as so politically aware. "Certainly no woman could ask for more than the throng gave her yesterday," the *News and Observer* reported, "and few men could ask for so much."[1]

The House chamber was jammed with legislators, reporters, and onlookers by the time mother and daughter arrived at the

State Capitol. Both of them wore tailored suits of Biltmore home-spun wool. Edith's was accented with a collar of rich, brown fur. She wore little jewelry, it was noted, but her choices were exceptional: a platinum and diamond wristwatch, a pearl bracelet, and an eyeglass chain with small emeralds and pearls set in platinum. Her hat was fashioned from a wrap of woven wool and a black veil closely covered her face. She wore no gloves.

The crowd was such that guests in the House gallery could scarcely see Edith until she emerged at the front of the chamber on the arm of Governor Cameron A. Morrison. Once in sight, the crowd found her appearance quite appealing. "It was almost with disbelief that they saw her when she came in. The throng was expecting a maturer woman, not this woman who looked not more than grown-up, who walked with such graceful sureness of herself."[2] At the time, Edith Vanderbilt was forty-seven.

The humility she expressed in her opening remarks was taken as genuine. While her hands trembled slightly, she spoke in a voice and accent that were easily heard and understood. She carried her audience with ease and an early joke. She said she had been told that a good speech "should be like a modern skirt: long enough to cover the subject, and short enough to attract attention." Men yelled outright, the paper said. "The women in the gallery laughed in high treble."[3]

Edith clearly had the measure of her audience that day. Her choice of an outfit made from homespun wool put the women at ease, while her charm and beauty captivated the men, including the governor, a widower, who later became a suitor. While her late husband had created a buffer of land at Biltmore to separate himself from his neighbors and ensure privacy, Edith seemed intent on connecting with the people in her adopted state. But then it had been that way with her almost from the start.

Before she married U.S. Senator Peter Gerry of Rhode Island in 1925, Edith Vanderbilt immersed herself in North Carolina affairs, becoming an outspoken advocate for good roads, the State Fair, and adult literacy. In this photograph she is wearing a suit made from Biltmore homespun, a handwoven woolen fabric from Biltmore Industries, an enterprise Edith began to encourage the production of handcrafts such as weaving and woodworking by mountain men and women.

*   *   *

Edith Stuyvesant Dresser Vanderbilt was a woman of strength and supreme self-confidence. She was tall—nearly six feet—with prominent features, brown hair, and dark hazel eyes. Giovanni Boldini's portrait of her presents a woman who all but walks from the canvas to command the room. She was one of four daughters of an army engineer breveted to colonel for bravery during the Civil War. Her mother was a direct descendant of the first Dutch governor of New York, Peter Stuyvesant. Edith was twenty-five, clearly independent, and living in Paris with an older, unmarried sister when she married George, who was then thirty-five. The two had spent considerable time together the year before when they saw each other in London at the Jubilee celebration for Queen Victoria. After the event, Edith returned to Paris and George headed to India. He cut his trip east short to return to Paris and proposed marriage to Edith in April. A wedding was announced for June 2, 1898.

As required by French law, they were married first in a civil ceremony in the office of the mayor of a Paris suburb. A well-attended but brief and simple religious ceremony followed the next day at the American Episcopal Church. Afterward, they dined at Edith's modest three-room apartment with a group of friends and family, then left on their honeymoon. They spent the summer in Italy and arrived at Biltmore in the fall with all the estate employees on hand to celebrate their arrival at the château.

Though she was raised in New York and Newport with no knowledge of the southern Appalachians, she came to share her husband's appreciation of the North Carolina mountains and the people who lived there. The two covered the farther reaches of the estate together on horseback, often stopping at remote cabins to purchase homespun fabrics that she shared with her society friends.[4] A yellow gown she fashioned from one selection created a brief "homespun fad" in New York City.[5]

Edith was friendly and approachable. Every worker on the estate and members of their families saw her at least once a year at the traditional Christmas party when her husband distributed presents from under the Biltmore tree. Preparations began in October, with Edith circulating among the farm families to update the names and ages of children so that each would have a gift. Some years she personally selected more than fifteen hundred presents for employees, former employees, and their families; saw that they were wrapped; and stashed them safely in one of the tower rooms until Christmas Day.[6]

She took a deep interest in the greater Biltmore community, where she was recognized more often than her husband. In 1906, when a fire broke out at a lumber mill just off the estate, she offered the estate's water supply to the firefighters, then stood by until the blaze was extinguished. Social programs sponsored by All Souls Church received Edith's special attention. With the Vanderbilts paying the church's regular bills, including the rector's handsome salary of $4,000 a year, Dr. Rodney R. Swope had at his disposal all the money collected at Sunday services where George himself passed the plate when he was in attendance.

All Souls' outreach included a ten-bed medical clinic that Vanderbilt endowed and named in honor of his late cousin and close friend, Clarence Barker. It was run under the watchful eye of the Vanderbilts' Asheville physician, Dr. Samuel Westray Battle. Swope supervised the Young Men's Institute, a Vanderbilt-sponsored educational and recreational facility he had built for the city's African American men, and he saw that Sunday school classes were provided for both black and white children. For eight years until public schools were established, the All Souls School conducted classes for as many as sixty children, including Cornelia. Edith had a farm wagon outfitted with seats and filled with hay to carry children four miles from the estate to the schoolhouse in the village.

The health and welfare of mountain families, especially women, most concerned Edith. She distributed maternity baskets that included items necessary for the care and comfort of mother and baby. With tact and diplomacy, she engaged women in talks about proper diet and child care. To encourage better health habits, she presented prizes to workers whose personal gardens produced the greatest variety of vegetables.[7] Recipients of her attention were gracious but also stubborn. She once bought a stove for a family she found huddled around a fireplace that filled the cabin with smoke only to return later to find the stove standing unused in a corner. She asked if there had been a problem. In reply, one of the elders told her, "If we had put in that thar stove, we would a had no whar to spit."[8]

Her work and that of her husband were closely aligned with the Social Gospel movement, which was a common theme of the sermons delivered by Swope from the All Souls pulpit. The movement's work was most often directed at relieving the distressing conditions of life in U.S. cities but was easily adapted to the conditions in the southern Appalachians, where Edith encouraged efforts to promote self-sufficiency among the poor. She supported a school to train young black women as domestic help and later lent her name to the so-called moonlight schools. This early effort at adult literacy utilized rural schoolhouses to which students were said to find their way once a month by the light of the full moon. One of these night schools was established in Biltmore Village for workers on the estate. Perhaps the most lasting contribution was Edith's investment in the work of Charlotte Yale and Eleanor Vance, with whom she created Biltmore Estate Industries.

Yale and Vance had already started a program for boys under All Souls sponsorship when they met Edith. The two were graduates of Moody Bible Institute in Chicago and arrived in Biltmore in 1901 inspired by Jane Addams's work at her Chicago Settlement Houses. With their own cottage as a classroom, the women created a school for boys, who learned the art of woodworking—a skill Yale and Vance hoped would grow into a sustainable source of income for their students. They began with a dozen students, and in four years the number had increased to twenty boys and girls. In time, the carvers became as accomplished as their teachers and were turning out bowls and picture frames that proved to be popular items for sale to tourists.

In 1907, the woodworking expanded into cabinetmaking. That same year, Edith encouraged Yale and Vance to experiment with dyeing and weaving with all wool instead of a blend of cotton and wool. To improve their skills, she paid their way to the British Isles—the ancestral home of many mountain folk—to study the work and styles of weavers there. They returned with a model for a loom that was duplicated by Biltmore woodworkers. Within a few years, Biltmore homespun was known around the country for its quality craftsmanship.

By 1916, Yale and Vance had moved on, and the demands of Biltmore Estate Industries were becoming more than Edith could support in the wake of her husband's death. Though the business had grown to eight looms, weavers still were unable to fill all orders. The carvers' walnut and mahogany items now included furniture, and all the products sold well at the shop in the village. More work space was needed when Edith faced even more troubling challenges in the summer of 1916.

Before dawn on the morning of July 16, the Swannanoa River began rising rapidly. Storms spawned by a hurricane out of the Gulf of Mexico soaked the mountains with rain. Creeks and rivers swelled to flood levels. This heavy weather passed and the streams had receded when more rain arrived a few days later boosted by an Atlantic hurricane that came ashore at Charleston. This second storm dropped more rain than the waterways could handle. Normally, the Swannanoa's excess would be absorbed by the French

Broad, but broken dams upstream turned the usually placid stream into a torrent filled with all manner of debris. When the Asheville bridge over the French Broad that held the measuring gage finally gave way, the river was nineteen feet over flood stage.

Biltmore Village lay in the floodplain just upstream from the confluence of the Swannanoa and the French Broad. Periodic flooding had always been a problem. Eight years earlier, a group of Biltmore workers, along with their horses and mules, barely escaped serious injury or death after the estate's ferry across the French Broad broke loose and overturned in rising water. The 1916 flood was the worst in years. Homes and shops were swept away, and the river inundated businesses and factories in the bottomland of the French Broad at Asheville. The city was isolated and dark. Generators at the power plants were awash. Rail service would be disrupted for weeks due to washed-out track and trestles. Altogether, about eighty people in western North Carolina lost their lives. The damage at Asheville alone was estimated at a million dollars.

Edith and Cornelia, a teenager at the time and a student at Miss Madeira's School in Washington, D.C., were at Biltmore for the summer when the storm hit and the flooded Swannanoa cut off access to Asheville. The flooded river swelled to nearly a mile wide to fill the Biltmore floodplain. As the waters receded, Edith pitched in where she could. She helped direct the search for bodies and sent food and clothing to those in need. Her limousine carried the bodies of three of the dead to the funeral parlor. Later, flowers from the estate's gardens were sent to cover the caskets.

Among the victims was James Lipe, Biltmore's superintendent of skilled labor, who had clung for hours with his daughters to a tree beside the Lodge Gate until he was swept away by waters that had risen nine feet above the roadway. Three people whom Lipe tried to save died as well.[9] His house, owned by the estate, stood long enough for a photographer to capture a picture of it surrounded by rushing water before it collapsed into the river and was carried away.

Edith and Cornelia with their mounts at the edge of the South Terrace in about 1917.

For Edith, the most costly loss was the estate's nursery and greenhouses located on the Swannanoa's north bank. The nursery was one of the first profitable components of the estate—bringing in $150,000 in good years—and it had grown in importance as a respected source of plants for the nation's gardeners. The details of plant material printed in the sales catalog—a 189-page hardcover book—were so complete that some botanists used it as a text in their classrooms. By the time the Swannanoa returned to its banks, the nursery buildings, greenhouses, and thousands upon thousands of plants were gone.

Flooded, too, were the workshops and retail store for Biltmore Estate Industries. A year after the flood, Edith sold the company to Fred L. Seely, who managed the Grove Park Inn for his father-in-law, E. W. Grove. Seely moved the business to a new, enlarged work space on the grounds of the hotel and resumed operation under a new name, Biltmore Industries.

The flood only compounded Edith's concern for the future of the estate, which her husband had left in the care of her and his brother, William, as trustees for Cornelia until she reached the age of twenty-five. The family clearly was not destitute, but the millions George Vanderbilt was reported to have on call simply were not there at the time of his death. He had borrowed heavily on a $1 million life insurance policy and still owed $65,000 on the house in Washington. Altogether, not counting the property in North Carolina, Vanderbilt's net worth was less than a million dollars, not the $20 or $50 million widely reported in 1914. When she came of age, Cornelia stood to inherit Biltmore, as well as $5 million from her grandfather's estate. But the $250,000 left to Edith in her husband's will had to be reduced by a third, along with all the other bequests that altogether totaled more than $1.2 million.[10]

Biltmore had never succeeded to George Vanderbilt's dream of self-sufficiency, which was made all the more difficult after his death with the imposition of federal income taxes. What had always been a luxury now was even more so. The estate's annual demand for cash was daunting. As many as five hundred people, including entire families, lived and worked on fourteen thousand acres of Vanderbilt land that straddled the French Broad River south of Asheville. Just beyond the luscious deer park and open woodlands that surrounded the house lay hundreds of acres of bottomland in cultivation with corn, silage, and grain that fed Biltmore's Jersey herd of more than 250 cows. Tenant farmers and their wives and children performed the twice-daily milkings at barns on both sides of the river. Farmers west of the river ferried their milk across the French Broad to a creamery near the main dairy barn with its distinctive clock tower.

More tenant farmers grew produce for the house and families on the estate with the extra yield going for sale at local markets. Other departments—the place was organized like a corporation—maintained the network of roads and tended the livestock. And then there was the considerable staff at the house. Maids, butlers and their assistants, cooks and their helpers, gardeners, and stable boys kept the place in order. There was even a police force; the rangers patrolling the property for poachers and trespassers were sworn deputy sheriffs.

The estate could survive only if Edith could find a way for it to pay for itself. With the income from the nursery gone, the trustees asked Junius G. Adams, an Asheville lawyer, to advise them on how to reduce expenses. Adams returned with a proposal to sell limited amounts of peripheral land to raise quick cash. The sales would reduce the estate's annual tax bill and capitalize on the growing demand for real estate in Asheville. He reported that a large tract on the estate's eastern boundary along Hendersonville Road would make a fine residential park, much like the one that E. W. Grove was building on the north side of Asheville near his popular hotel, the Grove Park Inn. He also urged the trustees to sell the two hundred acres of nursery property to the Southern Railway Company, which wanted to expand its rail yards.

The trustees made a deal with Southern Railway, which began building a new rail yard in 1917 just as the United States prepared to enter World War I. Fifty-three men from the estate marched off to Europe. Three never returned. Further land sales would have to wait as the nation's attention shifted to the war.

One of the footnotes to the war in Europe was the change in the traveling habits of wealthy Americans. Since submarine warfare had made Atlantic crossings dangerous, the rich exchanged their annual visits to European spas for luxurious hotels that had opened along Florida's east coast. They followed Henry Flagler's railroad south as it reached St. Augustine, then Palm Beach, and finally Miami. Asheville, too, had seen a steady growth in business from continent-bound tourists and seasonal residents. Immediately popular upon its opening in 1913 was the Grove Park Inn with its distinctive undulating red-tile roof and walls fashioned from huge boulders. Built by the St. Louis millionaire E. W. Grove, the hotel sat near the foot of Sunset Mountain and offered comfortable accommodations from spring through fall.

The new visitors were looking for relaxation and pleasure, and the city responded to the demand, eagerly shedding its reputation as a retreat for consumptives. Early advertising at the Grove Park impressed people that the hotel was not a hospital or a health resort, although they noted that silverware was boiled twice and even the coins in the register had been sanitized. As many as 250,000 visitors found Asheville in the summer of 1920. The Grove Park and the rental homes in the surrounding neighborhood were such favorites among North Carolinians that it often was easier to conduct state business along the five hundred feet of terraces at the hotel than in Raleigh.

North Carolina was emerging from an economic recession in 1920 when Edith Vanderbilt renewed her efforts to undergird the financial condition at the estate. That spring, George Stephens, a real estate developer who had recently completed the fashionable Myers Park subdivision in Charlotte, North Carolina, where James B. Duke had built a mansion, paid the estate a reported $500,000 for Biltmore Village, buying everything except the church, a two-story office building containing the estate's business offices, and the small hospital established by George Vanderbilt.

A few months later, in June, Edith pursued Adams's earlier advice and sold a well-placed fifteen hundred–acre tract extending from the estate's Lodge Gate south along Hendersonville Road. The trustees entered into a joint venture with a real estate syndicate that included Adams and Asheville businessman Thomas Wadley Raoul. Other investors included William A. Knight, a golfer and retired businessman from St. Augustine, Florida; and Burnham S. Colburn of Detroit, who was a retired director of the Canadian Bridge Company and a director in an Asheville bank in which Adams had an interest.

News of the sale squelched rumors that the château itself was to be sold and converted into a hotel.[11] Actually, that was never an option. The house remained a favorite retreat for Edith, who divided her time between Washington, D.C., and Asheville. Guests were often around the house from spring until fall. Edith even added an outdoor swimming pool on the South Terrace beside the library, where in earlier years the grassy surface was suitable for bowling. Fed by the estate's mountain reservoir, the water in the pool was stunningly cold even in the heat of summer. She seldom failed to be on hand at Christmas to continue the holiday tradition of gifts for all that had been started by her husband.

The developers announced plans for a residential park, which they soon named Biltmore Forest. They set out a subdivision of some small lots but mostly large plots—many were at least two acres, and the average was five—for a prospective clientele of lawyers, doctors, businessmen, and professional people. "Biltmore Forest is not a city," said a promotional brochure. "Neither is it a suburb. It is a sanctuary for the retired business man and the active leaders of the professions and of industry who wish to escape . . . the tumult, unsightliness and neurotic life of the modern city." Houses were to cost at least $15,000, nearly five times what an average homeowner paid for a comfortable bungalow in a North Carolina city.

Lots carved out of the heavily forested tract lined the fairways of a golf course designed by Donald Ross, the man who had helped Leonard Tufts turn his Pinehurst, North Carolina, resort into the golfing mecca of the South. A handsome clubhouse was built at the edge of the course. Over the years, a rumor gained sufficient currency that Edith had built the country club so that she could enjoy her cigarettes without the disdain of other ladies, but it held no substance. Biltmore Forest was strictly a business proposition.

The cache of Biltmore extended throughout the development. The roadways and grounds of Biltmore Forest were designed by Chauncey D. Beadle, Olmsted's protégé and estate superintendent at Biltmore. New homes were to be supplied with water from the estate's own supply of nearby Busbee Mountain. As a demonstration of their faith in the venture, the principal investors were among the first to erect houses along Stuyvesant Road, one of the development's major thoroughfares.

Adams and Raoul were in Edith's entourage when she arrived in Raleigh in February 1921 to address the General Assembly. Both men, as well as Stephens, were well connected politically and undoubtedly played a part in the arrangements for her Raleigh debut. Adams had served a term as a municipal judge before the war, and his law firm was one of the best known in the city. Raoul's father had been president of two major railroads before he had turned a thirty-two-acre farm on the north side of Asheville into the popular resort called the English Inn in America. This picturesque hotel was known as the Manor and preceded the Grove Park as a preferred hotel for wealthy and prominent visitors to Asheville. At least part of his share in the new venture came from his sale of the Manor to Grove just weeks before plans for Biltmore Forest were unveiled.[12] In addition to Stephens's interest in real estate, he was a founding director of the American Trust Company in Charlotte and a part owner of the *Asheville Citizen*. As a trustee of the University of North Carolina, he was a member of one of the most influential political bodies in the state.

While these three ushered Edith into North Carolina politics, once introduced, she fearlessly and enthusiastically set her own course. She told the members of the General Assembly—including the state House's first female member, Asheville's Lilian Exum Clement—that women should play a greater role in public affairs. From there she waltzed right into the biggest political fight of the legislative session by endorsing Governor Morrison's ambitious new road-building program. Charm, grace, and celebrity carried her a long way that day.

Her new state job was not window dressing; Edith came honestly to her election as leader of the state fair. Her husband's close friend and the estate's first manager, Charles McNamee, had presided over the agricultural association at the turn of the century. Now, Edith was the mistress of one of the largest agricultural enterprises in western North Carolina that over the preceding two decades had literally raised the standards of agriculture in the region. George Vanderbilt had sold his hogs and poultry at local markets for less than their full value, knowing that each sale helped improve the overall quality of local stock. His dairy herd of champion Jerseys was known around the country. The year before Vanderbilt died, one of Biltmore's Jerseys, Kola's Catherine, broke a world record for milk production. Even the produce from Biltmore farms altered local habits. Competitors started paying more attention to the presentation of produce they took to market after they found the estate vegetables tied with raffia instead of strips of dirty cloth. In addition, Edith had earned a reputation as a leader in the revival of native crafts. The weavers and woodworkers at Biltmore Industries were considered artists.

For those eager to spruce up the state's farm showcase, Edith was a superb choice. Her name alone was sufficient to make citizens take notice. Some also quietly expressed hope that she would match her interest in agriculture with some dollars to rehabilitate the state fairgrounds just outside of Raleigh, which had not seen any improvements since 1873.

Edith entered public life as North Carolina was being transformed from a state of small towns and farms into one of the most industrialized states in the South. Textile mills and tobacco factories were running full tilt in Durham, Greensboro, Charlotte, and Winston-Salem, where local boosters began to erect tall buildings and build residential areas called suburbs. Governor Morrison got his road money, and new concrete highways began connecting once-isolated municipalities, creating new business for the merchants and bankers on Main Street. A hard-surface, cross-state highway was planned to connect Asheville with the coast, and other routes were planned to ensure that tourists traveling north and south had ample opportunity to stop and visit.

Edith's endorsement of the governor's program added a fresh, exciting edge to Morrison's bold plans. She was talented, poised, and progressive. Her feminism undoubtedly shocked some old-timers in Raleigh who still referred to one another by their Civil War rank. She enthusiastically embraced her new duties and began paying call on counties from the mountains to the coast, traveling whenever possible by automobile. (She would later be elected president of the North Carolina Motor Club, the forerunner to the American Automobile Association, or AAA. Her car carried a large chrome AAA emblem on the front.) Ladies in Charlotte flocked to hear her promote the virtues of Biltmore homespun at a Made-in-Carolinas exhibition. She gave the opening address at a statewide conference on drainage convened in eastern North Carolina and made one of the first broadcasts over the fledgling radio station at the North Carolina State College campus. She attended county fairs and supported the creation of agricultural clubs for boys and girls—a forerunner of the latter-day 4-H clubs—as a way to develop a new generation of farmers. Biltmore's farm manager, A. S. Wheeler, took charge of the Buncombe County clubs, and once a year the youngsters were invited to Biltmore for a celebration.

Edith encouraged all manner of experimentation at Biltmore, from a potato crop planted to follow the market after the harvests farther south to the mining of various types of clay for use in the making of ceramics. At one point, she tinkered with production of a perfume.[13]

The state fair took on a new shine. She introduced a society horse show in 1921, and the following year a half-mile racetrack was opened. At her direction, games of chance and the sale of trinkets were banned from the midway and replaced with a broad range of new exhibits, from the state's coastal fisheries to apples and other fruit products harvested at the western end of the state. Exhibits of homespun woolens, pottery, woodcraft, and native arts were added. Displays of flowers and art gave the traditional livestock and produce competition a new dimension. The fair hours were extended into the evening and fireworks produced whopping crowds.

The fair lost money during Edith's first year when sideshows were outlawed, prompting a Raleigh man to complain, "People don't come to the fair to see flower gardens. They come to be humbugged. We do not want to make a Sunday school affair out of it." The courtly secretary of state, General Bryan Grimes, came to Edith's defense, and with Governor Morrison moved for her reelection. At the same meeting, the board approved the issuance of $100,000 in bonds to improve the fairgrounds.[14]

Her position seemed unassailable. "She is no longer merely the richest woman in North Carolina," Mrs. W. T. Bost wrote in the *Greensboro Daily News*, "but is reckoned one of the leading exponents on the development of North Carolina resources, agriculturally and commercially."[15]

More people flocked to the 1922 fair than had been seen since 1905 when President Theodore Roosevelt made an appearance. An exciting attraction was army chief of staff General John J. Pershing, who attended at Edith's invitation.[16] After the fair, Pershing, rumored to be a suitor to Edith, continued on to Biltmore with his uniformed retinue, where Edith entertained the nation's famous military commander. One guest reported later that the general sent junior officers to tap out his hostess's dance partners, who then relinquished her to the general. Another suitor seeking Edith's hand accused the general of cowardice for his deception.[17] One of Pershing's staff who left a calling card behind was Major George C. Marshall Jr. Twenty years later, he would be President Franklin Roosevelt's wartime military leader.

All of Edith's activities expanded the public perception of Biltmore. The château retained its allure as the largest private residence in the United States and the product of a rich man's fancy, but Vanderbilt's broader intentions for Biltmore as a productive, thriving agricultural enterprise now became more evident. Edith succeeded in carrying Biltmore beyond what her husband had seen in his day.

In 1924, she entertained delegates to an Asheville conference on waterpower and displayed an engineering study for a dam and hydroelectric plant on Biltmore land that would draw power from the French Broad. (The dam and the power plant were never built.)

Cornelia Vanderbilt found it difficult not to be swept up in her mother's wake. She had long been in the public eye and gamely but reluctantly fulfilled her role. She was still a child when her mother drafted her to lead a group of sixty Asheville and Buncombe County Civil War veterans in a parade through the estate. When her mother hosted a display of new Fordson tractors on the estate in 1918, Cornelia posed dutifully beside one of the new machines while her mother sat behind the steering wheel.

She was slender and tall like her mother. She had her father's dark hair and fine features, from long, delicate fingers to a deep chin and large, rather sad eyes. Most of her early childhood and schooling was at Biltmore or with tutors in Europe. When the family finally settled in Washington, D.C., she was enrolled at Miss Madeira's School, where she was remembered more for her shiny shoes than her grades or deportment. (She was warned once to leave her colorful argyle socks at home.) She placed well in French but performed poorly in most other subjects. Her graduation yearbook included a quotation from William Wordsworth: "Bliss it was in that dawn to be alive, but 'twas very heaven to be young."[18]

As a teenager in Asheville, Cornelia was lively and sociable. One summer, Robert Bunn saw an unattached young woman at a dance at the Manor—he didn't know it was Cornelia—and asked her to be his partner. "She was an excellent dancer. She was tall, real light on her feet and I was a pretty good sort of dancer. . . . And so, we danced right off and we had a good big dance before someone broke [in]."[19] Another who met her followed up with a passionate love letter.

Cornelia turned her talents to a variety of local projects, including a fund-raising event for Biltmore Hospital, the former Barker Memorial Hospital and Dispensary that had been opened by her father. In the early 1920s, she conceived the idea of a big gala and arranged for New York's Guy Lombardo Orchestra to be on hand for an evening at the Biltmore Forest Country Club.[20] Subsequent galas followed with mother and daughter joining in the painting of scenery for an event that raised as much as $15,000 a year. Cornelia enjoyed the outdoors, especially horses, and played polo and grew increasingly fond of art.

While Edith was called the richest woman in North Carolina, Cornelia's $5 million trust plus her claim to the estate made her clearly more substantial financially. She was obviously an inviting catch for an eligible bachelor, and after mother and daughter returned in 1924 from a trip to the Far East, they appeared to have found a suitable mate. He was John Francis Amherst Cecil, an Englishman who had only recently been posted to the British Embassy in Washington. The engagement was announced at a grand party at Biltmore in early March. The wedding was scheduled for a few weeks later on April 29, 1924.

The Cecils had been part of the English nobility since Queen Elizabeth I conferred the title of Lord Burghley on John's distant ancestor, William Cecil. John was one of four sons of another Lord William Cecil and third in line to the title. After finishing at Eton and Oxford, he joined the diplomatic corps and was assigned to Cairo, where a decade earlier his mother had traveled and studied. (She published *Bird Notes of the Nile* in 1904.) When England entered the war in 1914, John lost a coin toss with Anthony Eden (later Britain's prime minister), who was another junior member of the staff, and he remained behind in Egypt while Eden left to join

John Francis Amherst Cecil, an Englishman, was posted to the British Embassy in Washington, D.C., when he gave up a diplomatic career to marry Cornelia Vanderbilt.

a regiment. Cecil's service with the British Foreign Office continued in Madrid and then Prague until September 1923 when he was sent to Washington as first secretary. He was thirty-three years old.

Cecil was the proper English gentleman. Because he was the third son and the family title was destined for an older brother, he had chosen a diplomatic career. He was slightly balding, with a high forehead, a full, round face, and an ample dark mustache. He stood taller than six feet. His height and fully lidded eyes gave him an air of British coolness when in fact he was warm, friendly, and sociable. His friends called him Jack.

Almost ten years older than Cornelia, Cecil seemed a perfect choice to Edith, who was due to hand over full ownership of Biltmore to her daughter within the year. Cecil had grown up at Didlington, his family's estate east of Cambridge, and had some passing knowledge of the management of a large property, although his interests ran more to sport than farming. He was a fine shot, and on the eve of his marriage, estate workers gave him a complete set of fishing gear from the New York outfitters Abercrombie and Fitch. On his wedding day, he resigned his post with the British Foreign Office and said he planned to take a hand in the management of Biltmore, where he expected to spend the rest of his days.

The nuptials reflected Edith's long standing as a Washington hostess. Invitations for the wedding went out to President Calvin Coolidge and former president William Howard Taft, who was now chief justice of the Supreme Court. Sons of two former presidents, Robert Todd Lincoln and Theodore Roosevelt Jr., were on the list, as was Edith's old beau, General Pershing. Governor Cameron Morrison, another former suitor, would arrive with his new bride, the wealthy widow of George W. Watts of Durham. The largest group on the guest list—outside of the extended Vanderbilt family, of course—were members of the diplomatic corps, including Spanish ambassador Don Juan Riano, who had served as an honorary pallbearer for George Vanderbilt. The lineup of other nations included representatives from France, Great Britain, Italy, Egypt, China, Portugal, Denmark, tiny Romania, and, of course, Great Britain.

Asheville was absolutely giddy with anticipation. The president and first lady didn't attend, nor did Taft, Lincoln, Roosevelt, or Pershing. But there were enough Vanderbilts and European titles to impress. Guests were apportioned out to the Grove Park Inn, the Biltmore Forest Country Club, and the Kenilworth Inn. Forty-three stayed at Biltmore, where the Vestibule, Raphael, Earlom, and Sheraton rooms were redecorated for the occasion.

Well before the noontime ceremonies at All Souls Church, the streets of the village and the lawn outside the Lodge Gate filled with onlookers. A large wedding party and guests squeezed into the

Cornelia Vanderbilt and John Cecil were married at All Souls Church on April 29, 1924.

small sanctuary, where only 160 could be seated comfortably. Pews in the transepts were reserved for staff from the estate and Biltmore Hospital. The *Asheville Citizen* noted that one seat was saved for "Old Frank," the gatekeeper and a Biltmore employee for twenty-seven years. Edith sent him a new coat and ordered up a car to drive him to the church, which stood within a few hundred yards of his post in the Lodge Gate.[21] Cornelia's veil included blossoms from Chauncey Beadle's orange trees in Florida.

*   *   *

The Cecils honeymooned in Europe and returned to Biltmore in mid-August. Edith arrived from Europe a few weeks later. Reporters who greeted her in New York heard her tell the customs agent that she was "a plain farm woman." "I have no interest in society," she told reporters. "I would much rather live on a farm. I have been operating a dairy upon our estate since my husband's death. It seems to me that the next development in social life in America will be country life like that in England."[22]

Her declarations suggested a settled life in the dower house she was building in Biltmore Forest. Called the Frith—meaning "peace" or an "open space in the woods"—her new home of stucco was more Mediterranean than mountain and was the work of her Palm Beach architect, Bruce Kitchell, a protégé of Addison Mizner. A year later, Edith remarried; her husband was U.S. Senator Peter G. Gerry of Rhode Island. The religious ceremonies took place at Savoy Chapel of St. Martin-in-the-Field on Trafalgar Square with her daughter and son-in-law on hand.

Gerry was the great-grandson of Elbridge Gerry, a signer of the Declaration of Independence and vice president under President James Madison. Peter Gerry had served in the U.S. House of Representatives, lost his seat, and won election to the Senate in 1916. He was a Harvard-trained lawyer and wealthy in his own right. His marriage to Edith came within months of his divorce from a Washington, D.C., socialite. The union effectively ended Edith's immersion in North Carolina public affairs. She soon shifted her attention to Washington and to the affairs of her husband's home state, where he was up for reelection in 1928.

Edith's remarriage ended ten years of active participation in North Carolina. During that time, she had swept across the state, making friends and promoting agriculture, women's political participation, and Biltmore. She now devoted her attention to her husband and his political career.

The Cecils, on the right, with friends at the château in about 1925. Cornelia's twenty-fifth birthday party included three hundred guests.

The Cecils settled into life at Biltmore. John joined the Asheville Rotary Club and took up responsibilities as a member of the vestry at All Souls. Cornelia chaired the annual benefit for the hospital and played polo on a horse she named Commodore. Once again, the château became a family residence after the Cecils' son, George Henry Vanderbilt, was born on February 26, 1925. A second son, William Amherst Vanderbilt, was born on August 17, 1928. Both were delivered in the Louis XV room over her father's library, where Cornelia herself had been born.

The Louis XV room on the southeast corner was Edith Gerry's old bedroom. It is an airy, spacious, elegant chamber with an ivory and crimson wall covering of cut and uncut silk velvet and a mantle of white marble. Floor-to-ceiling windows on the south side provide an unobstructed view of the mountains beyond. On the east side, French doors open onto a shallow balcony, giving a full view of the esplanade below. William's delivery had been planned for the hospital, but when Cornelia went into labor, the Swannanoa was again in flood, and the estate was cut off from Asheville. As a result, William greeted life at Biltmore.

The inflated stock market of the mid-1920s fattened the portfolio held on Cornelia's behalf and enabled a life for the Cecils much like the one her father had enjoyed in his early days at Biltmore. The house was full of servants and activity. The Cecils often spent summer days at Buck Spring Lodge, where the air was refreshingly cool and the views as magnificent as any spot in the range.

In time, the Cecils also bought a home just off Connecticut Avenue in Washington, D.C. They both had friends there, and city living was an antidote to Biltmore's isolation, especially in winter when the big house was cold and damp. Even in the shoulder seasons, guests were forewarned about chilly nights. One year, some of the men at a costume party donned wool bathing suits under their outfits in an effort to be comfortable. As it turned out, the party was held in the basement near the château's huge boilers, where Cornelia and her friends painted the walls of the otherwise dark and inelegant chamber with images of characters from Alexander Pushkin's fairy tales. The room was so warm that those with extra clothing wished they had not come so prepared.

Construction of the Frith was completed just before the Asheville land boom reached its peak in 1926. The state's new roads had produced as expected; people were flocking to Asheville to buy a piece of the "Land of the Sky." Speculators had enjoyed a breathless run by selling lots in new subdivisions that sprouted like daisies north, east, and south of the city. During one 240-day period, the Kenilworth Company sold 283 homesites. Some homeowners never bothered to get comfortable in their new houses because they knew they were going to buy a bigger one sometime soon. Virtually everything was for sale. Two hundred thirty acres of an abandoned quarry on Sunset Mountain brought $7,000 an acre.

Boom times consumed the area. In downtown Asheville, E. W. Grove demolished the Battery Park Hotel, took seventy feet off the hill where it had stood, and put up a solid but unremarkable replacement made of brick. Directly in front, on new land created by the excavation, he built a commercial arcade that filled an entire city block. Plans called for it to be topped with a nineteen-story tower with space for offices and apartments. Scores of other new buildings were under construction nearby. The Jackson Building, a fifteen-story skyscraper, went up on the spot where Thomas Wolfe's father had once carved tombstones in a small building on Pack Square.

In 1921, a motion picture crew had taken over Pack Square to film a version of Booth Tarkington's novel *The Conquest of Canaan*. Locals scrambled for bit parts and jobs as extras while the stars lounged away their off hours on the veranda of the Grove Park Inn. Tarkington's story was well suited for the boosters' spirit of this mountain city. The hero is a small-town young lawyer who made good against great odds. The movie never captured the hearts of Americans, but it added to Asheville's luster as a city on the rise.

Folks just felt good about the future. Promoters figured it would be easy to convince a number of the hundreds of thousands of visitors to stay, and they did. During the 1920s, Asheville's population grew to more than fifty thousand, with a 79 percent increase between 1920 and 1928. Some said Asheville was on its way to rivaling Richmond or Atlanta.[23] City and county voters increased local bonded indebtedness tenfold—from $5 million to $56 million—to raise money to pay for a new city hall, county courthouse, high school, minor-league ball stadium, and extension of water and sewer lines to subdivisions that existed only on paper planned for miles out in the countryside. All told, Asheville's civic borrowing amounted to one-tenth of the bond debt of all one hundred North Carolina counties.

One of the liveliest promoters was J. T. Horney. In the summer of 1924, he offered a $250 cash prize for the person who came up with the best name for his latest development. Horney announced in his ads that he was so busy preparing the land and selling lots that he didn't have time to come up with a name on his own. "The tall trees, the wonderful effect of the broad, winding drives. To give it full justice, it must be seen," he declared.[24]

When Grove grew weary of selling expensive property near his hotel, he bought land east of Asheville near Swannanoa and began selling building lots that could be had for as little as $1,000. Buyers paid $250 down and promised the rest over four years. "I have heard it said," Grove announced in print, "that the subdivision business in Asheville was being overdone. In my opinion, men who take this view . . . do not stop to estimate the very large territory and millions of people Asheville has to draw from to build summer homes."

Promoters became absolutely lyrical in their efforts to entice buyers to what boosters called the "playground of America." One ad paid for by twenty-eight real estate agencies said, "Romance has been stirred in the breasts of thousands of people as they stopped their cars on the Dixie Highway along the shore of Beaver Lake and sat on the wide verandahs of the Tea House on the river, overlooking the beautiful sheet of water with the silver glint on the rippling surface as the moon emerges from the fleecy clouds or shines in its soft radiance from a clear sky over the mountain tops."[25]

Tourists came to play golf or tennis, swim in more than forty-five man-made lakes, ride horseback through miles of trails in Pisgah National Forest, or simply marvel at the high peaks, deep forests, and rushing mountain streams. So many Floridians crowded into nearby Hendersonville one summer that a candidate for governor from their home state showed up for a political rally.

"I just thought the boom was going to carry on forever," Frank Coxe said some years later. "And so did all of us and we carried right on, and we would buy and sell, and we would make obligations. We wouldn't see how we were going to take care of them, except we knew we would sell the property. Then, all of a sudden, you couldn't sell the property, when the thing stopped right in mid-air."[26]

The overheated real estate market was on the wane by 1927. Six-room bungalows that once rented for $125 a week could be had for $18 and $20. Barbecue became "free as water" as real estate promoters tried to draw crowds.[27] The city organized a Rhododendron Festival and Mountain Dance and Folk Festival to attract attention. As speculators ran out of new customers to meet their own financial obligations, they simply transferred their problems to banks, which had overextended credit. Asheville's financial base began to crumble, and insiders did what they could to minimize the damage. By 1929, western North Carolina's largest bank, Asheville's Central Bank and Trust Company, was declared insolvent by state examiners. Political influence kept the news from the public, however, and local officials used deposits of tax money to stave off outright collapse.

Even Edith Gerry's ambitions for the North Carolina State Fair turned sour. The new racetrack failed to pay its own way, and some of the notes cosigned by her to underwrite construction came due. The association had to sell its property to regain solvency and was folded into state government as part of the State Department of Agriculture.

In Asheville, one of the casualties was Biltmore Forest. Sales had gone well at first; more than a hundred homes were built. The development had never met expectations, however. After the first year, Junius Adams and the others prevailed on Edith for more of Cornelia's cash to complete construction of the clubhouse. They also trimmed their ambitions. A portion of the land was returned to the estate, and they put plans for a hotel on hold. When the bottom fell out entirely, ownership reverted to the Vanderbilt interests, who were left with unsold lots, the burden of operating a golf course and a country club, and strained relationships. Biltmore Forest was sufficiently weakened by 1929 that even the developers' considerable political muscle couldn't prevent annexation into Asheville as the city scrambled for new tax revenue.

It was an awkward time for everyone, especially Junius G. Adams. He had acquired a modest fortune during the heady days and was the president of a local bank. His new home in Biltmore Forest was a handsome Tudor-style that sat right on the golf course. As the financial and real estate markets collapsed, he scrambled to hang on to what he could, but his lucrative gains dwindled along with the rest of those who had held such high hopes for profits from the development of Biltmore Forest. A crowning blow came in 1929 when Adams was relieved of duties as mayor of Biltmore Forest.

Yet Adams would emerge in the coming years as the Vanderbilt family's most important and influential local retainer. In time, he would become the master of Biltmore Estate and run it like his own barony with virtually unquestioned authority. No other non-family member would do more to shape the future of the property as he continued Edith's transformation of an insulated private experiment in old-world living into a profitable financial enterprise.

CHAPTER 4

Judge Adams

When Cornelia and John Cecil opened Biltmore to the public in 1930, people were told that the couple had been prompted by civic duty and had answered the call of the Asheville Chamber of Commerce with hopes that the attraction would give a much-needed boost to the city's ailing tourist business. Indeed, there had been a plea from the chamber, and there was no question Asheville's financial future was uncertain. But so was Biltmore's.

In truth, the entire transaction was a delicate production orchestrated by Edith Vanderbilt Gerry's attorney, Junius G. Adams of Asheville. The chamber request relieved the family of any embarrassment that might accompany news that, in need of ready cash, George Vanderbilt's château and gardens had been turned into a tourist attraction. It was a business deal, plain and simple, with the chamber agreeing to underwrite the advertising expenses for the venture. At any rate, the story made good newspaper copy, the city's reputation as a resort town was burnished, and the Cecils had a new revenue stream to help defray the costs of maintaining the huge residence. Adams repeated the account of the family's generosity as litany, and the chamber's role became an established part of estate lore.

The arrangement was probably the best that Edith could manage under the circumstances. With the stock market in shambles and the Biltmore Forest developers in default, an annual maintenance bill of upward of $125,000 challenged even the resources of a Vanderbilt. Taxes alone amounted to more than $50,000 a year. Any income provided welcome relief.

For all her efforts since her husband's death, Edith had been unable to turn a profit from the Biltmore farming operations. The dairy was the one department that she had counted on to pay the bills, but it did not produce enough cash to sustain itself. There was some revenue from timber sales, but the most daunting problem was the burden of Biltmore's own heritage as a millionaire's experiment in grand country living. There was scant allegiance to the profit motive from managers who had never been penalized for losing money year after year. Aside from a few ads in the local paper and a glorious float prepared for seasonal parades, no one at the dairy went in search of new customers. Delivery routes simply evolved as customers presented themselves. Striving commercialism seemed out of place for the grandest house in the land, regardless of the fact that it had been built from the bounty of American capitalism.

Casual visitors to the estate probably did not understand the difficulties facing the family. Edith's fortune and that of her daughter had always been vastly overstated in the newspapers, and certain appearances were maintained. For any that caught sight of Vanderbilt's fabulous château before 1930, it looked much as it always had. Edith had made only modest changes since her husband's death, such as the installation of the outdoor swimming pool and a large canopy over the front terrace off the Winter Garden. Otherwise, the house appeared to be aging gracefully. It was all a facade, of course, and didn't accurately reflect conditions inside.

Biltmore's interior was losing its shine. Woodwork and leather once oiled and cleaned regularly by a large household staff was dry, cracked, and in need of attention. The upholstery was worn, faded, and, in some cases, in tatters. Draperies that had hung in place for more than thirty years were dusty and faded, and the rugs were frayed. Some rooms had been locked for decades and were used mainly as storage for unused and broken furniture, extra rugs, and the general detritus of an old house. On the last grand occasion—Cornelia's wedding in 1924—Edith had to overhaul entire rooms in order to make them presentable to her guests. Since then, entire sections had been dark. The Cecils spent most of their time in an apartment on the second floor of the Bachelor Wing on the north end, or at the Frith, Edith's home in Biltmore Forest that was far more manageable with a small staff.

A vexing question for Edith was how the estate would fare under the care of her daughter, who was supposed to come into full ownership when she turned twenty-five. If Edith's creative and determined promotion of Biltmore had not produced a profit, it was unlikely that Cornelia would do any better. She had no head for numbers or any inclination to business. Instead, she fancied a career as an artist and a writer. The spring after the house opened in 1930, she and John headed to the Florida Keys for a fishing trip. She then set off to New York and London in pursuit of a publisher for an illustrated children's story about a young girl from Elizabethan England who moves to the Carolinas. Cornelia's husband also was not up to the task. He had proved well suited to the life of a country squire but appeared to be of little help in running an operation the size of Biltmore. There was nothing in his background—Eton, Oxford, and the diplomatic corps—that had prepared him for such a challenge.

These questions and others clouded Biltmore's future. They also may explain why Edith and Frederick Vanderbilt—Cornelia's uncle who shared the trusteeship of Cornelia's inheritance with her mother (he had succeeded to the job upon William K. Vanderbilt's death in 1920)—delayed relinquishing full ownership of the estate to Cornelia for a full four years.

Finally, in the summer of 1929, not long before the wheels began to quietly turn toward opening the house as a tourist attraction, the trustees transferred title to the property to Cornelia. That was not the end of it, however. Over the next several months, Junius Adams negotiated a settlement between the trustees and the Cecils for the house and land to pass into a new corporation called the Biltmore Company. In addition, Cornelia agreed to put $3.8 million of her inheritance in trust to support the estate. In turn, she would take half the shares of Biltmore Company as her own and leave the balance for her sons, George and William.[1]

The negotiations were completed in March 1932, and the Biltmore Company was formally organized. Just before John and Cornelia left for several months in England, John told the *Asheville Citizen* that the changes were simply a more efficient way to manage the estate. Less than two years later, after the couple had gone their separate ways, Cornelia and John met in Paris and agreed to a divorce. Cornelia stayed in Europe with the children, never to see the United States again. John returned to Asheville to make his home at Biltmore.

The new master of Biltmore and the man who would run the estate for the next thirty years was not John Cecil but Junius Adams. His appointment as president of the Biltmore Company formalized a deep, trusting relationship with Edith Gerry that had begun in 1914. It was said that when Edith was in need of an

Asheville attorney Junius G. Adams assumed management of the estate after the Biltmore Company was organized in 1932 with Adams as its president. He lived on the estate at Farmcote, his home that sat within sight of Biltmore's famous dairy.

Asheville lawyer to handle her North Carolina affairs in the wake of her husband's death, she asked her New York counsel, Henry B. Anderson, to compile a list of the local talent. As soon as it was convenient, she invited Anderson's nominees to the château for dinner and an evening of socializing. While the guests focused attention on their hostess, Anderson circulated among the candidates and took a measure of the choices. When they all had departed, he told Edith that Adams was the best of the bunch.[2]

Called "June" by his friends and "Judge" by virtually everyone else, Adams was thirty years old when he received Edith's invitation in 1914. He was a partner in a firm that included his brother, John, and James G. Merrimon, who had replaced the Adamses' father, Joseph, a superior court judge, who had died on the bench in 1911. Junius was just about to complete a term as judge of the Asheville police court, where he was credited with cleaning out a nest of illegal saloons, but the firm's reputation was for its experience with business and civil law. Clients included leading businessmen such as the patent-medicine millionaire E. W. Grove, whose new hotel had just opened on the north side of Asheville.

Adams was a man of exacting thoroughness, precision, and attention to detail, all traits valued in a lawyer. "He never used two words when one would do," one of his friends later recalled.[3] He also was humorless, stern, and impatient with those who questioned his judgment. Years later, long after his era at Biltmore had passed, few of those who knew him related stories of warmth or compassion. He could be verbally abusive, dismissive, and curt. Most Biltmore employees kept their distance because crossing Adams could cost a man his job and a family their very home. Staying on his good side meant a worker's sibling, cousin, or good friend could find a place on the estate. "It was a family," one longtime employee said of that time. "It was just a big family and Mr. Adams would kind of sit in the head chair, and everybody worked."[4]

Adams could be charming to those he wished to impress. Edith enjoyed his unceasing cordiality and deference, and she responded with increasing confidence in his ability to handle delicate matters with finesse and creativity. Their relationship was clearly strong enough to withstand the Biltmore Forest fiasco in the late 1920s when Adams found himself financially indebted to his most important client. Edith's confidence in Adams remained firm through those difficulties. By that time, Adams was clearly the kind of flinty, hard-nosed manager that she needed if Biltmore was to be rescued from financial ruin.

Historic preservation was largely the hobby of amateurs as Adams prepared the château for its public debut in 1930. Most of those who took an interest in old houses were architects, not historians whose attention was focused on documents rather than old buildings. Enthusiastic laymen had met with some success, however. By the 1930s, there were about four hundred historic house museums in the United States, up from about a hundred in 1910. More than a third of them were in New England, although the Jamestown tercentennial in 1907 had ignited the interests of Virginians in protecting the homes of American heroes. The best-known among them was George Washington's home at Mount Vernon, which enjoyed about a half-million visitors a year.[5] Nothing, however, compared to what Adams was attempting with a huge château filled almost to overflowing with a treasure of art, furnishings, and other valuables.

Lacking any solid reference, Adams relied on his instincts and Biltmore's own traditions of grace and good breeding. In other words, if George Vanderbilt were alive, how would he treat those who came to his front door? Wouldn't he expect guests to exercise restraint and proper manners? Wouldn't he expect visitors who would appreciate what was inside? Wouldn't he expect such an exercise to pay for itself?

Given his personality, it is likely that Adams did not dwell long on philosophy. He was a practical man looking for workable solutions. And he had a deadline. With the aid of Herbert Noble, a butler the Cecils had sent south from Washington, D.C., to manage the house, Adams laid out a walking tour through the house that kept visitors contained to the areas most easily policed and accessible to the front door. He took tickets that had been issued for years to admit visitors to the grounds and made adjustments to include the house as well as the gardens. The admission price? If it had cost $1.50 to see the estate in days gone by, then two dollars seemed a reasonable figure that included a tour of the château. It was well above the quarter that most historic house museums asked for admission.[6]

Two dollars was not easy to come by in the spring of 1930, especially in the South, where the Depression had arrived earlier than in other parts of the nation. Two dollars bought a housewife a simple cotton dress or paid half the down payment on a new electric washing machine. For that amount some could feed a family for several days, even a week. A pound of butter sold for forty-five cents and would soon drop to thirty cents. Even a view from the top of Chimney Rock at nearby Lake Lure cost only a dollar. The working man and his family probably wouldn't be coming to Biltmore.

The admission fee looked excessive to the editors at the Greenville, South Carolina, newspaper who sniffed that two dollars was a lot to pay to see how rich folks lived. In one editorial, the paper said, "there are thousands of Nature's own masterpieces throughout western North Carolina which the tourist may see for nothing."

Adams was not dismayed. He sent the editors a couple of free tickets and responded saying the admission fee merely covered the cost of operation. At the same time, he clipped and savored another response to the editor. The letter writer said: "The comparatively few whose education enables them to appreciate Biltmore Place can well afford to make the visit. The purely curious can have no place there—nor should they be encouraged to come."[7]

Adams saw to it that visitors got what they paid for. Guests were treated with utmost courtesy by guards and gatemen outfitted in smart, tailored uniforms of black wool trimmed in gold. Their calves were bound in shiny black leather puttees; their caps and jackets bore brass buttons stamped with the letter V. In their outfits, they looked like the liveried staff who served the Park Avenue swells featured in the movies.

Adams dictated precise rules for employees: "Smartness, alertness and courtesy in the performance of his duties, and neatness and smartness in his appearance, are at all times required and most essential." Shoes must be kept at a high shine, and "every visitor must be treated with every courtesy and deference—departure from this attitude, or rudeness and incivility on the part of the Lodge Gate Keeper, will result in his immediate and permanent relief from duty." Even if a guest was found pocketing one of Mr. Vanderbilt's treasures, Adams instructed the guards—who were deputized by the Buncombe County sheriff—to apologize for putting the offender under arrest.[8]

The operational style was courteous but thorough. Visitors registered by name and address, and tickets were not transferable; Adams wanted to know who was coming to Biltmore's front door. The tickets were partitioned with perforations so that a portion could be collected at the Lodge Gate where the auto's license number was recorded on the stub. Another portion was removed at the house, and the final piece was collected upon exit. At the end of the day, guards were instructed to count the piles and account for every ticket. If there were any discrepancies, Adams wanted to know why.

The Billiard Room had been
rearranged as a first-floor
parlor and was called the Oak
Drawing Room by the time
the house opened to visitors
in 1930.

The Grand Staircase
in the Entrance Hall.

Once inside the château, visitors wandered unescorted along a route prescribed by boundaries of crimson velvet roping and dark brown rubber floor runners. Enter the front door, turn right, move to the Oak Drawing Room (later the Billiard Room) past the Palm Court (as the Winter Garden was then called) and into the cavernous Banquet Hall, and through the family dining room (later designated the Breakfast Room). After the Tapestry Gallery and the Library, the route led up the Grand Staircase, through the hallway salon and the bedrooms of Mr. and Mrs. Vanderbilt, down and out. A small booklet printed in black and white offered brief descriptions of the furnishings, the artwork, and the decor. "Pink marble Italian well head (15th Century)" . . . "fireplace is by Wedgwood" . . . "two Chinese vessels (Chou Dynasty, 800 B.C.)" . . . "portraits by Sargent" . . . "a large Ispahan rug (middle 16th Century)." The most talked-about item was the fabled chess set and small table owned by Napoleon Bonaparte. "Upon his death," the pamphlet read, perpetuating a fable, "his heart was placed in the drawer of this table."[9]

Visitors could enjoy the rooms where George Vanderbilt ate his breakfast and where he slept on the second floor. They craned their necks to take in the Pellegrini ceiling of the Library and then gaped, slack-jawed, before two stories of shelves containing more volumes than most could find in their hometown collections. One title dated to the sixteenth century, they learned. Altogether, only 12 of the 250-plus rooms were opened to viewing, but at Biltmore, a staircase, a hallway, or a corridor was worthy of attention.

That was the tour. There were no docents, interpretive labels, or descriptive signage. Guards stationed strategically in the house were versed in neither the history of the house nor the story of the family, nor expected to be. Any comments they made to visitors most likely reflected local gossip and hand-me-down yarns. Nonetheless, this rudimentary version of living history seemed to satisfy even discriminating visitors who passed through the front door for a garden stroll after finishing their tour.

Guests seemed to like the self-guided option, which for the penny-pinching Adams was both practical and inexpensive. "No keeping pace with a guide and listening to his monotonous chant," Chapel Hill, North Carolina, newspaperman Louis Graves wrote after a visit. "If you want to give half a minute to a painting and half an hour to a tapestry there is no one to say you nay. It is a comfort to be guided only by your own whims."[10]

During the first year, 38,913 came to call, producing nearly $64,000 in much-needed cash for the family. In fact, Biltmore became such a popular part of the Asheville tourists' schedule that Adams increased availability of house tours from four to seven days a week. The château was advertised as open every day except Thanksgiving, Christmas, and New Year's Day.

The financial return looked promising, and Adams made sure every available dollar was collected. He was stingy with free passes, but he made exceptions. Visiting newspapermen, who were likely to write about the house and spread the word for free, and a handful of local politicians passed through the Lodge Gate without charge. Discount rates were available to Asheville conventioneers, but Adams regularly denied requests for free admission for pleading schoolteachers and college students, no matter how earnest the requests.

The success was short-lived. Biltmore's first year as a tourist attraction was the busiest season the estate would enjoy until after World War II. A week before the house opened, President Herbert Hoover had predicted that hard times were only temporary. The economy would rebound in sixty days, Hoover said. But the economy wasn't listening. By the end of 1930, western North Carolina's largest bank, Asheville's Central Bank and Trust Company, had failed. Its collapse, delayed as long as possible by local intervention, set off a series of financial disasters among dependent correspondent banks in nearby cities and towns, which also closed their doors, leaving depositors empty-handed. When it was revealed that millions of dollars in public money was lost in the Central Bank failure, Asheville's mayor committed suicide.

Among the casualties was Asheville's National Bank of Commerce where Adams was a founding director and the president. The bank closed during the federal bank holiday in March 1933, failed, was reorganized, and eventually emerged as First National of Asheville. When it finally returned to full banking services in July 1933, Adams had been relieved of management. The new president was Burnham Colburn, one of the Biltmore Forest investors who remained solvent enough to buy Adams's Biltmore Forest home, which Adams was forced to sell to meet his obligations.

The bank failure, preceded by the collapse of the Biltmore Forest development, crushed Adams financially. After losing his home, he moved his family into a large two-story frame house on the estate that workers had been using as a community center and the site of weekend potluck suppers. During the week, dairy workers met their wives there for lunch, which was brought to them from home. The house was called Woodcote by George West when he built it before his home and farm were swept up in George Vanderbilt's buying spree. In the early days, the estate's first farm manager, Baron Eugene d'Alinges, had lived there. Later, it became the residence of Vanderbilt's forester, Dr. Carl A. Schenck. One of Schenck's guests was the noted American naturalist, John Muir. Situated on a knoll overlooking the farm and river valley, the house occupied one of the favored sites on the estate. Adams ordered up extensive renovations that were paid for by the Biltmore Company, and he renamed it Farmcote.

Unoccupied houses on the estate became a refuge for others as well. Adams's close friend and business partner, Thomas Wadley

Raoul, was forced to rent his Biltmore Forest home, and for two years his family lived in a ramshackle, estate-owned house with broken windows, no electricity, and only basic plumbing. A hydraulic ram supplied water. A few years earlier, Raoul and his wife had been able to tour France for six weeks. Another Biltmore Forest family, the Cecils' friends, David and Dario Morgan, moved into the gardener's cottage near the conservatory after Morgan's business in Black Mountain closed. They remained for ten years.[11]

As Asheville's fortunes declined, so did Biltmore's. Ticket sales for the house fell to an average of less than thirty a day in 1933. Despite the promotional efforts of the chamber of commerce and half-price rates at hotels, boardinghouses, and restaurants, there were few tourists anywhere that season in the Land of the Sky. Adams cut expenses beginning with the pay of the house staff, whose wages were reduced by 20 percent in 1931 and another 20 percent the following year. The wages of the butler, Herbert Noble, who had been hired at $175 a month with room and board, were slashed to $100 a month. The cook was told to prepare meals on a budget of sixty cents per head, per day.[12]

Some days, the only automobile at the château belonged to John Cecil. He had returned to Biltmore after Cornelia left to make her home in London and later in Switzerland. The divorce agreement included a provision for John to live in North Carolina and draw a modest income. His residence was the suite of rooms in the Bachelor's Wing that the family had used in the last few years they were together at Biltmore. The apartment was spacious and comfortable and included a recently added sleeping porch built off a second-floor bedroom on top of a one-story extension on the building's north side. John took his meals in a small room off the first-floor hall in the wing. His favorites from the kitchen included venison, duck with orange stuffing, tomato aspic, and Delmonico potatoes. From a window in his bedroom over the porte cochere,

John Cecil at the fountain on the esplanade in front of the château in the 1930s.
He remained at Biltmore after his divorce from Cornelia until his death in 1954.

Cecil could see a small flower garden beside the stable wall. In later years, it would become a favorite outing for a pitch-black terrier that he called Snowflake.

Visitors to the house seldom saw Cecil or evidence that anyone actually inhabited the château. The housemaids saw to it that any first-floor rooms that Cecil used in the evening for entertaining were neat and tidy before the gates opened at nine in the morning. Two of Cecil's favorite spots were the Smoking Room and the Gun Room, which he refurbished at his own expense. One of the mounted trophies was a recent addition. After Cornelia's parrot, Coco, died, John had the bird stuffed and installed in a cabinet along with other trophies.[13]

Cecil was thoroughly at home at Biltmore. Even before the divorce, while his wife was pursuing her art studies in New York and Washington, he enjoyed the life of a country gentleman. He had a deep appreciation for the treasures in the house and entertained his guests by translating the Old Latin woven into the tapestries. He brought a sense of British propriety to the château's new role as tourist attraction with an approach that was both Old World and Madison Avenue. For example, he insisted that the staff place fresh-cut flowers in the rooms opened to visitors to discount the appearance of a dusty museum.[14] His philosophy became a standard continued throughout Biltmore's public life.

Most of his suggestions were adopted by Herbert Noble, who frequently sought his advice. Cecil's notions of how the estate should fare elsewhere were not always well received, however. When he planted showy spring flowers on the Approach Road, he ran afoul of the estate superintendent, Chauncey D. Beadle. After Cecil's daffodils and crocuses popped up in the spring, Beadle moved them elsewhere to preserve the woody, green appearance of a deep forest that had been stipulated by Frederick Law Olmsted. Occasional blooms of snowdrops in the spring that appeared in later years were remnants of the Cecil-Beadle bulb war.

Cecil's influence dissipated once he got beyond the front door. In contrast to the crusty Adams, he mixed easily with the staff, most of whom learned to interpret his upper-class British accent. He often could call the workers and their children by their first names, a lesson he learned when he had played Santa Claus and dropped from the chimney in the Banquet Hall to pass out presents to all. He loved bird hunting and played golf regularly on the course at Biltmore Forest Country Club, where he had some minor managerial duties. He was also a devoted fan of American baseball. On weekends, he raised the volume on the radio in his rooms to the delight of the staff who gathered in the stable courtyard to listen along with him.

* * *

Herbert Noble was rejoining the Biltmore family when he accepted the job as the butler in 1930. He had worked in a lesser capacity before World War I before leaving to join the British army, which sent him home missing an arm. A small ribbon of decoration on his dark suit testified to his valor as a member of a special team of shock troops who saw frequent action in the Somme. He had a hospitable smile, blond hair, and an optimistic outlook. When Beadle once said something about the loss of his arm, Noble replied, "But just think, I might have had my bloomin' head knocked off."[15]

Despite his disability, Noble's forte was sewing. It was a talent that proved useful in a house where age, light, and neglect had faded and damaged all manner of fabrics. He also had an eye for detail and a resourcefulness largely driven by a limited budget and necessity. When visitors complained that the velvet roping on the grand staircase was a disgrace, Noble recovered the original with similar fabric he rescued from faded curtains in the Print Room. What he couldn't salvage for repairs from elsewhere in the house he replaced with orders from Bon Marche, an Asheville department store.

Noble pursued pieces of missing furniture with determination. Over the years, individual pieces had been shipped out to furnish Cornelia's apartment in New York and the Washington homes of the Gerrys and the Cecils. One consignment of furnishings, silver, linens, and artwork had followed Cornelia to London. Other pieces he found stacked haphazardly in out-of-the-way rooms where it had been stashed with a splintered leg or a cracked headboard. When possible, the broken pieces were reunited by Clyde Murray, an accomplished carpenter, who glued and stitched chairs and settees back together. A Jacobean settee that had been a favorite of George Vanderbilt, along with assorted other furnishings including two large rugs, was being used by the workers at Farmcote when it was a gathering spot for the farm families. "As all the doors were left open at Farmcote, I think every dog + cat on Biltmore Estate must have used them," Noble reported in his log of repairs he completed in 1936.[16] He cleaned the furnishings and set them out to air.

During the first six years that the house was open to the public, Noble and his staff upholstered fifty-eight chairs and seven settees, replaced curtains in nearly every room, including those closed to the public, and annually cleaned and oiled wood and leather to relieve cracks and restore the luster.

There was only so much that could be done. In addition to the carpenter, Noble's staff included electrician William Davidson, three housemaids, and a cook. Occasionally, two of the guards, Claude Austin and Boyce Jackson, helped wax the floors. It was a mere fraction of the help that had been available during Noble's earlier stint before World War I, yet the tasks remained just as large. It took Noble and his crew two months to wash, retint, and rehang curtains in the rooms on display on the first floor. Maids spent an entire day just waxing and polishing a single room. Rugs and delicate tapestries had to be cleaned annually.

Cecil, Adams, and Edith Gerry were the Biltmore Company. While Cecil's role was largely limited to the house and some oversight at the country club, Adams's influence extended across the entire range of Biltmore affairs. His power became even more pronounced after 1934 when the voters of Rhode Island returned Peter Gerry to Washington.

Senator Gerry had lost a bid for reelection in 1928 when Republicans swept the November general election. He had campaigned vigorously for Al Smith, the Democratic presidential candidate, as had his wife and Cornelia Cecil. When Smith made a tour of the South, he stopped at Biltmore, where news cameras were called out

*William A. V. Cecil as
a youngster at Biltmore
in the 1930s.*

to record him downing a bottle of Jersey milk as he stood outside
the entrance to the Biltmore creamery. Cornelia gave him a tour of
the estate in her open yellow Packard roadster, a sporty car that was
her favorite. The senator was stung by his loss and was determined
to regain a seat. In 1934, Edith campaigned beside her husband
across Rhode Island, engaging newly enfranchised voters with
speeches in Portuguese and French. The couple returned to Washington in 1935, and Edith resumed her role as a lively political
hostess.

Preoccupied with a progressive administration in Washington
that unsettled the conservative senator, the Gerrys had little time
for North Carolina. The Frith stood empty and unused. The Cecils
had stayed there for a brief time in 1932 after the kidnapping of
the infant son of Charles A. Lindbergh sent a scare through all
wealthy Americans. A bodyguard accompanied the Cecil children

when they were out of doors with their nanny. On one occasion, a Biltmore Forest neighbor reported some suspicious men in the neighborhood. If they had a plan, it was foiled when the Cecils left town.[17]

While Adams maintained overall control of the estate, he left the day-to-day management of the house and gardens to Chauncey Beadle, the gentle, scholarly Canadian who had come south in 1890 to work for Olmsted when the great landscaper's design for Vanderbilt's estate was just a vision. At the time, Beadle was a recent graduate of Cornell University, where he had taken courses in the developing art of what was called landscape engineering. His love of plants had begun in childhood when he lived with his grandfather, who ran an experimental test farm in Ontario. In his first twenty years on the estate, Beadle had pursued Olmsted's dream of making Biltmore a horticultural institution, complete with an extensive library and herbarium, but those dreams faded with the death of Vanderbilt and totally disappeared with the 1916 flood. If there was a flaw in Olmsted's plan, it was his siting of his beloved nursery in a floodplain.

Despite these setbacks, Beadle created a comfortable berth at Biltmore. He and his wife lived at Eastcote, a house tucked into the woods on a rise just inside the Lodge Gate. Beginning in the 1920s, he began building a collection of azaleas and woody ornamentals that he gathered from across the Southeast. He usually traveled with Sylvester Owens, his chauffeur and valet, who in time became a trusted friend and horticultural companion. Though Beadle clearly outranked Adams in seniority, he quietly accepted a secondary role in management, much to the relief of Adams, who was happy to move matters regarding the house and gardens off his desk. Adams believed the estate's real future was not as a tourist attraction but as a bottler of Jersey milk and a producer of fine ice cream and other dairy products.

Chauncey D. Beadle came to work for George Vanderbilt in 1890; by the time of his death in 1950, Beadle had been the superintendent of the estate for fifty years.

*   *   *

Most of the six hundred employees at Biltmore were required to run the estate's huge farm and dairy operation. By the 1930s, life at Biltmore proceeded much as it had since Vanderbilt brought the first of his purebred Jersey herd there from the family farm on Long Island. In the early years, he had enhanced the herd by importing prime breeding stock from the Isle of Jersey, the home of the breed. By 1901, Biltmore's Jersey cows were claiming prize ribbons at national and international expositions. A complex of handsome barns with twenty-five thousand square feet of floor space had been completed in 1902.

The backbone of Biltmore was the tenant farm system. By the 1930s, there were fourteen separate "farms" spread over twelve hundred acres, with each carrying a distinctive name such as Alta Vista, Inanda, Plateau, and Long Valley. Each farm included a cow barn, a horse barn, and a milk house. Tenants were given tools and implements to work the land and tend a portion of the estate herd. They paid their monthly rental by meeting a milk quota. If a tenant's cows produced more than was expected, the tenant received payment in cash for the overage. A fifteenth estate dairy was worked by hired hands, many of whom lived in the so-called Line Houses, a row of eight houses on a hillside near the horse barn.

Tenancy was an attractive alternative for hardscrabble mountain farmers, most of whom struggled to make a living. The two-story farmhouses on the estate were snug and secure. If they needed repair, there was a carpenter handy to nail down shingles or fix a broken window. Even the families in the Line Houses were given a garden plot that was plowed each year for them without charge. Once installed at Biltmore, it is easy to understand why families stayed from one generation to the next, with those inside giving a hand to relations looking for work.

The Biltmore families worked together, played together, and, for a time, even prayed together at special services conducted by Dr. Rodney Rush Swope, the rector at All Souls. Edith Gerry had become especially close to those on her husband's land. Little girls often ended up wearing Cornelia's hand-me-down clothing. She also encouraged a cooperative spirit among the families and created annual competitions for farmers and their wives. Prizes went to those who produced the fattest vegetables, the thickest jams, or the sweetest pies.

Over the years, farm managers had tended to choose tenants with large families because they knew that more hands around the barn meant more milk at the end of the day. As children grew of age, they married into other families on the estate. Sons succeeded their fathers or found other jobs on the farm, at the house, or in the dairy.

The main barn of the Biltmore Estate dairy operation that Junius Adams built into a successful enterprise. Profits from the dairy covered the expenses of operating the house and saved the estate from financial ruin.

A fleet of Biltmore trucks offered home delivery of dairy products in major cities in North and South Carolina.

Wives of the dairy workers who lived in the Line Houses peeled the peaches and capped the strawberries that went into the dairy's rich, fresh ice cream.

While the Biltmore families considered themselves the luckiest farmers in the world, their lives were separate from many in Asheville. Those who lived off the estate eyed them with suspicion that was tinged with jealousy, especially in hard times. Cash might not have been plentiful during the 1930s, but Biltmore families had plenty of homegrown food, free ice cream treats from the creamery, and ample supplies of milk. They also had steady work.

The dairy operation had evolved into wholesale and retail sales from the early days when George Vanderbilt shared extra production with the local hospital and his own clinic in the village. In time, the estate began supplying Asheville hotels and restaurants. Gradually, a local route system for home delivery to retail customers had been created. By the early 1930s, the dairy was selling its popular Jersey Creamline brand throughout Asheville, and trucks loaded with butter, cottage cheese, milk, and ice cream were dispatched daily to a depot 120 miles away in Charlotte. A bottling plant was opened there in 1934 with the expansion of home delivery in Charlotte's better neighborhoods.

Adams had grown up as close to the land as a lawyer's son could in the relatively rural environment of western North Carolina. Within a few years of assuming his new responsibilities at Biltmore, however, he was making a name for himself within the world of Jersey breeders, riding to his new career as a gentleman farmer on the reputation of the Biltmore herd of nearly a thousand head. While Adams would learn to recite the bloodlines of Biltmore stock as easily as Blackstone's law, it was after the addition of a new farm manager who understood the value of promotion that retail and wholesale dairy sales began to grow. In 1936, after years of losses, the dairy made a profit and began a period of thirty years of growth and steady revenue for the company.

*   *   *

The growing profitability of Biltmore proved a problem for Adams, however. One of the conditions in the trust arrangement with Cornelia Cecil called for the liquidation of the Biltmore Company if more than half of the estate property was sold or the costs of taxes and maintenance were less than $50,000 a year.[18] In 1939, Cornelia's London solicitor, T. E. Chester Barratt, arrived in Asheville to force the sale of Biltmore and recover what he could for his client from her shares in the Biltmore Company. Clearly, it was a proposition that Adams, John Cecil, and Edith Gerry received with trepidation.

Since leaving the United States, Cornelia was happy to have an ocean between herself and her mother. Her home now was London, although she spent considerable time on the Continent. The Cecil boys were in boarding school, first in France and later in Switzerland. The family had reunited in Paris for a visit in the summer of 1936. Cornelia was content with a life of relative obscurity. For a time, she even changed her last name to Baer, which was the name of an artist with whom she had an affair. She called herself Mary. Wealth seemed unimportant. In 1939, Cornelia took part of her inheritance and established the Mrs. Smith Trust in England. It made small grants to people in distress.

What actually transpired between Barratt and the directors of Biltmore Company is lost to time. Family lore says that upon seeing the château and the grandeur of the estate, Barratt became convinced that Cornelia was making a mistake to force a sale. He also may have been persuaded by the prevailing market for Gilded Age mansions, particularly those accompanied by twelve thousand acres of land and six hundred dependents. At about this same time, Frederick Vanderbilt's heirs were trying to sell Hyde Park, his estate on the Hudson River. The reduced price of $250,000 had attracted only one interested buyer, a New York radio evangelist named Father Devine. The wrecking ball had taken down the mansion at 660

Fifth Avenue in 1926. The Vanderbilt home at 1 West 57th Street was soon to be demolished to make way for a department store. Finding a buyer for Biltmore would not be easy.

In the end, Adams, Cecil, and Gerry convinced Barratt to return to England with $200,000 as payment for Cornelia's interest in her father's property on Staten Island, New York. A few months later, England was at war, and any further disposition of Biltmore would have to wait.

Asheville was a curious mix of politics in the months leading up to the nation's involvement in World War II. The city's best-known politician was Robert R. "Our Bob" Reynolds. He had been elected to the U.S. Senate in 1932 with a campaign that ridiculed the refined tastes of Edith Gerry's onetime suitor, the former governor Cameron Morrison. Once in Washington, Reynolds brayed about his support of Franklin D. Roosevelt's New Deal, then turned on the president. He caused a stir by kissing Hollywood starlets on the steps of the Capitol, and by the late 1930s was flirting with right-wing organizations such as the Silver Shirts, a quasi-Fascist organization whose national headquarters was in a former office of the Biltmore-Oteen bank.[19]

By contrast, at the same time Asheville boasted one of the largest North Carolina chapters of the Committee to Defend America by Aiding the Allies (CDAAA), a nationwide group sympathetic to the plight of Britain, which was under attack by Nazi Germany. The CDAAA gave support to Roosevelt's Lend-Lease program that resulted in munitions and other supplies going to the Allies.

Biltmore was virtually empty, with a reduced staff maintaining the house. In the summer of 1939, John Cecil sailed for England just weeks before Germany attacked Poland and England was drawn into the war. With many friends in the government, he was assigned to a sensitive position in the Ministry of Information. In the late summer of 1940, as Great Britain waited anxiously for word on support from the United States, Cecil's friends asked how he thought the U.S. Senate would react to Roosevelt's plans. Cecil said he didn't know for sure, but England could count on support from Senator Peter Gerry of Rhode Island.

In fact, Gerry opposed Roosevelt's efforts to align the United States with England. His votes effectively dashed any hopes that Edith and her husband might win an important ambassadorial post, perhaps to England. As for her own sentiments, she probably was closer to the British cause now that her family was in harm's way. Cornelia was in London, but Edith's two grandsons—George was fifteen and William was twelve—were not far from the German border at a boarding school in Switzerland.

In the summer of 1941, Edith was involved in her own war effort as she arranged for David E. Finley, the director of the newly created National Gallery of Art, to pay an unusual visit to Biltmore. About six months later, within days of the Japanese attack on Pearl Harbor, a heavily guarded rail shipment left Washington for North Carolina. When the Railway Express cars reached Asheville, they were pulled onto a siding. A few hours later, armed guards watched as the contents were quietly unloaded onto trucks that headed off to the estate.

CHAPTER 5

The National Gallery's
Wartime Vault

D avid E. Finley had been a guest at Biltmore on at least one
other occasion before his visit in the summer of 1941. The
year was 1926. He was a young attorney in Washington, D.C.,
soon to become an assistant to Andrew Mellon, the legendary treasury secretary for three Republican presidents. Politically astute and
socially well connected—Finley's wife was the granddaughter of
William Wilson Corcoran, founder of the Corcoran Gallery in Washington—he blended well in the social stew mixed by the Cecils and
the Gerrys.

Finley had not come south in 1941 to appraise the Biltmore art,
which he found exceptional, especially the John Singer Sargent
portrait of Mrs. Benjamin Kissam hanging in the château's second-
floor Oak Sitting Room. This trip was of greater urgency. With war
already consuming Europe, Finley was concerned for the safety of
the collection of Washington's new National Gallery of Art, which

had just opened under his leadership as director. At the gallery's inauguration a few months earlier in March, Finley had approached the Gerrys with a question: Could his trustees count on Biltmore as a safe haven for the gallery's most precious holdings in the event of a national emergency? They told him yes.

The château offered all that Finley could hope for. It was well inland and safe from harm. It also was secure within its own boundaries. The château's stone and masonry construction made the space reassuringly fireproof. Moreover, the owners would appreciate the gallery's specifications for the care and protection of works of art. His July visit confirmed all this and more. Inside the house, he found a perfect spot to store the nation's art treasures—Biltmore's first-floor broom closet.

Architect Richard Morris Hunt had designated the space that Finley selected as a music room. Yet forty-five years after the "completion" of the house, the large room—roughly fifteen hundred square feet—remained unfinished. The walls were bare brick. The rough tile of the fifteen-foot-high vaulted ceiling had never received a final coat of plaster. The fireplace was unadorned. A simple wooden door hung at the arched opening while some of Herbert Noble's homemade curtains covered windows that opened to the loggia and the terrace. Over the years, the house staff had found the space convenient for the storage of mop buckets, odd plants, and cleaning supplies.

Finley's advisers told him the room could easily be made secure with a steel door. Bars on the windows could be installed on the inside to avoid defacing the limestone exterior. Other work would be necessary but not costly. Plans called for wire mesh all around to discourage mice, and a plaster finish was requested for the ceiling to prevent loose mortar from falling onto the paintings below. New fire extinguishers would be required. Dry rot of the forty-year-old fire hoses in the house had rendered them useless.

Priceless paintings and sculpture from the National Gallery of Art in Washington, D.C., were secreted away to Biltmore Estate during World War II for safekeeping. Workers removed them in 1944 for their return to Washington.

Junius Adams arranged for the preparation of the room, ordering the repairs in the name of the Biltmore Company to avoid raising suspicion. By the time of the Japanese attack on Pearl Harbor in December, the new vault was all but complete. After the gallery in Washington closed for the New Year's Day holiday, curators began packaging carefully selected treasures for shipment to Biltmore. For purposes of morale, Finley was determined to leave a portion of the collection on display throughout the war. A shipment of sixty-two paintings and seventeen works of sculpture left Washington in a heavily guarded Railway Express car and arrived at a siding across the Swannanoa River near the estate's Victoria Bridge on Thursday morning, January 8, 1942.

Temperatures were the coldest that Asheville had experienced in years as trucks carrying the steel cases enclosing the collection eased up Olmsted's curving Approach Road to the house. The trucks swayed from side to side. Riding close behind, Finley imagined an accident with Raphael's *Alba Madonna* crashing on the road.[1] The trucks arrived safely at the front door where the cargo was carried inside.

Secrecy had covered the summertime negotiations, and the shipment south was all under guard and hush-hush. Secrets were hard to keep within the coziness of the estate family, however, and by the time the Railway Express cars reached Asheville, workers and their families were on hand to witness the unloading. Adams did keep the story out of the newspapers, and no photographs were taken.

There was really little to see. Paintings by Botticelli, Goya, Rembrandt, Gainsborough, Titian, Van Dyck, Velázquez, and Vermeer arrived in containers. Among the most recognizable would have been Gilbert Stuart's portrait of George Washington, an image imprinted on the minds of schoolchildren across the land. The paintings were tucked safely into the first-floor room while sculpture by Agostino di Duccio, Donatello, and Verocchio were carried downstairs to former living space that had been evacuated by the house staff.

Despite Biltmore's new high priority in the national defense, Adams kept the house open to visitors throughout 1942. It isn't known what explanation was offered about the uniformed guards with holstered revolvers and gas billies who stood outside the heavy steel door just across the entrance hall from the front vestibule. No one explained to visitors why Mr. Vanderbilt's bedroom directly above on the second floor was closed.

A year after the collection arrived, however, the issue became moot. On January 8, 1943, Adams suspended visitation for the duration of the war. Clearly, in the face of a national emergency and gas rationing, tourists would not be coming to the estate. Attendance in 1942 was only a third of the year before, with an average of twenty-eight guests a day.

The war cut short a revival of interest in the estate. Attendance in 1940 and 1941 had been strong and had almost reached the levels that Biltmore had enjoyed in 1930. The recovery was largely the result of word-of-mouth promotion. Adams continued to rely on the Asheville Chamber of Commerce for modest advertising placements in newspapers. He also had become adept at generating free publicity through his courtship of newspaper editors around the country. In the late 1930s, he hired an unemployed journalist to write a flattering article about the house, got it placed in the *Asheville Citizen* for legitimacy, and circulated reprints freely to newspapers all around the country. He also made sure reporters knew of the odd and interesting, such as the appearance of a pair of bear cubs named Mandy and Jane who were put on display by the estate's gamekeeper, J. C. Shackleford. He fed them with meat and corn bread from John Cecil's dinner table at the château.

The national emergency brought a new kind of visitor to Asheville's hotels and boardinghouses. In April 1942, the government requisitioned the Grove Park Inn to house diplomats of the Axis powers, pending their exchange. Most were relocated by midsummer of that year, and the hotel management scurried to recover its lost tourist business. Regular guests with standing reservations had been shut out. A few months later, however, the navy leased the property as a rest and rehabilitation center for wounded officers. Later in the war, the Grove Park was one of four Asheville hotels used as a redistribution center for returning combat veterans.

As for Biltmore, the château had perhaps reached its highest and best use for the duration as a safe repository for valuable works of art. Adams retained the house staff who did not leave for defense jobs. Some found better-paying jobs at the nearby Enka mills that were turning out rayon for parachutes and tire cording. Production reached full capacity, and for a time the plant drew additional water from the French Broad River in a line that ran across the estate's west side. Those who remained on the property tended to the house. For a time, the front of the château was obscured by scaffolding as carpenters and painters rehabilitated the exterior woodwork.

The only outside visitors to the estate were the curators from the National Gallery who arrived from time to time to inspect the condition of the collection. The house had no air-conditioning—which had been considered as a precaution—but Chauncey Beadle regulated the huge boilers to achieve an environment that met the inspectors' requirements. The routine was exceedingly dull, broken only by the changing of the guards at the Music Room and the rooms below.

With no visitors loose on the grounds, Beadle turned his attention to the cultivation and planting of an azalea garden in a forested ravine between the Bass Pond and the conservatory at the Walled Garden. Olmsted's plans called this space the Glen. On April 1, 1940, it had become the Beadle Azalea Garden after Edith Gerry unveiled a bronze marker mounted on a hip-high boulder. The ceremonies dedicating the spot recognized Beadle's fifty years at Biltmore. That spring, he started planting selections from more than three thousand azaleas that were part of a vast collection of rare species he cultivated at his farm in nearby Oteen.

As soon as the war in Europe came to an end in the spring of 1945, John Cecil purchased the first berth he could find and headed back to the United States. Before he left London, he and his two brothers scraped together a few pounds and threw a party celebrating the Allied victory in Europe. The highlight of the evening was the uncorking of an old dusty selection with a faded label they had found in the wine cellar of their father, Lord William, who had died in 1943. The bottle was one of two set apart from others, suggesting a special vintage. Since there were only two bottles and not three, they chose to savor them together at the end of the war. Midway through their victory celebration, John's eldest brother opened one of the bottles and poured the contents all around. One sip was enough to tell there was some mistake. Upon closer inspection, they found a notation on the smudged and dirty label that the bottle was not wine at all but water from the Jordan River, where they had been baptized.

Cecil resumed the life of a country gentleman that he had enjoyed before the war. This time, however, he was joined by his eldest son, George, who had just turned twenty-one when he arrived at Biltmore upon his release from the British Navy in 1946. Young William, George's brother, remained in England, where he had begun military service and appeared to be set on a career as a naval officer.

The war had united the Cecil family in the same country, if not under the same roof. Cornelia had a house in Kensington, while John lived at his club. George had entered the navy in 1943 as soon as he was of age, while William was enrolled at Bradfield, a proper British boarding school that had set many a young man on a track to serve the empire. The stuffiness didn't suit William, who finished with an unremarkable record. Even years later, he cringed at the crushing reports from his Welsh schoolmasters, one of whom wrote, "He must find it boring to sit for so long and do so little."[2]

William and his brother had virtually been raised in boarding schools. At the onset of war, the boys were stranded at a school in Switzerland. William had just turned eleven and George was fourteen in September 1939 when the hostilities officially began. They remained in school for the coming term. It wasn't until after America entered the war in December 1941 that they finally were recalled to London. Traveling alone in the summer of 1942, they boarded a train in Geneva and crossed German-occupied France into Spain. The two arrived without incident in Madrid, which carried the marks of a destructive civil war, only to find that no one would accept either their British pound notes or their U.S. dollars. The Bank of Spain even turned down the bills they carried out of concern that they might be counterfeit.

William and George were fluent in French and German as well as English. Unfortunately, neither knew Spanish, and they could find no one whom they understood to give them directions to the British embassy, where they might find help. Then they stopped a priest on the street. After some linguistic gymnastics involving schoolboy Latin and ancient Greek, the priest sent them on their way to the British compound, where their arrival was expected. Some of their father's former companions—he had served there in the 1920s—solved their currency problems. The embassy also sent word to London that the two were safe.

With their finances refreshed, the boys made their way across the Spanish border to Lisbon, Portugal, the departure point for the only air service from the Continent to England. They waited several weeks before they could finally secure passage, only to be bumped at the last minute by the arrival of an unidentified VIP. They watched their flight take off on schedule but learned later it disappeared over the Bay of Biscay. It was several more weeks before seats became available on a flight that carried them safely to England.

William experienced an eerie footnote to this astonishing trek. One evening a few months after he had arrived in London, he left his mother's house to post a letter and discovered a woman on the street who insisted she had information essential to the conduct of the war. The fog was thick, the night was dark, and the woman could not locate a pay station, so William invited her to use the telephone in his mother's house. She accepted the offer and, after insisting on secrecy, put in a call to the British Air Ministry. She told them she had a message from Leslie Howard, the British actor whose plane from Lisbon—the one that the Cecil boys had been scheduled to board—was shot down over the Bay of Biscay.

William spent most of the war years at Bradfield and had enlisted for twelve years in the British Navy, thinking he wanted to be an officer, when he responded to his father's urging that he come see his inheritance in the United States, of which he knew little. After completing his basic training, he took a three-month leave and in the summer of 1947 headed west on a trip of discovery.

William Amherst Vanderbilt Cecil had left the United States with the innocence and limited perspective of a six-year-old. He retained little recollection of life at Biltmore, which, after all, had been a passing residence, just one of the homes occupied by his parents in the years the family was together. In 1947, his brother picked him up in New York and they drove to North Carolina together. As the car turned into the esplanade, he experienced the same awe and surprise as any first-time visitor. "The first time you see that . . ." he said some years later, his voice drifting off. "It had the same effect on me as it does everybody else."[3]

As he headed down the drive by the leafy green of the tall tulip poplars, he saw the château with fresh eyes. He passed the fountain, a Biltmore-size plate of shallow water where he had splashed about in the hot summertime, as had his mother before him. He and George had ridden their feisty ponies on the broad lawn. Ahead, in his father's rooms over the porte cochere, he found the "schoolroom" where he and his brother had endured their early tutors. Another room stored his toys. Though his memory was

William A. V. Cecil was twenty-one when he left the British Navy following World War II to return to the United States and Biltmore Estate before enrolling at Harvard University in preparation for a career in banking.

thin, there were those who remembered him. Edna Sales, a nurse first for Cornelia and later for the boys, was still on the payroll as a housekeeper.

John Cecil had convinced William that he should at least see what was available to him in the United States before he grew firm in his intent for a naval career. Nothing the young man had been told to that point had given him any appreciation of what lay across the sea. He had attended boarding schools, but he had never considered his circumstances equal to those of a Vanderbilt heir. While waiting to be called to the navy, he had taken a factory job making artificial ice cream for a chain of British teahouses. As an ordinary seaman, he had supplemented his pay by repairing shoes and converting canisters of cut tobacco into packets of rolled cigarettes that he sold to his shipmates. His only indulgence was photography. A camera was part of his kit on board the HMS *Montclair*, a submarine tender, where he was a signalman. When he did hear of Biltmore, it was from a Scottish tailor who was familiar with Biltmore homespun, not the château.

For three months—from late summer to fall in 1947—William bunked with his father and brother in the Bachelor Wing. George was already enrolled as an understudy at the dairy, where it was assumed he would one day take over. He turned out for daily chores on the farm, learning the business from the field to the barn. William got only a taste of the estate's agricultural ventures. Before he returned to England, he traveled to Atlanta with his brother and Adams to attend a Jersey show where he discovered that Adams's title of judge covered cows as well as the law.

William explored the estate with Chauncey Beadle and, using his father's Packard convertible, learned to drive an automobile. It was a beast of a machine to manage, and he plowed it through a fence before he finally got the hang of handling a heavy American car.

If there was no job for him in the dairy business, William thought that perhaps his future was as Beadle's successor as superintendent of the house and gardens. He roamed about the château, poking into rooms unoccupied for years where armoires still held clothing belonging to his mother and his grandparents. Many rooms remained just as they had been upon the departure of the last guest. He understood the château's daunting size one day when his father left after lunch saying he planned to visit each room. John Cecil did not return for four and a half hours.

Each morning, the housemaids swept up behind the three bachelors if they had used the first-floor rooms the night before. Paying visitors had returned to Biltmore.

Beadle reopened the house to tourists on March 15, 1946. The National Gallery had removed the paintings and sculpture in the fall of 1944 after the threat of invasion had long passed. The return of the artwork to Washington was accompanied by a parade of police cars and sirens. Even before the collection was removed from Biltmore, Beadle had opened the house periodically for veterans recuperating at the area hospitals. The tours for servicemen and their wives were offered in appreciation for the sacrifices they had made for their country. One sailor rounded the corner at the base of the South Terrace totally dumbstruck by the forty-foot-high western base of the house. "This wall is about as high up as a ship's deck above water," he told a reporter.[4]

Beadle's generosity came early in the government's stay in Asheville. By war's end, Asheville was growing weary of the limits that the military's use put on the tourist accommodations. Guests with standing reservations were eager to return to their favorite hotels, some of which remained under contract to the government. Ancillary businesses were suffering. Shop owners and other vendors who depended on the annual flow of tourists found themselves in serious financial difficulty. Business didn't return to normal until 1946.

By that time, Americans were eager to get on with their lives after years of war. Even though automobiles, tires, and fuel remained hard to come by, tourism enjoyed a revival. More than forty-two thousand visitors paid the two dollars for admission to the estate in 1946, four times the number in 1940. To Adams's surprise, admission income exceeded expenses for the first time ever. Summertime visitation added needed cash and even sustained other operations for a short time. However, the $5,909.50 profit barely offset the losses that had been incurred since 1930.

Biltmore deeply impressed the young William Cecil. First was the grandeur and magnificence of the place. And the breadth of the countryside on his first drive through the United States was as overwhelming as the house itself. But there was more. "I found Biltmore and Biltmore found me and that was the end of it," he said many years later. As imposing as his grandfather's château was to visitors, the huge pile of chiseled limestone—from the angry gargoyles near the roofline down to the foundation that stood as solid as the mountain underneath—looked like a home to William. By the time his leave was over, he was sure his future was in the United States, at Biltmore, and not with the British Navy.

Before he left for England, William talked over his future with Adams, his father, his brother, and his grandmother. The brothers shared an equal claim to the estate, which would become theirs upon William's thirty-fifth birthday. (After the experience with Cornelia, who came into her inheritance at age twenty-five, the trustees had added ten years as an additional measure of comfort.) While their shares were equal, their status was not. As the eldest, George was expected to assume the leadership, which prompted questions from both the young men. Adams assured Edith Gerry, however, that by the time the two were thirty-five "they will have been able to work themselves into smooth grooves and get along without difficulty. In the meantime of course there would be the trustees to iron out any differences and keep them in line."[5]

Besides, said Adams, George's interest was in the dairy while William seemed happy as Beadle's successor as superintendent of the house and gardens. The judge told William he would do a fine job in that role after he had finished some courses in horticulture, landscape gardening, and engineering, probably at Beadle's alma mater, Cornell University.

"I was made painfully aware that the future was drab and while I might be a fifty-percent stockholder of the company, the only thing of value, other than the contents [of the house], was the dairy," Cecil later wrote. "Furthermore, I was informed that there was no room, nor any funds for salaries, in the dairy operation."[6]

Even when presented with these limited prospects, William left for England to negotiate his release from the navy, which he accomplished on totally unexpected terms. He secured a discharge for medical reasons. During an examination, doctors discovered a curvature of his spine that should have precluded him from being enrolled in the first place. In the late spring of 1949, he was back in the States. One of his first stops was his grandmother's home in Providence. Upon seeing her tall, lanky, and exceedingly thin grandson—he was six-four and weighed 135 pounds—she ordered up a feast to put some meat on his bones.

On the advice of his father, he headed not to Cornell but to Harvard University. John Cecil told his son if he was to succeed in the world, he would need more than a few courses in horticulture. No one, including John Cecil, seriously believed that managing a historic house was much of a career path.

CHAPTER 6

A Curiosity or a Treasure

Chauncey DeLos Beadle was the last of Biltmore's founding family when he died July 4, 1950. He had invested most of his adult life in the estate as the faithful and meticulous curator of the landscape design created by his mentor, Frederick Law Olmsted. A handful of other employees had decades in service at Biltmore, but at midcentury only Beadle could say he had stood beside George Vanderbilt as the walls of the château rose stone by stone in the early 1890s.

Beadle had experienced the full rush of Biltmore's creation. He had arrived April 1, 1890, for a thirty-day assignment as Olmsted's assistant. He never left. When Vanderbilt's close friend and attorney, Charles McNamee, departed Asheville in 1904 for other duties, Vanderbilt appointed Beadle superintendent. The development of the house, the gardens, and the farms all took shape on his watch. He had seen the scarred and rutted countryside renewed under the vast landmark reforestation conceived by Olmsted and perfected by Dr. Carl A. Schenck. Those early plantings had matured into deep pine forests. Beadle's legacy was bringing to maturity in twig and blossom, branch and leaf what Olmsted had seen mostly only on his detailed design drawings.

In the early years, Beadle's single-minded passion had been directed toward the realization of Biltmore as a preserve where horticulturists would find every plant that could accommodate the climate and soils of the southern Appalachians. These plantings were to be given focus along a nine-mile arboretum drive and the subject of study at a research library. Beadle nudged Vanderbilt gently and persistently to fulfill Olmsted's dream but to no avail. Vanderbilt's deteriorated financial condition cut short that part of the landscaping master's plan. Beadle did raise to national attention the estate's nursery, which produced a dazzling array of plants. He created an extensive catalog and supervised a profitable enterprise only to watch, undoubtedly brokenhearted, as the 1916 flood carried all his years of devotion away in an angry, muddy torrent.

He was revived by the 1920s when Edith Gerry gave him the woodlands of Biltmore Forest as his own horticultural canvas. As the developers' landscape designer, he laid out the roads that followed the contours of the land in a design that complemented Olmsted's work next door at Biltmore. Widowed and remarried, Beadle also resumed his scholarship with a determination that drove him to the far reaches of the southern Appalachians. Accompanied by William A. Knight and Frank Crayton, and with Sylvester Owens, his chauffeur, at the wheel, Beadle and the "Azalea Hunters," as they called themselves, went in search of new species and subspecies of azaleas and rhododendron, which grew in wild profusion in the region. The collection became his extended family. Edith Gerry rewarded his efforts in 1940 with the dedication of the Beadle Azalea Garden and a $5,000 check to underwrite publication of his research by the Smithsonian Institution. The book was still a work in progress at the time of his death. His lasting signatures in the horticultural world were species of azaleas and rhododendron that bore his name.

Beadle's passing at age eighty-two came just as the prospects of the great houses of the Gilded Age, including his beloved Biltmore, were the most dim. Progress had overtaken all the Vanderbilts' Fifth Avenue mansions. George's 640 Fifth Avenue had been the last to fall, in 1947, for the sake of an office building. Idle Hour, the Long Island residence of George's brother, William, had gone through several iterations after William's son sold it in 1922. Heirs had turned Elm Court, his sister Emily's summer home outside of Lenox, Massachusetts, into a country inn. Woodlea in Scarborough, New York, had been a country club since 1910. Frederick's Hyde Park was secure in the arms of the National Park Service, which had taken it as a gift at the encouragement of Frederick's next-door neighbor, President Franklin D. Roosevelt. Of the dozen mansions and summer palaces erected by the children of William Henry Vanderbilt in their frenzy of extravagant construction, only Biltmore, George's sister Lila's Shelbourne Farms in Vermont, and the Breakers in Newport were still owned by the family.

The second-generation heirs had shown little interest in their patrimony. In the case of Biltmore, Cornelia Cecil had remarried in 1949 and was settled in London, where she was awaiting a cash payment on the agreement she had made in the creation of the Biltmore Company and the trusts for her sons.

As soon as the war had ended, her London solicitor had contacted Adams with an offer. Since the estate couldn't be sold without "irreparable loss," Cornelia would accept eight dollars a share for her half interest in the Biltmore Company. She proposed that the $2 million for her 2,500 shares be paid in two installments, with the first due in the spring of 1947. The balance would be due a year later.[1]

Fortunately for all concerned, the dairy had produced respectable profits during the war years. It ran at near full capacity, and at one point Adams had plans for an expanded processing facility off the estate on property closer to downtown Asheville. It was never built, however, because the War Allocation Board refused to approve the necessary building materials.[2] In the years immediately after the war, the estate also began a wholesale harvesting of timber as the nation's demand for new houses for returning veterans rejuvenated the housing market.

Working with Edith Gerry, Adams arranged to make the payments to Cornelia, which included the sale of some of the investments that had enjoyed substantial growth since the end of the war. There was some delay in the final payment, but by 1950 Adams secured the cash necessary to purchase Cornelia's interest in the company. Thus, Edith's intervention in the 1930s assured that the estate would pass into the hands of Cornelia's sons, George and William, once William reached the age of thirty-five.

The settlement with Cornelia also secured Adams's own future. He had turned his law practice over to his sons after the war and was devoting his full time to the management of the estate. He continued to live at Farmcote, where he enjoyed the life of a country squire, comfortable in his confidence that the estate's prize herd of Jersey cattle represented the future of Biltmore.

Adams's casual approach to the château and its possibilities was held by many. Americans, especially New Englanders and southerners, had developed a keen interest in historic preservation but their attention was on houses that dated to the seventeenth or eighteenth century, or, like Mount Vernon, held some patriotic significance. There was little affection for houses that were the residue of ostentatious wealth. None had done more to shape this fascination with the patriotic past than a determined antiquarian named William Sumner Appleton of Boston and the country's best-known millionaire, John D. Rockefeller Jr., whose millions were re-creating Colonial Williamsburg.

By midcentury, the town of Williamsburg, Virginia, was more than two hundred years old, yet, by a strange turn of fate, still in its teens. Benjamin Franklin had walked the streets of this center of tidewater commerce and politics three decades before the American Revolution. By the late nineteenth century, however—at about the time George Vanderbilt paid his first visit to Asheville—the old town was known more as the location of a nearby mental hospital than for its place in American history. The handful of remaining colonial structures were in disrepair or worse. In the mid-1920s, however, a resolute local minister convinced John D. Rockefeller Jr. that he could save Williamsburg and give Americans a gift of their own heritage.

The restoration and re-creation of Williamsburg's colonial structures began under the watchful eye of the Reverend W. A. R. Goodwin of the historic Bruton Parish Church, who almost single-handedly created Colonial Williamsburg Inc. In the early days, the minister served as Rockefeller's agent and purchased available properties, optioned others, and bought more when the time was right. By the time Goodwin was through, he had accumulated more than three hundred acres and assembled what would become the core of the nation's best-known historic district. In September 1932, the first tourists stepped inside the reconstructed Raleigh Tavern on Duke of Gloucester Street. By that time, Rockefeller had spent $7 million, and the two notable re-creations, the Governor's Palace and the colonial capitol, were still in the planning stage.[3]

Even incomplete and lacking its signature buildings, Colonial Williamsburg drew thirty thousand visitors in 1934, about the same Biltmore had seen four years before. That number tripled with the completion of the capitol and the palace. By the early 1950s—and more than $25 million of Mr. Rockefeller's money later—visitation had grown to more than a half million annually as Colonial Williamsburg surpassed Mount Vernon as the nation's favorite historic site. The city's most important guest remained Rockefeller himself, who maintained a home on the grounds within sight of the re-created capitol, which had been resurrected largely from an artist's rendering of the exterior. Rockefeller's vision of neat gardens, bowing servants, and bewigged actors in civil discourse was a romantic tableau and the nation's largest historic preservation enterprise.

Goodwin had first approached Henry Ford about his plans for Williamsburg. He got nowhere. Ford was not to be distracted from his own desire to re-create an America he believed was fast disappearing at his own historical park, called Greenfield Village, on a campus outside of Detroit. Ford accumulated an impressive collection of buildings there, some historic and others just old, which he uprooted from around the country and plopped down around a village green. Ford did not bother with historians to certify historic relevance but relied on his own agents who scoured the countryside in search of icons of the past. At Greenfield Village, he installed houses from New England, slave cabins from Georgia, the Wright brothers' Dayton, Ohio, bicycle shop, Thomas Edison's Menlo Park laboratory, and even the schoolhouse that Ford himself had attended as a boy. There was a country store, a windmill from Cape Cod, a watchmaker's shop, a post office, a railroad station, and a carding mill. He dismantled the aging Postville Courthouse in Lincoln, Illinois, where Abraham Lincoln had once practiced law, even as townspeople were scampering about to keep the building on its original foundation. When President Herbert Hoover arrived at Greenfield Village for a visit in October 1929, a Lincoln impersonator strolled the grounds. Ford's "animated textbook" of early

American life even came with a complement of real students for the schoolhouse.

Ford's approach was anathema to the purists, some of whom considered his removal of structures from their context a sacrilege. Organized vandalism, they called it.[4] The world-famous automaker didn't care. He once told his secretary, "All this history is mostly bunk anyhow."[5] He declared that he would show folks how life really was.

Greenfield Village was followed by other outdoor museums, such as Old Sturbridge Village, a fictional town filled with a collection of New England structures set around a shady green. It was the creation of a wealthy businessman and collector, Albert Wells. First called Old Quinebaug Village, it opened in 1946 near Sturbridge, Massachusetts, with Wells eager to see it pay its own way from the admission fee of a dollar and revenue from items made in the village shops.

These outdoor museums and re-creations, Colonial Williamsburg included, were a dramatic departure from earlier preservation efforts. They were directed at educating a fast-growing audience of American tourists about a lifestyle and period in American history rather than simply saving an old building that enjoyed patriotic significance. The first of these single-structure efforts had been at Mount Vernon, George Washington's home on the Potomac. In the years before the Civil War, Ann Pamela Cunningham, a South Carolinian, formed the Mount Vernon Ladies Association of the Union to save Washington's estate from speculators, who were said to be ready to use the estate as the site of a racetrack and accompanying saloon. During the Depression, the federal government built a parkway from Alexandria, Virginia, to the boundary of Washington's estate along the banks of the Potomac River.

Boston's Appleton mounted the effort to save Paul Revere's house in a campaign that eventually led to the creation of the nation's first broad-based preservation effort, the Society for the Preservation of New England Antiquities (SPNEA). Appleton's missionary work in favor of old houses carried over into other communities and inspired scores of local historic house museums. Whereas there were but ten historic house museums in 1895, the number had grown to more than a hundred by 1910. Sites in New England accounted for more than a fourth of the nearly four hundred historic house museums that were open in 1933.[6] At the time of his death in 1947, Appleton's SPNEA owned nearly fifty of these properties. An enduring result of his efforts was a loosening of the preservation movement from its patriotic anchor to allow enough swing and sway for the inclusion of structures of architectural significance as well.

While Appleton inspired the movement, the work at Colonial Williamsburg set the standard for historic preservation, despite the irony that the signature buildings were what one writer called "a beguiling mixture of the preserved, the restored and the reconstructed."[7] Nonetheless, Rockefeller's investment attracted the architectural talent and later the historical and archaeological professionals whose early work institutionalized preservation. In the beginning, the architects were in charge. Trained archaeologists were scarce, and historians were more interested in documents than structures. Colonial Williamsburg's first historian was hired to record the work of the restoration, not poke into the past of the community or its way of life. That did change, and by the end of World War II, the work at Colonial Williamsburg had virtually created a new academic discipline.

In addition, Colonial Williamsburg had become *the* clearinghouse for preservation. South Carolinians drew upon the work there to craft a zoning ordinance and create the first historic district in Charleston. Charlestonians had developed preservation fever after it was reported that old houses were being replaced by filling stations, including some from Rockefeller's own Standard Oil Company. The staff at Colonial Williamsburg helped draft the 1935 Historic Sites Act, and congressmen who needed convincing of the value of such efforts were whisked away to see the place for themselves. After twenty-five years, Colonial Williamsburg's position as the leading effort in historic preservation and interpretation was secure.

The preservation movement had largely ignored Biltmore. A directory of historic houses published in 1933, three years after the opening of the château to the public, listed four historic sites in North Carolina—two in Raleigh and two in Winston-Salem—but included no mention of Biltmore.[8] One of the most comprehensive histories on historic preservation in the United States, Charles Hosmer's two-volume chronicle of the movement in the first half of the twentieth century, took notice of Biltmore only once. It appeared as a passing reference in an account from the late 1940s related to the newly formed Preservation Society of Newport County and its preparation for the opening of another Vanderbilt mansion, the Breakers.

The $7 million, seaside "cottage" had been built for Cornelius Vanderbilt II in 1895 and was the largest and grandest of these seasonal mansions. It was still occupied by Vanderbilt's daughter, Countess Laszlo Szechenyi, who had talked with the National Park Service about taking the house. When those discussions stalled—the government couldn't guarantee money to underwrite the venture—the countess herself was having second thoughts about "all sorts of people running through the house and prying into the intimacy of her father's home and its possessions."[9]

The Newport Preservation Society, not the Park Service, finally struck a bargain: The society would lease the house for a dollar a year and pay for the annual upkeep of the property—about

$22,000—while the countess would remain in residence in a portion of the house that was well away from the crowds. The bills would be paid with admission fees. One of the society's early leaders, Katherine Warren, noted that if Biltmore's admission was $2, then visitors would pay a comparable amount to see the Breakers. Others advised a lesser amount. Warren finally settled on $1.25. Public response was overwhelming. The house had twenty-six thousand visitors that first summer.[10]

The formative years of the preservationist movement culminated in October 1949, just as William Cecil was beginning his first year at Harvard University, with President Harry Truman's signing of legislation creating the National Trust for Historic Preservation. This quasi-public organization picked up where Colonial Williamsburg had begun as the source for preservation information and advice.

North Carolinians had joined the preservation movement with money and enthusiasm. Christopher Crittenden, the director of the state's Department of Archives and History, was one of the organizers of the National Trust. A statewide preservation society called the North Carolina Society for the Preservation of Antiquities had been organized in the 1930s and was firmly in the control of Ruth Cannon of Concord. Her husband, Charles A. Cannon, presided over Cannon Mills Company, a sprawling textile empire whose huge mills and company-owned housing made up Kannapolis, the largest unincorporated town in the United States. Like enthusiasts elsewhere, however, the attention was focused on the colonial era, not the late nineteenth century. Ruth Cannon's fascination with the architecture of Colonial Williamsburg had shaped the design of the retail and commercial buildings in Kannapolis, from the cornices of the structures down to the town's signage.

Private and public money in North Carolina flowed into the reconstruction of the palace of William Tryon, the colonial governor whose Georgian mansion had once stood on the riverbank at New Bern before it burned in 1789. At the same time, a movement was afoot in Winston-Salem to restore Salem, the colonial-era settlement of Moravians. The first structure, Salem Tavern, had opened in 1929. Winston-Salem's aldermen created the nation's third historic district—after Charleston and New Orleans—to save Salem and put an end to plans of a developer who wanted to build a grocery store on what local preservationists considered hallowed land.

Biltmore was considered more of a curiosity than a treasure. It was well regarded within the state but not as a tribute to Hunt's architectural style, Olmsted's landscaping genius, or the art treasures found inside. Rather, Biltmore was appreciated as one of the leading tourist attractions—a sight to see when in western North Carolina, just like the view from Mt. Mitchell or a drive through the new Great Smoky Mountains National Park. None of the literature about the house or countless newspaper articles referred to Biltmore as a historic house museum. And there was no evidence that relegating it to the status of tourist attraction bothered anyone in Asheville or at Biltmore.

For Junius Adams, the house was little more than a loss leader. He could rhapsodize over the estate's lush pastures and the dairy's Jersey cows that produced oceans of milk. Perhaps his proudest year—aside from his presidency of the American Jersey Cattle Association during World War II—was 1952 when standouts in the Biltmore herd won national championships for both cows and bulls. But the house was a financial drain. It gave the dairy business cache but failed to produce enough income to offset the expense of the staff of fifteen that in 1950 was responsible for cleaning, maintenance, and guard duty.

In the wake of Beadle's death, Adams relied on John Cecil to keep an eye on the house and to report anything that needed attention. Cecil's contribution was limited, however. About two years after Beadle's death, Cecil fell ill with cancer. He died in October 1954.

Tourists still found their way to the estate. There was a steady growth in ticket sales after the house reopened in 1946, and visitation reached a peak in 1950 when nearly fifty thousand paid for admission to the house. Among those on the property that summer were aging graduates of the Biltmore Forest School, the first school of forestry in the United States, which Carl Schenck had organized at the turn of the century. The alumni included George W. Merck, the president of Merck Chemical Company in New York.

Schenck did not attend, but a nephew represented him. A year later, Schenck made a grand tour of the United States and stopped in North Carolina to see some of his former students. He also returned in 1952 to receive an honorary degree from North Carolina State College, which named a demonstration forest in his honor to mark his contribution to forestry in the United States. (Adams also received an honorary degree on the same occasion in recognition of his support of the state's dairy industry.)

The tourist business had not seen such success since the boom times of the 1920s. This was a new generation of travelers, however. They roamed farther afield in their automobiles on paved roads that had not existed twenty and thirty years earlier. New cross-mountain national highways opened where there had once been wilderness accessible only on horseback, if at all.

A new destination was the town of Cherokee at the edge of the boundary of the reservation belonging to the Eastern Band of Cherokees. In the summer of 1950, an outdoor drama titled *Unto These Hills* opened to overwhelming success. The story portrayed the history of the Cherokee nation from 1540 to the removal of the tribe from western North Carolina in the early eighteenth century. Two years later, the Oconoluftee Indian Village, a re-creation of the early life of the ancestors of the Cherokees, opened to tourists. Both became popular destinations.

Cherokee was one of the North Carolina gateways to the Great Smoky Mountains National Park, a vast area south and west of Asheville that included some of the most rugged country on the eastern seaboard. It had been acquired and preserved during the Depression with help from John D. Rockefeller Jr. Tourists now could reach mountain peaks standing higher than six thousand feet and enjoy breathtaking vistas from the edge of concrete and asphalt overlooks. Then they hurried down the western slope to Gatlinburg, Tennessee, a one-time crossroads that was emerging as a mountain playground. In 1945, the park drew more visitors than any other national park in the nation.[11]

Tourism was becoming a regional industry. Asheville remained a well-known spot, but now it shared billing with attractions throughout western North Carolina, from Cherokee in the southwest to Grandfather Mountain fifty miles to the northeast where Hugh Morton had installed his "mile-high" swinging bridge in 1952.

Americans on wheels were looking for weeklong vacations in the new motels and motor courts that welcomed them in casual style for a day or two in contrast to the formality of the old establishments such as Battery Park where guests had once stayed for months at a time. In 1946, only a dozen tourist courts were open in Asheville. By the mid-1950s, more than fifty were offering rooms to traveling families at rates half of what they would pay at a hotel. Changes in travel habits drained business from the Grove Park Inn, where the current owner had been trying to sell the old hotel for five years.[12]

The national magazine *Better Homes & Gardens* published a round-trip tour of the southern mountains complete with suggestions for inexpensive motels, sights to see, restaurants, and highway routes. A family of four could make a ten-day loop through the mountains of Virginia, North Carolina, and Tennessee for $350 and see just about everything there was to see, including Biltmore, which received prominent mention.[13]

The war had produced an entire resort on the edge of the national park. Fontana Village was built in 1942 to house five thousand workers building a 7,400-acre lake and power plant to supply energy for aluminum production. After the war, the village was converted into a tourist destination that offered square dancing, boating, horseback riding, and relaxation in the cool of the North Carolina mountains.

Many visitors arriving in Asheville came by way of the Blue Ridge Parkway, whose southern segment from Mt. Mitchell ended at the city's doorstep. Construction on the so-called mile-high scenic road linking Shenandoah National Park in Virginia with the Smokies had begun during the Depression. Before the war halted work, 350 miles of the 470-mile route was under construction, with 250 miles open to cars. A final North Carolina section linking Linville south to Asheville opened in time for the rush of the growing number of tourists in the 1950s.

After a banner year in 1950, Biltmore began to feel the competition from other attractions and the expanding options for travel. In 1954, tourist spending in western North Carolina was up by as much as 30 percent; Biltmore visitation had declined by about 10 percent.[14] The operation came close to breaking even in that year—for the first time since 1946—but only because of a change in the federal tax laws. The 20-percent federal luxury tax imposed during the war was reduced, but Biltmore continued to collect $2.40 for admission rather than give visitors the benefit of the tax cut. Biltmore picked up an additional eighteen cents per ticket without announcing a price increase.

There were periodic flurries of interest in the estate. In 1949, portions of a Hollywood movie titled *Tap Roots* were filmed on the grounds. Photographs of the house appeared in *Life* magazine in 1950 as part of a half-century retrospective of grand American houses. The château also appeared as the backdrop for another photo display of society wives in *Town and Country* magazine in 1954.

Yet the business was entering an awkward period—caught between growing competition for the tourists' dollars and changing attitudes in Asheville—that was soon complicated as Asheville began making plans for a new airport to serve the city and the region's expanding economy.

CHAPTER 7

The Airport Fight

B old entrepreneurs had helped the railroads open Asheville and western North Carolina, with tourism paying part of the cost. In the years following World War II, many argued that the same vision was needed with air transportation. Prominent men at City Hall and within the chamber of commerce warned that unless Asheville improved air service at the landing field the city shared with Hendersonville twenty-five miles to the south, Asheville would return to the isolation it had known a hundred years earlier before the railroad.

There was ample evidence that the Asheville-Hendersonville airport needed attention. The military had improved the facility during the war, but it was still fit to operate only about six hours a day. Heavy morning fog prevented airlines from scheduling regular service before noon, and a lack of field lights and instrumentation made nighttime service impossible. Nearby Burney Mountain was such a hazard that if a pilot missed his approach by as little as 3 percent, the result would be disastrous.

By 1954, a group of energetic boosters within the chamber of commerce and the city's business community said they had the perfect site for a new facility. An exhaustive engineering study of potential sites focused on eight hundred acres on Biltmore Estate's west side directly across from the château in a rolling plateau of the French Broad River valley. According to the report, it was the only site that met all the criteria for twenty-four-hour all-weather operations. At the time, the land was part of the dairy and farm operations of the Biltmore Company and set apart from the main body of the estate by the river. It was accessible by road from U.S. 74, the main highway into Asheville from the west. Direct access to the dairy farms from the estate was by way of a simple flat-bottom ferry that used the river current to carry it across the French Broad.

Proponents argued that the new airport would not detract from the estate. The runways, the control tower, and support buildings would all be hidden from the château by a ridge along the river's west side. The leading argument, however, was that the airport was essential for Asheville to remain competitive among cities in North Carolina and across the mountains in Tennessee. Both Knoxville and Charlotte had superior facilities.

Despite the disclaimers, there was no mistaking that development of the west side would interrupt the magical vista from the château to the mountains on the western horizon. A visitor standing at the window in George Vanderbilt's bedroom on the second floor would clearly see and hear the rumbling four-engine airliners on takeoff as well as in their glide pattern to the airport. The view of Mt. Pisgah that Richard Morris Hunt had saved for his patron's chambers would never be the same.

Taking the Biltmore land for the new airport had been proposed first in 1948. Junius Adams had held off proponents at that time, and the plan had not gained widespread official endorsement. Now the plans were incorporated into a formal proposal

The tall, mature tulip poplars lining the esplanade had created a corridor of green by the late 1950s, when visitors were allowed to park their cars right at the front door.

endorsed and promoted by the city and county governments. A referendum to approve the sale of local bonds to finance half the estimated $3 million cost was scheduled for early May 1955. Adams girded for a fight.

The bond campaign enjoyed the enthusiastic support of Asheville's newspapers, the *Citizen* and the *Times*, now owned by the same company. The *Citizen's* influential editor, Don Elias, had little sympathy for Adams's objections. He and the lawyer had been at each other for more than twenty years when Adams represented a financial interest that had lost a bid for ownership of the papers and had been left with a minority stake. As the editor of the largest newspaper in western North Carolina, Elias was one of Asheville's leading figures. It was said that he, Asheville city manager Weldon Weir, and Buncombe County Sheriff Lawrence Brown could determine the outcome of elections in Asheville, and their influence extended into the region as well. Joining these three in support of the airport were a majority of the membership of the chamber of commerce, a group called the Asheville Business Council, and the Junior Chamber of Commerce, or the Jaycees, who were known for their hard work and the long hours they put into civic projects.

This was a formidable array of political talent. Proponents pegged their entire campaign on progress. One editorial in the *Asheville Times* concluded, "Let's 'think big' and for a bright and more prosperous future get this new all-weather 24-hour airport NOW."[1]

Adams and the Cecils were in a difficult spot. Heretofore, the interests of Biltmore and Asheville had always accommodated each other. The chamber of commerce still handled virtually all the advertising for the estate under the arrangements made in 1929 with John and Cornelia Cecil. During the tussle with Tennessee over the final route of the Blue Ridge Parkway, Adams had pitched in and used his own political contacts to boost North Carolina's interest and help swing the decision in the state's favor. As a result, the parkway passed through Asheville.

Even when problems arose, they were handled quietly. Such was the case with the location of the broadcast tower of Asheville's new television station, WLOS-TV, at the top of Mt. Pisgah. The station's steel needle reached well above the tree line atop Pisgah and was visible from virtually every point on the compass, especially from Buck Spring Lodge. There was no mistaking human intrusion upon pristine forest. The Cecils kept their silence, however, in deference to John Cecil's admonition to his sons that to object for their own personal interests was simply bad form.[2]

This time the stakes were clearly higher than a tower that disturbed the view of a few family members. The construction of the airport on estate land would alter the landscape, disturb the setting of the château, and have other serious consequences. Further development would inevitably follow the airport, thus increasing pressure for Biltmore to release additional property.

The deference to Biltmore that had once existed among the city's establishment wasn't as firm with the new generation of leaders. Perhaps Asheville had begun to take the estate for granted, or perhaps it was that younger promoters in the city saw industrial development as a more promising golden goose than tourism. Biltmore was no longer Buncombe County's largest employer. New industries, such as American Enka, whose huge plant sat on the outskirts of Asheville, now employed five times as many workers as the Biltmore Company. And there was a determined new effort to find more industrial citizens.

The threat of the loss of eight hundred acres of prime land on the estate aroused all the family, but they left the organization of the opposition to Adams. Edith Gerry and the Cecils—George and William—remained silent during the campaign. To meet the challenge, Adams organized a front group with a clumsy but clearly defined name: the Committee Opposed to Bond Issue for Another Airport. Adams took no public role after issuing a statement in opposition to the proposed site. He left the appearances at civic clubs and public forums to Harry L. Nettles, a nurseryman with ties to the estate, and Kingsland Van Winkle, a leading attorney and one of Adams's fellow vestryman at All Souls.

The campaign grew especially heated in the final days before the referendum. Proponents recruited airline executives to plead the case for a facility designed to accommodate the new four-engine airliners that were fast replacing the lumbering twin-engine DC-3s. The famed World War I flying ace Eddie Rickenbacker, who was now the head of Eastern Airlines, paid a call on the city five days before the vote. He told a civic club luncheon audience, "Don't, I beg you, let Asheville become and stay 'a village.' We've all seen them—the little villages that refused to let the railroad come through—and they're still villages."[3]

The speech sent Adams's blood into a perfect boil. As Rickenbacker left town, the bond opponents were crafting a newspaper ad pointedly telling Rickenbacker to keep his opinions to himself. "Goodbye, Captain Rickenbacker. It was mighty nice of you to come down from Eastern Airlines—but the voters hereabouts didn't really need you."[4]

For the most part, both sides tried to keep the attention of voters focused on the financial costs of the proposed venture. Proponents said the investment would be returned quickly by increased business and growth in Asheville. Adams and his allies reminded voters of the heady years during the 1920s when public officials had issued millions of dollars in bonds in the name of progress. It was a debt that had humbled the city and remained unpaid. In fact, the bonds for the airport would have to be issued by the county government because Asheville's city government bond rating was still not respectable.

The most stinging rebuke to Adams and Biltmore came two days before the election in a newspaper advertisement that raised the skirts on some of Biltmore's affairs. The ad claimed that the estate's twelve thousand–plus acres were valued at an average of $50 an acre, and the Biltmore Company had enjoyed preferential treatment for years. It was inferred that the loss of the eight hundred acres was a small price for Biltmore to pay in exchange for such a favorable tax bill over the years. The inference to foreign ownership was also dead wrong. There was no missing the advertisement. It was topped with an illustration of an alligator shedding tears. "Would the same tears flow out along the French Broad and lap over some pasture land of a property, in part owned abroad, that the community wishes to make use of at a fair price."[5]

While Adams was up against the strongest political coalition imaginable, the old lawyer knew his community and called in his chits, some of which had lain uncollected for fifty years. The Vanderbilt interests may have lost some of their clout downtown—otherwise the issue never would have gone this far—but in the county, personal ties to the estate were exceptionally strong, especially among farmers who sold their milk to the dairy. Adams also made sure that preachers in west Asheville, whose churches sat under the proposed flight path, understood the disturbance that landing airliners might cause in the middle of their Sunday sermons.

The bonds were defeated by a two-to-one margin, with voters in the county and in west Asheville giving Adams the overwhelming margin. He was so pleased with the results that he had one of the estate's best-bred heifers taken to Nettles's farm in appreciation. He wired William: "We beat the bastards, two to one."[6]

In a letter to William's brother, George, who was traveling in France on his honeymoon, Adams later reported that the outcome was a resounding defeat for the newspapers. "I think they got the shock of their lives and have learned a lesson."[7]

It was also a resounding endorsement of the estate's place within the community. After more than fifty years, local residents appeared to be happy to have the estate as a neighbor and did not want to do anything to disturb the relationship.

Ten days before the election, the windows of the château were filled with light and the Vanderbilt silver was brought to a high shine as the family made ready for the celebration of the marriage of George Cecil and Nancy Owen of Asheville. George had finished his role as an understudy to the farm manager, E. D. Mitchell, and had joined Adams as an officer of the Biltmore Company. His primary focus was the dairy, which had expanded with the acquisition of a dairy processing plant 150 miles east of Asheville in Winston-Salem. Plans also were afoot to build a $1.2 million plant just outside the Lodge Gate on Hendersonville Road to replace the aging creamery on the estate.

The wedding party enjoyed the trappings of the kind of festivities that had once been commonplace at the château. Edith Gerry arrived from Rhode Island with an entourage of attendants, including two butlers, a chef, a chauffeur, and a nurse. The former mistress of Biltmore was eighty-two years old. A stroke five years earlier had left her confined to a wheelchair, but she retained much of her flair for life. She and her husband had made their way to Asheville in a private railcar that had been loaned to them by the president of the New York, New Haven and Hartford Railroad Company. The trip south included a stopover in Washington, D.C., where they entertained old friends at a cocktail party on a siding near the Capitol.

The Gerrys had become only intermittent visitors to North Carolina in the years since Peter Gerry had retired from the Senate in 1947. Before her stroke, Edith had made at least one trip a year to settle business matters with Adams, including balancing the books at the Biltmore Forest Country Club, where she wrote a check to cover the year's losses. Her allegiance was to Rhode Island, not North Carolina, although she and her husband spent considerable time at Gerry's country house, Lake Delaware Farm, in Delhi, New York.

The wedding was Edith Gerry's last visit to Biltmore. She died in December 1958 at her home in Providence, a year after the death of her husband. Missing from most accounts of her full and vigorous life was mention of her role in securing the preservation of Biltmore. At the time of her death, the château and the main body of the estate—less the lands that were part of Pisgah National Forest—was much the same as the day she and George Vanderbilt returned from their honeymoon to be welcomed by a huge floral horseshoe and a host of estate workers. The toll of the years, compounded by occasional indifference and petty theft, had reduced the furnishings, and smaller objects such as pieces of china and silver were missing. At the same time, however, the foundations of the château were as solid as the day they were laid. Olmsted's gardens had come to life. The forests had restored the land. The combined efforts of Beadle and Adams, reinforced by the determination and sheer force of will of Edith Gerry, had kept intact George Vanderbilt's collection of art, books, and other treasures. There was nothing else quite like it in America that remained in private hands.

Whether Edith's grandsons, George and William, could or even would continue to maintain the château and gardens for another year, another decade, or another generation was an open question. The upkeep of the house remained a serious drain on the company whose main business was milk and ice cream, not tourism. Maintenance of the house and gardens now cost the Biltmore Company more than $158,000 a year. After thirty years, gate receipts from tourists had produced a profit in only one year, although they had come close in others. Without the support of the dairy (producing gross revenues of nearly $12 million by the late 1950s), the farm operations, and the renewed timber sales, the château would long ago have been forsaken as more of a burden than anyone would wish to bear.

Most people—nearly everyone in fact—believed that the private preservation of the château was impossible in the long run. But no one had a firm plan for the future. One suggestion floating in the 1950s was that the château and some property be placed in the hands of a foundation. Writing to William Cecil in 1958, Junius Adams Jr., the judge's son who had succeeded his father as the company's legal counsel, described Biltmore as "nothing more nor less than a successful property management trust, which by force of circumstances has built up a rather large dairy operation."[8]

William may have been the only person who saw any hope for the future of the house and gardens. His attraction to Biltmore had not diminished from his postwar visit in 1947 or in 1950 when he argued that he should leave Harvard and come to North Carolina to replace Beadle as superintendent of the estate. His father and Adams convinced him to stay at Harvard. Afterward, William took a job at Chase National Bank in New York, and upon completion of a rotation for junior executives through the bank's departments, he landed a slot in the foreign department.

Nearly ten years later, in 1959, Cecil was thirty-one, just four years shy of coming into his inheritance, when he happened upon Chase President David Rockefeller, who asked what the family planned to do with that "white elephant" it owned in North Carolina.

"I'm going to turn it into a black elephant," Cecil replied.

"Can't be done," said Rockefeller. "I've tried it at Williamsburg."[9]

Thinking back on the encounter some years later, Cecil said, "This would undoubtedly have discouraged a less stubborn man, but all it did was to convince me that I had to try and that, more importantly, I had to succeed."[10]

CHAPTER 8

Homecoming

A few years before William Cecil moved south, a publicist at
the Asheville Chamber of Commerce responded to an adver-
tiser in the *New York Times* who was seeking a castle to use as a
backdrop for a motion picture. Lou Harshaw rushed off a packet
of photographs of the Biltmore château, and a few weeks later, she
was showing Hollywood director Charles Vidor around the esplanade as his crew measured the house and grounds for camera
angles. In September 1955, the estate closed for three weeks for the
filming of *The Swan*, a romantic comedy starring Grace Kelly and
Alec Guinness.

MGM was in a hurry to get the motion picture into theaters.
The period piece of a royal romance set in 1812 Austria closely
mirrored Kelly's own plans to marry and become Princess Grace of
Monaco. When *The Swan* was released in 1956, it was overshadowed by another Kelly hit, *High Society*. Nonetheless, the estate received a starring role with generous scenes of the house, the grounds,
the terraces, and a final, lasting image of a swan gliding on the

lagoon with the château behind on a distant hill. The impact was immediate; ticket revenue at Biltmore jumped 30 percent in 1956.

The elegant house that appeared on the silver screen was polished and scrubbed. Light spilled from the windows. The interiors were brightly furnished, and the gardens and terraces were neat and trim. That image was more Hollywood than reality, however. The château itself was still sound enough. The roof didn't leak, and the heating system, lights, and plumbing were in reasonable condition considering their age. Richard Morris Hunt had used the latest technology in his design, and the basics still met the demands of modern usage. Even the telephone switchboard, the first in Asheville, handled calls with clarity. At the same time, the house was not the grand palace featured in *The Swan*.

After more than fifty years, Biltmore carried the stain of time, the elements, and in some cases, benign neglect. Visitors walked through rooms that were dark and gloomy. The once-golden hue of the oak trim in the Winter Garden, then called the Palm Court, was hidden under a dull accumulation of dirt that had hardened after years of polish and oil. Some of the flags in the banquet hall clung to their staffs by little more than a thread. Common everyday wall-to-wall carpet covered the floor of the Morning Salon, which was called the Print Room. Some pieces of furniture were in need of repair. The housekeeping staff, reduced to a bare minimum by Junius Adams's budget cuts, never kept up with the demands at hand. Harshaw said it reminded her of a "sad house."[1]

"It was run down, but only of old age," William Cecil recalled. "It was beginning to be shabby. Not much had been done to it since 1915. There wasn't much money here. There wasn't much going on. No one was particularly interested in it."[2]

Beyond the immediate gardens, which had seen more attention during Beadle's reign as superintendent, the grounds needed work as well. The grass along the Approach Road was often shaggy and overgrown. It was mowed only three or four times a year. The lawn on the esplanade was cut with only slightly more frequency. If a stone fell out of one of the bridges, the gap was left open or, at best, poorly repaired. The paint on the farm buildings was faded, and the barnyards were becoming overgrown with weeds. The creamery had been abandoned in favor of the new processing plant just outside the Lodge Gate on Hendersonville Road. The Biltmore Dairy Bar that adjoined the plant on the busy highway was on its way to becoming a landmark for a new generation of tourists.

Visitor accommodations at the house were inconvenient or worse. The public toilet was downstairs adjacent to the gymnasium and accessible by way of a narrow, winding staircase. The booklet for the self-guided tour was dull and had not been updated in years. Accommodating the public seemed an afterthought or unwanted burden. Some prospective guests never made it onto the estate grounds because it was simply too inconvenient to buy a ticket at the Biltmore offices in Biltmore Village, then cross a busy intersection to reach the entrance at the Lodge Gate.

The boost in attendance occasioned by Hollywood's attention had begun to fade by the time William Cecil and his family arrived in Asheville near the end of 1959 to make their home at the Frith, the Biltmore Forest home that Edith Gerry had left to her grandson. It was going to be another money-losing year on the house and gardens side of the ledger at the Biltmore Company. So far the family's grand gesture in 1930 had cost hundreds of thousands of dollars. No one believed William could reverse a thirty-year trend, and most told him so.

William had every reason to remain with a comfortable and promising career at the nation's leading bank, Chase Manhattan. When he joined the family business, he took a cut in pay—only Junius Adams and farm manager Everett Mitchell made more than

$10,000 a year. Cecil's expense allowance in Washington, where he was Chase's man on Capitol Hill, was four times that amount. Opportunities with the company were limited. His elder brother, George, was in line to succeed Adams as president of the Biltmore Company.

What none had taken into account was that William considered Biltmore to be his home. He didn't expect to live or raise his family in the huge house. He had learned about the pitfalls of château living during his visits over the past ten years. Life on the estate isolated one from the neighbors, and accommodations in the mansion were not that luxurious without the support of a host of servants, which he could not afford. The food was generally cold by the time it reached the table from the kitchen down below. The stairs were steep and the heat never seemed to warm the rooms. And one had to be forever mindful of appearances with early-morning tourists wandering about the main floor.

For William, the estate was home in the broader, deeper meaning of the word. Biltmore was where he planned to put down roots after a lifetime of dislocation. In his thirty-plus years, he had accumulated a long list of addresses that included boarding schools in France and Switzerland, a flat in London, the navy, Harvard, New York, and most recently Washington. Biltmore was permanent, enduring. It was the first real home he had ever known, and his patrimony drew him south like a magnet. His wife, the former Mary Ryan of Long Island, New York, or Mimi as she was called, knew soon after they were married in 1957 that they would eventually live in Asheville. When the bank posted William to Washington, which proved to be an unfulfilling assignment, his attention turned to North Carolina long before the car was packed. That was fine with her. She liked the open spaces and thousands of acres over which to roam on horseback. Her enthusiasm made the move all the more exciting for the family.

Cecil was bound by a deep-seated, very English devotion to the estate that would soon come to him and his brother under the terms of the family trust agreement. "Place is very important in England," Cecil said sometime later. "[Americans] don't give a damn about place. We are expected to move about four or five times in our lifetime."[3] He planned to stay put.

His obligation reached back to the 1930s when his grand-mother, his parents, and Junius Adams had set out to preserve for him and his brother their grandfather's magnificent house, his gardens, and his noble experiments in agriculture. Now it was time for William to assume responsibility for their efforts on his behalf. In 1963, when William turned thirty-five, the estate would belong to the brothers.

Could he make a difference? William didn't know, but he was enough of a Vanderbilt to believe that hard work, common sense, and an entrepreneurial spirit made a good combination. He was determined to make a go at seeing that his inheritance was in good shape when it left his hands for the next generation, regardless of what he was told of the impossible nature of his task.

"There was always this negativism that it can't be done," he said. "If you ever want me to do something, just say, 'It can't be done,'" Cecil said. "Everyone told me it couldn't be done, so I just stuck my feet in it and I said, 'We'll see about that.' And that is what motivated me."[4] In his private moments, however, he believed that the best he could hope for was to break even by the time he retired.

William Cecil took an office in the company headquarters on Bilt-more Plaza in the complex of village buildings just outside the Lodge Gate. It was the same building where his grandfather's agents had once conducted business. The early months were discouraging. The existing management was focused entirely on operation of the dairy and the farm, and they received him with benign disdain. "Any stupid question I asked was answered with a tolerant smile and then it was made quite clear that I was better off not lingering around. Everyone knew that the dairy was famous not only for its milk but for its ice cream and that this enterprise kept the estate together. They subscribed to the common wisdom that nothing could be done to make the estate and house self-sufficient."[5]

"Nobody gave a damn about the house," he said, "except it was the cross we have got to bear. I took it off their hands and they knew it was going to fail."[6]

As he explored the operation of the estate, he found that little had changed in the thirty years since the company was formed. The paternalism of the estate remained intact. Entire families continued to work the individual dairy farms, taking their pay in milk and cash for any production over their quotas. William was astonished to see estate employees lined up outside the company office each Saturday morning waiting to receive their pay envelope. Inside, a clerk wearing a green eyeshade and hunched over the desk called each person forward and recited aloud their itemized deductions in a voice that filled the room. If a man was short on his deductions, all knew about his financial embarrassment.

Visitors to the house and gardens were still bound by rules and regulations adopted in 1930 that were printed on the back of the ticket stubs. Admission not only required a fee of $2.40 but visitors were asked to supply their name, home address, and a local contact—conditions that Adams had imposed at the outset for an abundance of security. Now this anachronism was honored in the breach. "Who gave a damn where they were staying?" Cecil said some years later. "We had more Mr. and Mrs. Smiths than you could shake a stick at."

Just buying a ticket required persistence if one didn't know the rules. Sales were handled at the Biltmore Company offices, which were separated from the Lodge Gate by a busy highway. In 1957, George Cecil had tried to convince Adams that the awkward arrangement was driving customers away. He had found that about a third of those who arrived at the Lodge Gate seeking admission drove on rather than ford the heavy flow of traffic on U.S. 25, then endure the limited parking at the company offices. Adams was unmoved.

Adams was not in a mood for changes. Shortly after his own arrival, William had proposed a less complicated ticket that he argued could be printed at a lower cost. The company was still using check-proof paper—another Adams security measure—that exposed any erasures and was very expensive. "Well William," Adams told him, "in 1930, I worked out the wording on the tickets and the rules and regulations. I can't remember why I did it that way but the reason was valid then and it still is."[7]

In 1960, Adams was well past seventy years old. Age had slowed his step and his eyesight was all but gone. Nonetheless, the brothers approached him with deference, and the elder Adams remained the baron of Biltmore, his position all the more secure since Edith Gerry's death in 1958. He continued to live at Farmcote, ruling by fiat and almost by whim. He once told farm manager Everett Mitchell that any employee seen driving without both hands on the wheel was subject to dismissal. "I am convinced that if God gave a man two hands and arms for any particular purpose it was for the purpose of driving an automobile," Adams wrote Mitchell.[8] When a security guard prevented Adams's daughter-in-law from entering a road closed temporarily for the shooting of a scene in *The Swan*, Adams had the man dismissed. The guard was later reinstated at William's insistence, since the man was simply following orders from the moviemakers, who had authority to limit traffic.

Whatever might be thought of Adams and his flinty reputation and high-handed manner, he had played a pivotal role in the modern story of Biltmore. He had been a devoted guardian of the integrity of the estate property, and tough, hard-nosed decisions had saved Biltmore from sale, financial ruin, and division. His most significant achievement was the success of the dairy. Working with Mitchell, Adams had restored Biltmore's stature as a model farm and a financial success. What was valued at less than a quarter of a million dollars in 1930 had grown into a $12 million enterprise.[9] Dairy profits had secured the estate, unencumbered by debt or outside ownership, for George and William Cecil. After such a personal investment in the property, it is not difficult to see why he held fast to the title of president of Biltmore Company to the day he died in January 1962.

Upon Adams's passing, George succeeded to the presidency of the company. He was thirty-five and well liked about town. He had recently been named to the board of directors of one of the state's newest banks, First Union National Bank, which was formed from the merger of Union National of Charlotte and First National of Asheville, the bank that Edith Gerry had helped underwrite at Adams's behest during the Depression. George and his wife, Nancy, had begun raising a family of six children at Eastcote, the turn-of-the-century residence that had been Chauncey Beadle's home for nearly fifty years.

William had been in and out of the city for more than a decade, but his circle of acquaintances was small and centered on friends who belonged to the Biltmore Forest Country Club. He was tall, thin like his brother, and had his father's receding hairline and high forehead. His height and reserved nature, along with a pronounced British accent, suggested he was detached and aloof, but those who engaged him in conversation discovered his wit and charm. He had a generous smile.

William was an unknown among most of the employees on the estate and was at a decided disadvantage to his brother, who had proved his worth in his own early days by sweating and digging ditches with the farm help. Cecil said, "I had, after all, a Harvard education and an English accent and had served in the British Navy and was a New York banker corrupted by Washington."[10]

William was elected vice president of the Biltmore Company. The restlessness between the two brothers that Adams had warned their grandmother about some years before remained, but they could pull in tandem. Nothing less than total cooperation was required in the spring of 1962 as the estate faced a threat to its boundaries at least as serious as the uproar over the location of the Asheville airport.

As the airport fight was building in the mid-1950s, government surveyors were already prospecting routes for public roadways across the estate. This time, the loss of Biltmore land for public use was not an option. It was inevitable. For the Blue Ridge Parkway to reach its final destination at the town of Cherokee eighty miles southwest of Asheville, the route would have to cross Biltmore land. More troubling, however, was the proposed intersection of two interstate highways in Asheville. All these roads promised profound change to the existing landscape both for the estate and for the community. The question for the Cecils was not how to block construction of these new roads, which they knew were important for the economic future of Asheville and Biltmore, but how to minimize the impact.

Government right-of-way engineers had selected a tentative route across the Biltmore property for the parkway by the late 1930s, shortly after U.S. Secretary of the Interior Harold Ickes had settled the dispute between North Carolina and Tennessee over which side of the Smoky Mountains tourists would see. The Biltmore segment was the first in a series west of Asheville that would carry the parkway through Pisgah National Forest to Mt. Pisgah where it ultimately would pass close by George Vanderbilt's lodge at Buck Spring. In fact, the proposed route west of the French Broad River roughly followed an early horse trail that wound along the ridgeline up to the site of the lodge.

As negotiations for acquisition of right of way commenced, Adams's earlier enthusiasm for the parkway was put to the test. Survey teams got a warm welcome at first, but the reception became less so as the actual taking of land grew imminent. The government wanted a strip of real estate from U.S. 25 at the southern tip of Biltmore Forest, where the roadway was to pass within a hundred yards of the Frith, along a southwesterly route through the estate's forestland to the French Broad River. Altogether, the government wanted 308 acres of land that was owned by either the Biltmore Company, the Biltmore Forest Company, or Edith Gerry.

The proposed route was relatively benign. The roadway would cross the southern end of the estate's lands, well away from the house and gardens, and two lanes of low-speed traffic did not appear to create much of a disturbance. Adams's concern, first raised by Beadle in the 1940s, was access to the estate's farm roads that intersected with the parkway. Most would be closed. The government's plans also included an overlook on the Biltmore property at the river's edge. Adams argued that the overlook would become a parking lot for poachers eager to bag a deer in the deep forests south of the château. Negotiations finally concluded in 1956. The government got its overlook, but put it on the west side of the river on national forest land.

The greatest loss to the estate and to preservationists occurred in 1962 when Buck Spring Lodge was demolished. Edith Gerry had left the lodge and surrounding land to her grandson, George, who lost the lodge to the parkway that passed within a stone's throw of the complex of Hunt-designed log buildings. Rather than preserve the buildings, the National Park Service dismantled them.

Some of the chestnut logs that had become impossible to find since the American chestnut forests were destroyed by a blight were eventually used by George in a new home. Forty years later, the only evidence of Vanderbilt's mountain hideaway was a set of steps leading away from an overlook.

However, the plans for high-speed four-lane interstate highways with wide, grassy medians and ample shoulders would never be hidden in the deep forest of pines and oaks like the parkway's two lanes of blacktop. And Biltmore was caught in the intersection of two of these superhighways.

In a significant way, Asheville was blessed by the plans for the nation's new interstate road building program announced in 1957. Early plans called for an intersection of two routes at the edge of the city. One was Interstate 26, which originated in Charleston, South Carolina, and ended at Asheville. It promised easy access to the mountains from the southeast, especially for visitors and residents with summer retreats in western North Carolina. The other was Interstate 40, which then began in Greensboro, North Carolina, and crossed the breadth of the United States to end on the Pacific coast in San Diego. This route would provide full, easy passage through the Smokies, open the North Carolina mountains to the Midwest, and create a long-awaited transmountain commercial link between Asheville and Knoxville, Tennessee.

Early maps introducing the two routes to the public in 1958 were speculative and proved totally unreliable in the long run. For example, at the outset the entrance of Interstate 26 into the city was parallel to the existing U.S. 25 on the estate's east side. When construction began, however, the route followed the western bank of the French Broad River. This new roadway caused some dislocation for the estate as it severed long-established farm roads, but it was well west of the château, the gardens, and the portion of the estate visited by tourists. Years later, it would be difficult to even catch a glimpse of the house from I-26.

Interstate 40 was more problematic. The engineers' first choice called for a corridor along the north bank of the Swannanoa River valley. This was the preferred route in the 1960s for the same reason it had been chosen by railroad builders before the turn of the century. The valley floor was fairly level and free of geological obstacles. There were a few manufacturing plants and businesses alongside the railroad tracks across from the Biltmore property, but the route was relatively free of private residences, thus reducing the threat to the highway department of pesky condemnation suits. The consequences for Biltmore were horrendous. The Lodge Gate, Biltmore's front door, would have been left in the shadow of a huge overpass.

Two riverside corridors were considered, and both were bad as far as the Cecils were concerned. The one that followed a course along the north side of the river passed within 125 feet of the Lodge Gate before crossing the river near the site of old Victoria Bridge, an early farm entrance to the estate. An alternative route came into the valley the same way and crossed the Swannanoa farther west. It also would have required the destruction of a Hunt-designed farm cottage and produce-packing complex that had once been the center of the estate's truck farming operation. A similar route continued farther down the river's north side before connecting to I-26 on the west side of the French Broad River. Either would have dramatically changed the character of the visitors' introduction to Biltmore. Instead of a pastoral view of open farmland, visitors would have been confronted by acres of concrete roadway and speeding traffic. (If this route had been chosen, it was later discovered, the pavement would have covered several important archaeological sites.)

The Cecils protested and proposed a route that was south of the house and gardens in the general vicinity of the Blue Ridge Parkway. They argued that this path would reduce land acquisition costs, require fewer bridges, and do less harm to the estate. Highway planners turned them down. Such a route would require expensive changes to the construction of I-26, which was already under way. This proposal was discarded as no more practical than a very early plan to take I-40 around the north side of Asheville, thus avoiding the estate land altogether.

Negotiations continued for more than two years. While the brothers talked with highway officials in Raleigh, William tried to find some relief in Washington, where his wife's first cousin, Jacqueline Kennedy, was the wife of President John F. Kennedy. Before William could secure an appointment with federal highway officials, however, Lyndon Johnson had succeeded the assassinated president. He finally secured an appointment at the Federal Bureau of Public Roads. A deputy administrator kept him waiting for more than an hour, then dismissed his concern as nothing more than an effort to save what the highway official believed was an old mountain hotel.

William returned home. He was still fuming but responded with restrained indignation when he sent a brochure to Washington from the house along with a copy of the designation of Biltmore Estate as a National Historic Landmark by the U.S. Department of the Interior. The landmark designation had not been sought, but it was well received in the spring of 1963, just as the negotiations for the interstate routes were becoming contentious. Biltmore was named one of twenty-two sites among the new additions to the nation's 404 Registered National Historic Landmarks. Added at the same time were the Santa Fe Trail; the Kit Carson House in Taos, New Mexico; and the U.S. frigate *Constellation*, the aging wooden warship floating in Boston harbor. Biltmore's recognition was in honor of its place as the nation's "home of conservation" and

Highway engineers designed special rock-faced supports for the interstate highway bridges that crossed Frederick Law Olmsted's Approach Road on the estate.

George Vanderbilt's farsighted support of forestry and the establishment of the nation's first forestry school. In light of recent developments, it was ironic that the house received only a three-sentence mention in the three-page documentation supporting the nomination.

The nomination followed close on the heels of an impromptu but determined effort by U.S. Secretary of Agriculture Orville Freeman to celebrate Vanderbilt's early efforts on behalf of forestry. In 1961, Freeman had visited Asheville as part of a fiftieth anniversary celebration of the Weeks Act, which had expanded the national forest program. On a trip to the Pink Beds and the site of Dr. Carl Schenck's forestry school, Freeman had declared, "We intend to make it a real kind of mecca for those who love the outdoors." Late in 1962, a historian arrived at Biltmore and prepared the documentation that led to the designation in 1963, along with the homes of Gifford Pinchot and Frederick Law Olmsted.

"They wanted us to have it," William Cecil said some years later of the recognition. "It was not just the house. It was the whole estate." Unfortunately, he said, the designation provided little protection against highway development as it would in later years. "It was virtually worthless," he said, but it helped to remind road builders that the estate warranted some special attention.[11]

The final I-40 route was about the best that the brothers could hope for. The highway entered the property south of the Lodge Gate rather than beside the river, and the roadway was tucked below a ridge where trees would eventually hide it throughout most of the year. The most significant loss was a quarry that had been the source of the rock used to build many of the low bridges along the Approach Road and elsewhere. After construction ended, Olmsted had turned it into a landscaping feature that included a waterfall. The Cecils did win a major concession from the federal road builders who agreed to face the interstate bridges with stone rather than leave them in bare concrete. The government also paid for extensive landscaping, thus softening the visual impact of the overpass on the Approach Road. Altogether, I-40 came to occupy 124 acres while I-26 took nearly 190 acres of the estate's land. An agreement was announced in August 1964.

"They thought we didn't want the interstate," Cecil said many years later. "We wanted the interstate, but we wanted it to go where it wouldn't harm us. We wanted the highway to open up the mountains."

CHAPTER 9

Mr. C

In later years, William Cecil liked to say that all he needed to know about preserving and managing a historic house he learned from his forebears. The combination of the Cecil and Vanderbilt lineage produced a genetic code aptly suited to private preservation. "The Cecils were all diplomacy, all gentle aristocracy, no business whatsoever," he said. "The Vanderbilts, on the other hand, just go out and make the money and you find a way to do it."[1]

Cecil's entrepreneurial talent had emerged early enough. As a teenage seaman in the British Navy, he had rolled cigarettes on a small machine and sold them to his shipmates for some extra spending money. It is a stretch to imagine a Vanderbilt strapped for cash, but Cecil declares, "I didn't have a nickel. The pay in the navy was three pounds a week. So, if you wanted anything you had to hustle. I learned how to repair shoes and roll cigarettes, and I rolled a hell of a lot of them."

That was the sort of creativity that Cecil brought to bear at Biltmore after he arrived in Asheville in midwinter with his wife, Mimi, and their toddlers, Bill and Dini. At the time, the house and gardens were open year-round, closing only on Thanksgiving Day, Christmas Day, and New Year's Day. Attendance averaged about three thousand visitors a month, but most of them arrived in the summer. On some of the cold, dreary days of January and February in the winter of 1960 Cecil did not see a single paying guest.

The quiet days were unnerving. The winter lull gave him an opportunity to take a measure of the place and become acquainted with the forty to fifty employees who were assigned to the house and gardens. These included a housekeeping staff, guards at the house and Lodge Gate, as well as gardeners and others at the greenhouse, where a successor to Chauncey Beadle was nearing retirement age.

As Cecil explored the château, he was encouraged. What the house needed most, he decided, was someone to attend to routine maintenance and upkeep. Thankfully, whatever flaws he discovered were mostly cosmetic and did not require major expense to repair. No one had given the house much attention since the mid-1950s when George and Nancy Cecil had moved out. Eager to have someone present night and day, Junius Adams had hired a curator to manage the inside staff and prepare an inventory of the twenty-thousand–volume library. An apartment had been provided on the second floor for the man and his wife, but the engagement was short-lived. Thereafter, the curator's salary went to the hiring of a horticulturist whose specialty was roses.

Cecil brought a fresh and appreciative perspective to Biltmore. He saw the château not with the eye of a curator hired to present and explain a historic property but as a devoted family member who was proud of what his grandfather had left for him and others to enjoy. Like his father before him, William believed that visitors should be made to feel like guests rather than ticket holders and should be welcomed warmly and treated with courtesy.

He wanted visitors to stroll at their own pace, unencumbered by guides, and see a residence that met his grandfather's standards for hospitality as well as appearance. Details were important. If a lightbulb was dark, Cecil had it replaced immediately. He insisted that the clocks be set to the correct time, and fresh flowers from the garden were placed strategically along the tour. In the bedrooms, a book was left open on a table. Clothes were visible in the armoires. When the weather cooperated, the windows were opened to allow fresh air to circulate freely and remove any mustiness. No photographs were allowed inside. The flash of cameras was an annoying distraction to visitors, and, Cecil said, it was just something you didn't do when you were visiting in a private home.

The basic tour route he found in 1960 had not changed since Adams laid it out in the 1930s. "If you came to visit," he said, "what you saw was the front entrance and you went through the ground floor—the Oak Drawing Room, Palm Court, Breakfast Room, Banquet Hall, the Tapestry Gallery and the Library. There was no flow to it.

"You went upstairs, saw the Red Room or the hall on the second floor. Then Mr. Vanderbilt's bedroom, the in-between room, his mother's room, the Gold Room on the end and down and out." Most guests then headed to the gardens. "That was pretty good," he added.

Cecil's early attention to detail became the standard for the years ahead. It not only enhanced the visitors' experience but also reminded staff members of their responsibility. If something relatively minor such as a broken lightbulb was ignored, said house manager Richard King, whose apprenticeship began in the early 1970s, "then it's easy to let dust gather here and then it's very easy for these things to become acceptable. When the little things become acceptable, it doesn't take long until a lot of things become acceptable that really shouldn't be."[2]

Cecil also gave the legends of the house a thorough cleansing. "It was well-rumored that Mr. Vanderbilt had Caesar's bathtub," Cecil said. The story was not true—the alleged tub was old, but it came with relatively modern plumbing fittings. Yet the story was passed on as gospel. "Somehow or another, if a palm had been greased, you got to see that. We put a stop to that by putting up a mirror [that allowed all to see the tub]. And chewing the hell out of the [guards]."

"You have to be absolutely honest," Cecil said, reciting one of the lessons he was taught in his early years. "You cannot fool people. You don't want to. It is bad business."[3]

He believed that fanciful stories simply undermined the integrity of Biltmore's remarkable collection. There was no need to fabricate legends when there was enough awesome truth in the art, furnishings, and sculpture that visitors encountered by simply walking in the front door of the largest private home in the United States. Unlike many historic houses, whose owners struggled to recover lost furniture and family heirlooms, every item at Biltmore was original to the house. It may not have been the best of a particular period, and some of it was even gaudy, but it reflected the tastes of the collector and therefore was unique to Biltmore. In addition, the clothes that George and Edith Vanderbilt wore on their mountaintop rides were at hand. His desk was filled with letters to the writers, artists, and other friends who had traveled widely with him as he collected the treasures that filled the house. Edith's 1913 Stevens-Duryea convertible remained in running condition and was stored in the stables. In short, Biltmore was real.

Antique dealers and owners of period furnishings often offered their holdings up for sale, and they all received polite replies. In answer to one proffer of a handsome empire sofa, Cecil wrote, "Unfortunately, we have no interest in purchasing furniture since Biltmore House is completely furnished."[4]

Cecil punched up the maintenance schedule outside as well. In the spring, the mowing crew became more attentive to the appearance of the Approach Road, Olmsted's landscaping masterpiece, and the lawn on the esplanade was kept in presentable condition. The handmade brooms that workers had produced during the slack periods under Adams's reign were replaced with more serviceable commercial models.

During William's first summer as overseer of the house and gardens, the estate welcomed its one-millionth visitor, C. M. Vernon of Danville, Virginia. Vernon posed for a picture standing alongside George Cecil, and it appeared in the local papers.[5] The summer attendance showed no improvement over the previous year, however, and as William made plans for 1961, his second year, he looked for economies. He announced that the house and gardens would be closed to visitors from December 15 to January 1. Employees would take a two-week vacation to enjoy the Christmas holidays, then return January 2 to clean and make repairs for the coming season. As he did with most ideas that popped into his head, he had carefully worked out the numbers on an adding machine that he kept close at hand on his desk. The company would lose $1,400 in ticket sales but recover that and more in savings on wages.

There were only so many dollars to be shaved from Junius Adams's already thin budget, however. What Cecil needed most to make Biltmore profitable was more visitors.

"There was no a, b, c," Cecil said some years later of his early experience. "There was no book to go by. We wrote the book."[6]

Biltmore's primary market had always been close at hand. More than three-quarters of the visitors to the estate came from the Carolinas or neighboring states as well as those in the Deep South who flocked to the mountains in the summertime. Over the years, the company's most important advertising had been word-of-mouth and local support by Ashevillians carrying their out-of-town guests to see the place. More importantly, hotel and motel owners made admission tickets available for purchase by their guests at the front desk, keeping a modest discount on the ticket price for themselves. Some even provided transportation to the front door. Convention-eers recruited by the Asheville Chamber of Commerce also received discounts.

As it had since the 1930s, the Biltmore Company depended almost entirely on the Asheville Chamber of Commerce for its advertising, promotion, and overall exposure to the traveling public. This included promotional brochures produced at the chamber's expense and distributed around the region as well as membership for Biltmore in the Southern Highlands Attractions, a trade association that included more than a dozen tourist venues in the mountains of Virginia, North Carolina, and Tennessee. When Cecil arrived, the company's direct out-of-pocket advertising expense for the house and gardens was no more than $1,000 a year.

Biltmore was enjoying a growing reputation beyond its traditional market thanks to North Carolina governor Luther Hodges, who began to promote the state as a tourist destination in the late 1950s. That campaign was continued by his successor, Governor Terry Sanford, and by 1963, tourism revenues exceeded $1 billion and had begun to challenge tobacco as the state's leading cash crop. More than 30 million visitors came to the state that year, and nearly 90 percent arrived by car.

Those who came to Biltmore found it easier to gain admission to the estate. In 1962, a new ticket office had been opened on the green just outside the Lodge Gate. It was a modest building that Cecil had built for half the amount that the company had given him to spend. The company easily recovered the $10,000 investment and was relieved of the aggravating traffic jam at the offices on Biltmore Plaza.

The office opened just in time for Biltmore's second Azalea Festival. Cecil had shamelessly copied the event from a similar floral attraction in the city of Wilmington, North Carolina. The coastal city's production came with a beauty queen and parade that attracted tourists in early spring to a display of natural color. Since the spring floral season in the mountains tracked several weeks behind the weather on the coast, Cecil scheduled Biltmore's festival for early May. The flowers were equally dramatic and drew attention to Chauncey Beadle's dazzling collection of varieties and colors that came into bloom in the gardens just above the Bass Pond. In 1961, the two-day affair, which included a discounted ticket, brought seventy-five hundred visitors to the estate.

As visitation began to inch up and revenue increased, Cecil tightened controls on the expense side of the ledger. He imposed a new financial discipline on the managers of the estate departments, who were given a budget and were expected to live within it. Each area of operations—the house, the greenhouse, the landscaping— was expected to hold its own. If managers didn't give the numbers the attention Cecil thought they deserved, he called them to account. "The pressure of budgets on specialists was evident and in cases of failure resignations began to come in."[7]

"I began to think of other things," he said. "We couldn't afford all our grass mowers, so I got outside contracts. We would go and do landscaping and gardening work for various and sundry companies [off the estate]. That helped fill in."

The success of the Azalea Festival provided an early lesson: visitors from Asheville and nearby cities and towns would return to see Biltmore, but they needed a reason for the trip. It was a message that Cecil reinforced with a new advertising program that began with a visit to the office of the publisher of the Asheville newspapers.

When Cecil joined the Biltmore Company, the entire advertising budget for the estate was invested in two pages of space in special sections. One was devoted to the summer tourist season and the other featured the estate's agricultural enterprises, especially the dairy. Cecil called the newspaper advertising department and canceled both. He then paid a call on the publisher and, feigning ignorance, said he was unaware of the contentious history between the newspaper and Adams. But, he said, whatever had happened in the past, he was ready to start fresh.

"I don't know what the fight was about," he told the publisher, "so why don't we bury whatever hatchets there are. I cancelled all my ads and if we shake hands and come out friends, I'll double my ads. If we don't we'll leave it as it is. And he laughed, we shook hands and became quite good friends."

The cordiality of the new relationship soon spread throughout the paper. Cecil cultivated a relationship with reporters and editors and developed a keen appreciation for the daily flow of the news. For example, when he learned that editors scrambled each week to fill the Wednesday paper, which was usually a large one full of grocery ads, he saw to it that the layout desk had plenty of pictures and copy about Biltmore that they could use as filler. When visiting dignitaries came for a tour of the estate, Cecil alerted the editors ahead of time so that a reporter could be on hand for an interview.

As an accomplished amateur photographer, Cecil got along especially well with the newspaper's photo staff. He had picked up his first camera when he was a teenager and had never put it down. Among his collection of photographs were many taken during his tour with the navy, including one that was particularly meaningful. His ship had made one of the first peacetime stops at Antwerp, Belgium, and while on leave he had visited a cemetery for British soldiers killed in the battle at Arnheim. Upon his return to England, he was talking with a painter working in his mother's home and learned the man's son was buried in the very cemetery he had visited. He pulled out his prints to show the father the cemetery and discovered that among the close-ups of headstones was one that stood over the grave of the painter's son.

Cecil brought his hobby with him to Asheville. He installed a darkroom in the Frith, where he processed his own film and made black-and-white prints. If he captured an interesting shot on the estate, he made sure a copy went to the newspaper's photo department. The editors soon had a generous inventory of images of the house in the summer, in the winter, and everything in between. He also filled in as needed for special duty. On one occasion, the newspaper's own photographers were reluctant to shoot an eclipse of the sun, fearing damage to their lenses. Cecil found protection for his cameras and took the shot for them. He made sure a silhouette of the house was well positioned in the frame.

Cecil was clever in his approach and trusted the editor's judgment of what made a good picture. He always sent along a selection of prints—not just one—but he saw to it that the picture he wanted used was accompanied by two or three others that included some obvious flaw that a good editor was likely to see.

Each Sunday for several years running, the Biltmore name appeared in a free gardening column called "Trowel and Dibble" that Cecil supplied. The Biltmore garden staff wrote the column, but it passed under Cecil's pen before it was sent to the newspaper. "Trowel and Dibble" was discontinued after an editor objected to Cecil's use of the space to lobby against the highway department's intrusion into Biltmore lands. "The publisher said, 'I don't think this has anything to do with gardening,'" Cecil recalled.

Cecil combined his talent as a photographer and the lesson of the Azalea Festival to create a print advertising campaign that won regional attention from newspaper publishers. He called the series the "Alice" ads, and they were created in cooperation with William Guillet, a freelance advertising man who also handled advertising for the dairy.

The "Alice" or "Mountain Queen" ads created conversations between Alice, a curious visitor to Biltmore, and the Mountain Queen. The ads occupied a full page and engaged the reader with photographer Bert Shipman's expressive photographs and simple dialogue written by Cecil. In one, the queen mutters that there is nothing to do in the mountains. "Of course there is," replies Alice. "Biltmore is always exciting and it's a castle, and there are 'things' in the castle and 'things' in the gardens." Cecil called his Alice campaign, the "hard, soft sell."

"We have to motivate readers to get off their duffs and drive here," Cecil told a writer in 1967.

The creative approach distinguished Biltmore from the other tourist attractions in the mountains whose promotion was mainly directed to travelers looking for entertainment for children. This wasn't Ghost Town. "We're selling a national shrine," Cecil told a reporter a few years later, "not something one could wrap up and tie a string around and carry home. We wanted plenty of good art; short, inviting copy in a new and different type layout. Since we were in the mountains, the Mountain Queen was a logical character. Alice more or less evolved in the straight role. There was no intended similarity between our Alice and Lewis Carroll's."[8]

Cecil himself made good newspaper copy. The idea of a Vanderbilt rolling up his sleeves and pitching in to manage the estate was a good story, and Cecil's media platform provided him with an early opportunity to campaign for private preservation. "There are fewer and fewer places like Biltmore surviving today," Cecil told the *Charlotte Observer* in 1965. "The only way a place such as this can be preserved is by the private enterprise system. Once it leaves private enterprise, it goes to pot."[9]

Before his success with the vineyards, William Cecil (left) tried other agricultural enterprises, including the wholesale production and marketing of tomatoes grown on Biltmore fields and by area farmers. Sorting through this delivery of salad tomatoes is one of the area extension agents who worked with Cecil on his effort to expand agricultural opportunities in the region.

By the middle of the 1960s, Cecil had expanded the estate's advertising budget to nearly $90,000 a year. It had increased each year as ticket sales began to climb. His rule of thumb when preparing the budget was to include money for advertising equal to a minimum of 25 percent of each year's expenses. He once joked that he would lay off staff before he cut back on advertising. The investment was paying off. In 1965, more than ninety-four thousand visitors came to Biltmore, up from about thirty-five thousand a year in the late 1950s.

Building traffic at the house was a consuming interest. "You never stop thinking about it," Cecil said. "It is not just an eye [on the business] but a working eye. I call it common sense."

Cecil wasn't blinded by his own success in creating alluring ads. Early on, he wanted the best and wrote David Ogilvy, at the time the country's leading advertising executive, to ask if his New York agency would take on Biltmore as a client. Ogilvy declined the offer, saying Biltmore's $90,000 advertising budget was too small for consideration by his firm, Ogilvy and Mather. He did tell Cecil about a château he had bought in France that had about ten thousand visitors a year. Cecil responded:

> Partly in jest, and definitely with understanding, may I suggest the following. Since your 10,000 visitors will probably not support the advertising budget required to use Ogilvy and Mather, nor will they make your château a paying proposition, we might be able to increase the visitations to 200,000 with our promotion methods. Then both of us may be clients of Ogilvy and Mather.[10]

Biltmore's reputation was growing. In 1967, NBC's *Today* show produced a one-hour segment from the estate. The year before, the producers of the popular television series *Lassie* used Biltmore as one of its locations. Asheville's WLOS-TV filmed a series of Christmas concerts that were broadcast in 1963. Governor Terry Sanford and his arts adviser, novelist John Ehle of Asheville, asked to use the house for a summer arts program, but the idea never got beyond the talking stage. Ford Motor Company started filming its advertising on the Biltmore grounds while a Scandinavian cigarette manufacturer with a Biltmore brand also asked for location rights.

Cecil's stature was improved. The man whose key employees had begun to call "Mr. C" was now a familiar figure around Asheville. He cultivated the estate's relationship with the community and took a turn as the chairman of the city's Metropolitan Planning Commission. When the Southern Governors Conference met in Asheville, he entertained the governors with a dinner in the Banquet Hall. Years later, he remembered the occasion with some disappointment over the manners of elected officials. He said Georgia governor Lester Maddox was the only one who sent a proper thank-you note even though he was considered a country bumpkin and electoral fluke after being swept into office on his segregationist politics.

The family's position within the community was enhanced by Cecil's wife, Mimi, whose gregarious, relaxed, and approachable manner took some of the edge off her husband's reputation for a chilly demeanor. She was passionate about politics, the environment, and horses. She introduced a hundred-mile ride for horse people on the Biltmore grounds and was a regular competitor, along with her son, Bill. In time, her interest in politics led her to put her name on the ballot for the school board.

"I wondered if I should be Mrs. Cecil of Biltmore or Mimi Cecil," she said, and was anxious about how she, a New Yorker, would be received. "I discovered that when I got talking to people, [they said] 'Well, my uncle worked for Biltmore, my grandfather worked at Biltmore.' Everybody who was born here and not an outsider, which I definitely was, had something to do with Biltmore and they were proud of it."[11]

Cecil's vision extended beyond the immediate vicinity of western North Carolina. He considered Biltmore a national treasure with something to offer everyone and began marketing reproductions of prints of birds found in the rare books of his grandfather's library. "I thought it was a good idea to use the library as cash," Cecil said. " The prints were attractive and superb quality, but they did not sell well. Oh, we made a few bucks on them." In 1967, he proposed to Colonial Williamsburg, the White House Historical Association, and the management at Mount Vernon that the three join Biltmore in a first-class, full-color book featuring the four historic sites. He got polite but negative replies.

Cecil's promotional style clearly set him apart from the management of other historic properties and fueled suspicion of Biltmore as too commercial. The label came more from the admission charge that had increased to $2.50. (Cecil had raised the fee from $2.40. He said it didn't make sense for Biltmore to leave a dime on the table with each ticket it sold.)

He made no apology for the admission price. As a private enterprise, Biltmore had a tax bill and other expenses that public or nonprofit operations could ignore. Public sites were supposed to have lower fees to encourage visitors at all economic levels. Basically, Cecil believed Biltmore was worth the charge. When travelers added up their vacation expenses, admission was a small part of the overall budget.

Beyond the admission price, critics had little to support the objections. Commerce on the estate was virtually nonexistent. A small stand offered sleeves of slides with images of the house interior and a new guidebook, but the small shop didn't even carry camera film, although the photographers who snapped away in the gardens and before the château's grand exterior usually ran out. "Not in keeping with the place," Cecil said.[12] Visitors could purchase a soft drink from machines, but there were no other snacks. Cecil explored the idea of establishing a picnic area near the lower end of the Approach Road, but it never got beyond the talking stage. The money Cecil used to pay for improvements, such as new restroom facilities and additions to the staff, came almost entirely from admissions.

Underlying the continued popularity of Biltmore was nothing more profound than location. The estate was within an hour's drive of the Great Smoky Mountains National Park, which attracted more than 3 million visitors in 1967. Many Asheville tourists also arrived by way of the Blue Ridge Parkway that crossed the estate's southern boundary. In 1968, after the opening of Asheville's interstate connections, the parkway traffic jumped to 5 million visitors. Biltmore's Lodge Gate admitted ninety-six thousand paying guests, a number down slightly from the year before an increase in ticket prices from $2.50 to $3.00.

At the Biltmore Company's annual meeting in 1969, William Cecil announced the house and gardens had made a profit of $16.34. It wasn't much, but in less than ten years he had accomplished what he believed might elude him for his entire business career.

"It took us three, four or five years to get over the hump. We were within $10,000 of making a profit for two or three years," he said. "We were beginning to build up visitation and then you had to put in an extra guard here. Finally, we broke through."

CHAPTER 10

The Music Room

In the fall of 1973, a war in the Middle East disrupted the world's supply of cheap oil and threw a mighty scare into the U.S. travel industry. Virtually overnight, the cost of a tank of gas doubled. Drivers parked their cars and curtailed travel while government officials advised against any trips that weren't absolutely necessary. Businessmen such as William Cecil who depended on a traveling public for their livelihood scrambled to do what they could to mitigate the damage.

National response was immediate. Daylight savings time was introduced nationwide. Highway speed limits were capped at fifty-five miles per hour. Sunday gasoline sales were prohibited. In an effort to reduce the dangerous congestion at service stations, drivers with license plates ending in an even number were told to buy gas on even-numbered days. Those with odd numbers followed suit as well.

The consequences for the travel industry were immediate. Travel destinations in Florida, a popular winter haven for tourists, reported a drop in attendance of 45 to 50 percent. The prohibition on Sunday sales was equally devastating to tourist destinations closer to home, since most leisure travel fell on the weekends.

Gasoline prices began to recede in the early months of 1974, along with the long lines of frustrated drivers that had formed at service stations across the land. At the same time, however, the message from Saudi Arabia and other oil-rich nations was brought forcefully home: the United States could no longer rely on cheap gas to carry mom, dad, and the kids to far corners of the nation on what later would look like pocket change. As a result, American tourists—70 percent of whom traveled by private automobile—were going to be more selective in their travel destinations. They would require convincing that their next trip would be worthwhile.

Fortunately for Cecil and Biltmore, the more severe energy restrictions came during the deep winter months when the house was closed to visitors and normal traffic was low. Economy measures were introduced. The thermostat in the house was lowered, and Cecil gave up his Jaguar sedan for an American-made economy model. Cecil knew the consequences for the estate if conditions continued, however. He was just completing a term as the president of the Southern Highlands Attractions and was active in the Discover America Travel Organization. Early in 1974, he traveled to Washington twice to present the travel industry's case to Congress.

He also pushed the creation of a new promotion campaign for Asheville. Even though Biltmore received only five cents of every tourist dollar spent in the city, the company put up $3,500 of a $50,000 budget to promote travel to the region. He also increased his own advertising budget by 50 percent.[1]

Leisure travel was not a frivolous waste of energy, Cecil argued. It supported the $61 billion travel industry that was just as important to the nation's economic welfare as American steel. The jobs and profits from hotels, motels, restaurants, and attractions such as Biltmore made it possible for people to buy American cars and other products. At the same time, he argued, "The need to resolve our short-term petroleum problem thus gains far greater urgency than just a selfish desire to survive on behalf of the travel industry.

"We must and indeed we will conquer the disrupting energy problems facing us today, and with leadership from our leaders and with unity from us the people, we will be prepared to welcome the travelers on January 1, 1976, to the shores, to the mountains, to the plains, to the cities, and to the hamlets of these United States of America."[2]

The spike in oil prices caused a slight dip in ticket sales at Biltmore in the spring of 1974. Fortunately, the condition was only temporary. By summertime, visitation at the château returned to a new high. In fact, nearly 30,000 more visitors came to Biltmore in 1974 than the year before, pushing ticket sales to 283,000. While Biltmore gained, many other destinations did not fare as well. Cecil attributed Biltmore's good fortune to an aggressive advertising campaign and an increase in southeastern travelers who took their vacations closer to home.

The results were satisfying, particularly in light of increases in ticket prices to $4 for adult admission. While growing numbers of visitors kept coming to see the estate, Cecil believed that for Biltmore to capitalize on the expanding travel industry—Disney World had opened in Florida a few years earlier—it needed something new to remain competitive. He looked no further than the first floor of the château as the place to begin.

Stepping through the doors of Biltmore had always been a breathtaking experience. First-timers usually stopped in their tracks, craned their necks, and stared upward more than seventy feet to the four-story height of the spiral staircase and ascending columns of windows that spilled light onto the limestone floor. Once past the stairway, however, visitors entered one of the darker recesses of the house. While the morning sun filled the entrance with light, the entry was in shadow by afternoon with the western sunlight blocked by a room that had been closed for years. For Cecil, it was time to complete the work his grandfather had left undone eighty years before.

No one had ever determined why George Vanderbilt did not finish two large first-floor rooms immediately adjacent to the grandest spaces of his château. There was one notion that he and Edith had simply tired of living amidst the shuffle and noise of construction. There also was evidence that he had run short of money. Vanderbilt and Hunt traveled throughout Europe looking for furnishings for the château. By the time he came to the two rooms in the middle of the west side, however, his bank account may not have been able to withstand major acquisitions. Another theory held that Hunt had died before he and Vanderbilt found the right pieces to serve as focal points for these two rooms.

The larger of the two was the Music Room, which had been fortified during World War II by the government to protect the National Gallery's art collection. The bars over the windows had been removed after the war, but twenty-five years later the government-issue steel door remained in place, although hidden from view behind one of the Richelieu hangings. The housekeeping staff used the room for storage. Stacked inside were mops, buckets, brooms, and other utensils along with a resupply of the slides and photographs of the house that were offered for sale at a counter just inside the front door. At one point, it had been suggested that the room be outfitted as a shop for the "sale of views," as this photography sideline was discreetly called, but nothing came of it.

Immediately adjacent to the Music Room was the room Hunt designated as the Salon, but it became known as the Print Room when the house was opened in 1930. This long, rectangular space featured tall French doors to the west that offered a magnificent view of the mountains. On the inside wall, two archways opened onto the Winter Garden.

Edith Vanderbilt had disguised the unfinished state of the Salon by covering the ceiling with crimson-colored woolen fabric that hung in billows from corner to corner. She put Turkish rugs on the rough subfloor and folded them at the edges to get a correct fit. Guests were invited to lounge about on overstuffed cushions. All in all, her decorations gave the room something of a Bohemian atmosphere. Her grandson said a Middle Eastern hookah wouldn't have been considered out of place.

When the house opened for visitors in 1930, the fabric was left on the ceiling, but assorted pieces of furniture were exchanged for the puffy cushions. It was called the Print Room in the visitors' brochure to draw attention to the ten-by-ten-foot Albrecht Durer wood-block print recounting the reign of Holy Roman Emperor Maximilian I that covered most of one wall. Other assorted prints from Vanderbilt's extensive collection were also on display. Situated prominently near the center was the chess set and table that had belonged to Napoleon. It was an ever-popular sight for visitors. For a time, a scale model of the château was available under a case. These eye-catching items tended to distract visitors from the common wall-to-wall carpet that had been installed after World War II and was showing signs of wear by 1970.

Producing a profit in 1968—modest though it was—had encouraged Cecil to begin thinking about expanding the offerings for guests. No major changes had been made to the interior of the house since work concluded in his grandfather's day. During his own time on the estate, Cecil had concentrated on more pressing needs such as the new ticket office, additional restrooms, and an overhaul of a garden shop outside of the Lodge Gate across from the ticket office.

There were many demands for his time and money. As visitation had increased, so had traffic congestion. Parking was a headache, especially during the peak travel periods during the summer. Some days, cars overflowed the space available on the esplanade onto the shoulders of the Approach Road. Cecil was concerned about the condition of the Pellegrini canvas that covered the ceiling in the library. It had come loose in various places and was beginning to sag. Among the choices for major investment, however, the completion of the Music Room and the Salon showed the most potential for increasing visitation. If Biltmore could offer something new, those who had visited before would have a reason to return. A new parking lot and repairs to the ceiling were important, but Cecil did not see them as adding much to the bottom line.

As Cecil considered the possibilities, he proceeded cautiously. Making changes to the château was no casual affair. He decided to first test his resolve with the installation of a new floor in the Salon. It would be a relatively easy task to complete—certainly not irreversible if he made a mistake—and it could be accomplished at relatively modest expense. It would also give him a chance to bolster the confidence of Biltmore's craftsmen. "I wanted something to reinforce the quality of work that our staff could do," he explained some years later. "I wanted to show that they weren't just a bunch of carpenters sitting around hammering nails in an old building."[3]

He assigned Wexler Ogle Plemmons, Biltmore's head carpenter, to the job. The Plemmons name was familiar among the estate families, but WO, as he was called, came from the Madison County Plemmonses and had been on the staff for less than ten years. He was a big, broad-shouldered man with large hands who spoke in a thick mountain brogue. He was a first-rate mechanic and an

The Music Room remained unfinished until the 1970s, when William Cecil used Biltmore craftsmen to complete the fifteen-hundred-square-foot space that had been used as a broom closet and storage area for seventy years.

accomplished craftsman with wood. Though it wasn't required for the job, he even carried a union card. Cecil's confidence in Plemmons's ability to produce a flawless floor was based on what he had seen of his work on other large jobs, including the construction of the new garden center. But he wanted Plemmons himself to buy into the project.

"I said, 'Tell me which is the hardest parquet floor in the house to duplicate.'" Plemmons looked about and suggested one of the chevron patterns that Richard Morris Hunt had used in other rooms. "'So,' I said, 'duplicate it.'"

"North Carolina mountain people are naturally good craftsmen and I really thought the risk was small that the job would be botched," Cecil said. As visitors passed through the house in 1973, they paused beside the Winter Garden and looked through the archways to the Salon to watch Plemmons and his assistants carefully measure the oak flooring that had been cut, dried, and finished from trees in the estate forest. Each piece was sawed to a precise miter, then nailed into place. The care that Plemmons and his assistants put to the job was such that nary a scar, a knot, or a nail disturbed the surface of the floor when it was stained and shined to a rich, warm finish. Years later, Cecil chuckled at the thought of guests stopping on their way through the magnificent château to watch as the noise of the new carpentry work filled the air. The public viewing served two purposes, he said. It put Plemmons and his helpers on stage, raising their self-esteem, plus it discouraged them from dawdling.

While Plemmons worked on the floor, Cecil waited on the results of the cleaning of the ceiling fabric. Richard King, a twenty-two-year-old who was new to his job as house manager, had carefully dismounted the fabric and found that even after more than fifty years, the woolen material remained remarkably strong, albeit very dirty. Repeated vacuuming produced mounds of dust and bits of mortar that had dislodged over the years. To Cecil's relief, however, the fabric survived this vigorous cleaning with no damage.

With the new floor in place and the ceiling fabric rehung, the completion of the château's new Morning Salon encouraged both Cecil and Plemmons. "Except for it being 'new,'" Cecil said, "no one would be able to tell that it had not been laid by the original installers. Our people selected the furnishings and we were in business. The comments of our visitors were enough reward, apart from the now flowing pay increases, to ensure that this job would not be the last."[4]

The next stage would prove to be a more difficult challenge. The Music Room would require not only a floor, but the walls would need to be finished and a new ceiling installed. In addition, it needed a personality. Just what did Hunt have in mind for this space anyhow? What period did it reflect? As of 1974, the room was a fifteen hundred–square-foot architectural blank. Cecil recalled a conversation with his father, who told him he had looked into finishing the room in the 1930s. The cost was prohibitive, John Cecil had decided.[5] He said it couldn't be done. His son never accepted such advice.

When Cecil contacted architectural historian Alan Burnham of the New York Landmark Preservation Commission in 1974, Burnham was considered the foremost authority on Richard Morris Hunt. Trained at Harvard and Columbia University, Burnham had devoted nearly forty years to a study of Hunt's work that included cataloging the architect's correspondence. Cecil had been told that there was no one who could better interpret Hunt's intentions for the unfinished room at Biltmore.

Burnham accepted Cecil's invitation with enthusiasm and without a fee. He came to Biltmore, looked at the empty space, and studied page after page of plans that Hunt had left behind in North

Carolina. Unfortunately, the early drawings proved to be of limited use. Nothing Burnham found provided a clue to Hunt's plans for the room other than it was to be a music room, thus suggesting to Burnham a reason why Vanderbilt had left it incomplete. Burnham reasoned that Vanderbilt's passion was for literature, although he had a keen appreciation for opera. If he had indeed found himself short of funds or patience or both, this room would not have been a high priority. After all, he also had failed to install an organ in the Banquet Hall.

If the room had been finished in 1895, it would have offered the Vanderbilts and their guests a large, comfortable space in which to relax. Windows on the south and west offered views of the deer park below and the mountains beyond. The sheer size of the room would have allowed the staging of recitals or solo performances. It was large enough to accommodate a small chamber orchestra. Rough and unfinished, it was not fit for use as a parlor, so the family had used the Oak Drawing Room (originally designated as the Billiard Room) on the château's east side.

The size of the room presented unusual challenges. It measured fifty-five feet from the doorway off the entrance hall to the windows that opened to the west. From the roughed-in fireplace on the north wall, it was thirty-three feet across to the windows on the south side. Short angled walls at each corner produced an elongated octagon, indicating that Hunt may have intended the room to be oval in shape. The ceiling was twenty feet high.

Burnham dug into Hunt's designs of Renaissance reproductions that had been drawn for other rooms in the house. What he found especially useful in George Vanderbilt's library was a copy of the work of Viollet Le Duc, an influential nineteenth-century French architect who had compiled information on fifteenth- and sixteenth-century French design. Under Cecil's instructions to finish the room in materials from the estate—meaning wood—Burnham arrived at a presentation that reflected the French Renaissance style and borrowed heavily on the Gothic design of the adjacent Tapestry Gallery. He sketched a design for twelve-foot-high wood paneling carved in a linen-fold pattern. Wood also encased the exposed steel beams in the ceiling, which were to be trimmed with a delicate painted pattern. To decorate the walls above the paneling, he created an interlocking stenciling that featured the acorns found in the Vanderbilt crest.

"His drawings, many of them done during his vacation in Maine, were marvels," said Cecil. "I had asked him to limit the handwork to decorative designs that could be done by machines, such as routers. We have drawings done on the back of supermarket paper bags. These had pictures of the machine [tools] sketched to show our people how he intended the paneling to be accomplished and by what machine."[6]

Burnham's sketches were just the start. It was up to Asheville architect John Cort to translate his sketches into working drawings. That proved a bit of a challenge. While Burnham was an architect, he had never actually designed anything that was ever built. Cort said Burnham's sketches were often the wrong scale for the room and had to be interpreted to fit the large space. During the months of work, Cort became something of a translator between Burnham and Plemmons, who manufactured the cutting blades needed to shape the raw wood into Burnham's moldings.

Most of the first-floor rooms were designed around an important architectural feature or work of art, such as Karl Bitter's sculpture in the Winter Garden, the Pellegrini ceiling in the library, and the expansive sixteenth-century Flemish tapestries in the Tapestry Gallery. At first, there appeared to be nothing immediately at hand for the Music Room until one of the estate's longtime employees, Warren Moore, told Cecil about a large mantel that was stored in the dust and dirt of the stables.

The mantel installed in the Music Room was found in perfect condition packed in the same crate that had brought it to Biltmore more than seventy years earlier.

Cecil knew the spot. When the stable was in regular use, the room was always heavy with manure. After the horses were retired, John Cecil had used the space to hang ducks to age during the winter shooting season. With Moore in the lead, Cecil discovered underneath the dirt and detritus of seventy-five years a mantel of carved stone still in the original crate that had carried it to Biltmore long ago.

The mantel proved to be more than leftover furnishings. Everything about it, especially the design and size, indicated that Hunt had created it with this room in mind. It was carved with the initials of Albrecht Durer and his life dates, and when placed with Durer's massive print of Maximilian's accomplishments, the combination of the two would fit in no other room in the house. The only missing parts for completing the installation of the mantel were pieces of matching stone for the flanking. Cort searched sources in Europe, then found a match in a Tennessee quarry.

As the details of the room came together, Cecil proceeded with a series of other changes to the first-floor rooms. He found that with the completion of the Music Room—which he planned to furnish much like a sitting room—he now had the opportunity to return the Oak Drawing Room beside the Banquet Hall to its original service as a Billiard Room. Located adjacent to the Gun Room and the Smoking Room, the Oak Drawing Room had really never suited as a proper parlor. At some point after Vanderbilt's death and before the Cecils made their home at that end of the house, it had been turned into a first-floor sitting room, or living room, where the family and guests could relax in the evening.

Cecil retrieved the billiard tables from below stairs where employees had given them regular use over the years during their lunch break. They were reconditioned and equipped with balls and cues. To complete the transition, the Steinway piano was relocated to the Tapestry Gallery. The shifting, sorting, and restoring produced a handsome men's room featuring wildlife prints, mounted hunting trophies, leather furnishings, and the handsome felted tables, one for pool (with pockets) and the other for carom billiards.

"It was really a three-ring circus, one ring dependent on the other, until it was all sorted out," he said, describing the experience.

In early 1975, Cecil publicly announced the Billiard Room, the Morning Salon, and the ongoing work on the Music Room.

Also highlighted for the coming season were plans for changes on the second floor where a bedroom, a sitting room, and a bath—partitioned into an apartment for the curator in the mid-1950s—were to be returned to their original use as guest bedrooms. The Music Room remained incomplete, however.

Plemmons refused to rush his work. The construction of the floor proved far more difficult than the one in the Morning Salon. This room was larger, but the challenge was adjusting delicate miter cuts to accommodate the room's odd shape, where Cort found the walls were not parallel. To compensate for the odd measure, Plemmons had to taper each board so that the pattern complemented the corners and the windows, presenting a uniform centerline.

The installation of the paneling went slowly. Each piece was secured so that if the wood split sometime later, the broken piece could be removed and replaced. Cecil wanted to preserve an electrical panel on one wall, which he had used from time to time to provide power for photographic lights. Cort fashioned one section of the paneling so that it was held in place by magnets to allow for easy removal. Switches for the lighting were hidden in the woodwork.

Also troublesome were the arches over the windows; the arc of each varied from one opening to the next. The differences were such that each window would have required the construction of a separate mold to produce the plaster roping that Burnham called for in his design. As an alternative to building individual molds, Cort purchased heavy rope—such as that used as a hawser on a tugboat—and had it secured in the arches over the windows and doors, and then covered it with plaster. Rather than plaster imitating rope, it became rope in plaster imitating rope.

Included in the finished design was an alcove with shelves to hold a rare collection of porcelain sculptures of the twelve apostles produced by Johann Joachim Kandler, the master modeler of the Meissen factory near Dresden. Burnham's paneling mimicked the hand-carved woodwork elsewhere in the house.

The cost of the creation of the room was between $180,000 and $200,000, depending on the financial accounting of the work of Biltmore's own carpenters and staff. To pay for the work, Cecil and his brother, George, sold a portion of their grandfather's collection of Whistler prints that had been left to them by their grandmother. Aside from George Vanderbilt's own sale of art during his period of financial distress, this was the only time a part of his collection was ever put up for sale.

The final result of the room's creation was a stunning contrast of dark wood and bright, almost electric, colors. One writer said the room "allowed Burnham to dream in a different way, to create a room that embodies self-indulgence and pretense, a lot of formality and a huge dose of nostalgia for earlier days—just like the rest of the house." As Burnham himself described the house: "Hunt obviously had fun with Biltmore."[7]

On the evening of June 15, 1976, William Cecil presented the room to 155 special guests, with his grandfather's ebony Steinway prominently restationed from the Tapestry Gallery. The guests joined William and his brother for a dinner of tenderloin beef and some of the estate's early wine in honor of Burnham and Plemmons, who Burnham called "a master craftsman." (Plemmons had reluctantly pulled on a rented tuxedo for the special occasion.) After the meal, guests adjourned from the Banquet Hall, where the twenty-one-piece Piedmont Chamber Orchestra from the North Carolina School of the Arts offered forty-five minutes of selections from Bartok, Rossini, and Mozart.

The following day, sixteen hundred visitors strolled through the château. When they reached the Music Room, they could see the peak of Mt. Pisgah through the windows that now brought sunlight to Biltmore's entrance hall.

A few weeks before the formal opening of the Music Room, William Cecil led a group of English visitors through his grandfather's château. Most of his guests were associated with Great

Britain's National Trust for Places of Historic Interest or Natural Beauty (the National Trust), which had been founded the same year George Vanderbilt had moved into Biltmore. Since its early days, the trust had become the largest landowner in England, with 150 houses, a dozen castles, a hundred gardens, ten deer parks, about a dozen sites containing Roman ruins, and nearly four hundred miles of coastline in its care. Among those at Biltmore in May 1976 was Cecil's cousin, John George Vanderbilt Henry Spencer-Churchill, the eleventh duke of Marlborough. The family called him Sunny.

Cecil's guests were on a tour of historic sites in the United States. They had come to Biltmore to see what Cecil was doing with the largest private residence in the country. It was one of only a few grand homes that offered a comparison to the great houses of England, which included the duke of Marlborough's own Blenheim Palace. The Cecils' private management of Biltmore was also the closest thing to the British style of preservation, where family use of the properties was maintained rather than shifted to a public and nonprofit ownership as had become common in the United States.

As he presented his finished work as Biltmore's offering for the bicentennial of the United States—Cecil timed the opening to capitalize on American tourists' renewed interest in their national heritage—it was not lost on Cecil that a delegation from the British Trust had found their way to Biltmore's doorstep while their peers at the (U.S.) National Trust for Historic Preservation had never come to call.

CHAPTER 11

Presentation versus Preservation

T he public had never known what to make of Biltmore. Many
assumed that since it was a National Historic Landmark, it was
owned by the government. At the very least, it was believed, the
estate enjoyed the support of a foundation or a trust fund established by George Vanderbilt. Forty years after the château was
opened to the public, visitors were still surprised to learn that the
estate—house and all—remained in private hands and that one of
the owners, William Cecil, was making a career of caring for a historic house.

Clearly, Biltmore was the exception within the preservation community, where the bottom line was usually secondary to the curatorial mission. Such thinking was disastrous, Cecil believed, and he
was not bashful in proclaiming his contrary view. "I preserve for
profit a French château," he told a 1972 preservation conference.
"If for one instant we forget that our goal is to make a profit on

that which we preserve, that profit will disappear." And, he added, so would the property under their care. But, he said, his motives were not selfish. He didn't preserve Biltmore to make money. He made money to preserve Biltmore.

It was a startling declaration to many. Conventional wisdom held that preservation did not make money. In fact, it could not even support itself. The most successful preservation venture—Colonial Williamsburg, with nearly a million visitors a year—depended on income from a hefty endowment, individual and corporate donations, as well as revenue from a hotel, a golf course, and rent payments from retail shops that sold reproductions licensed by the landlord. To Cecil's knowledge, Biltmore was the only privately owned property making its own way.

The attitudes went beyond disbelief to disdain. If William Cecil was operating Biltmore for a profit, the critics argued, he could not possibly be serious about preservation. The implication was that the Cecils were simply draining Biltmore of its value before they finally disposed of their tourist attraction and turned it into a real estate development, thus consigning it to the same fate as many other Gilded Age properties.

The criticism of Biltmore's for-profit management rang hollow when, upon closer inspection, the operations of the estate were compared to Colonial Williamsburg with its myriad of commercial, for-profit operations. The only items that had ever been offered for sale at Biltmore were photographs of the château and its interior, along with a four-color guidebook. It was not until the early 1970s that soft drinks and snacks were made available to visitors. Ticket prices were a step or two ahead of most properties open to the public, but most were not burdened with annual levies of local, state, and federal taxes.

Cecil made no apologies for the way he did business. "Well, we pay our bills, if that makes us commercial," he said. He believed that private preservation was far superior to anything he had seen under government management. Still hanging in his craw was the decision of the National Park Service to dismantle his grandfather's Buck Spring Lodge rather than preserve it. In addition, Biltmore contributed more to the Asheville community as a tax-paying, private employer than if the property were held by a foundation or otherwise taken off the tax rolls. And if Cecil was successful, then that success flowed directly into the community many times over in the money that Biltmore visitors spent for food, lodging, and other entertainment. Moreover, private enterprise spawned creativity and motivated management—something missing in most government operations. "It must support itself. If it doesn't, I don't get my two eggs for breakfast," he said.

Cecil further startled managers of large nonprofit operations when he told them that they should be as inspired as he was to generate more revenue than they spent. These "profits" could be put back into the property and ease the demand of public and private dollars that might flow instead to the benefit of smaller historic house museums whose prospects for breaking even were less promising.

The skepticism of preservation purists was made clear to Cecil by none other than Carlisle H. Humelsine when he was the chairman of the National Trust for Historic Preservation and the president of Colonial Williamsburg. Cecil had just seated himself at the president's table at a National Trust meeting in Williamsburg when Humelsine approached and asked who he was and what he was doing there. Cecil introduced himself and explained that trust president James Biddle had offered him a chair. "He shouldn't have," Humelsine huffed.

"Well," Cecil said, "that set the tone for the meeting. Private enterprise was not welcome and 'commercial' historic houses had no place in the preservation world of the National Trust at that time."[1]

Cecil chafed under the criticism from the established preservation community. He had long admired Colonial Williamsburg, envying the national and even international recognition that had been achieved under Humelsine's leadership. A former State Department deputy undersecretary, Humelsine had turned Williamsburg into a popular diplomatic waystation through which protocol directors routed many visiting dignitaries before they made their way to Washington, D.C.

"I always thought Williamsburg was an incredible place," Cecil said. "If I had the visitation that Williamsburg had, [I thought] I'd be in hog heaven, especially with the State Department staying there with all the VIPs."[2]

Preservationists didn't understand Biltmore because virtually everything Cecil practiced was contrary to the way most historic properties were run. The differences were apparent as soon as a visitor entered the front door.

At most historic sites, guides or docents, often dressed in period costume, conducted tours of the property. Groups of visitors moved together from one room to the next, where the styles of furniture, the artwork, or the architecture was explained in detail. Most historic properties were on an educational mission. In the case of Colonial Williamsburg, it was the essence of its existence, both intellectually and practically. The profits earned from Colonial Williamsburg tourist operations were tax exempt since the site fulfilled an educational purpose.

Cecil steadfastly remained with the European model. Britain's Hampton Court and France's Versailles did not have guides, and neither did Biltmore. For Cecil, experiencing the world of George Vanderbilt without interference was more important than being taught facts along the way. Visitors were not expected to understand every item but to absorb the sum of the house and the collection it held.

Occasionally, Cecil heard from visitors who wanted to know more. "As we looked through the rooms," a Wisconsin woman wrote Cecil in 1966, "we felt that a guide who could point out interesting details about the furnishings, members of the family, history of the art objects would be very valuable."[3] Cecil was unmoved. He believed a packaged monologue by a guide often left some guests shortchanged. A canned spiel could not accommodate all interests. "You might be interested in mirrors and I might be interested in chairs," he said.

There were practical reasons behind Biltmore's more casual presentation. Hiring and training guides was expensive and, Cecil believed, unnecessary. Unlike most historic houses, where space was cramped and rooms were small, Biltmore had ample room for visitors to wander at will and not disrupt the flow of traffic. Cecil also believed that canned presentations led to excesses. A tour guide delivering a pat lecture over and over again was tempted to embellish, he said, and that was how rumors started that could mushroom into embarrassment.

Cecil also discouraged any signage in the house that warned visitors not to touch particular objects or sit in the chairs. He believed they detracted from the impression of the house that he wanted to convey. His restrictions were subtler. Objects and furniture were put out of reach of passing guests, and a rope was draped lightly over the back of a chair to indicate it was not to be used. His ambition was to present Biltmore as it was when his grandfather slept on the second floor or sat with a book in the library. His grandfather wouldn't have had signs labeling rooms or describing his art collection. Nor would he have had velvet roping along the corridors, and Cecil kept such traffic control measures to a minimum.

Preservationists could be a prickly bunch and often didn't agree among themselves. Purists believed that historic properties should remain untouched; intervention was acceptable only when the integrity of the structure was in peril. The best example of this philosophy was Drayton Hall, one of the prize properties of the National Trust, which was built between 1738 and 1742. This Ashley River mansion near Charleston, South Carolina, was the only great plantation palace to survive both the Revolutionary and Civil wars. After Drayton Hall was acquired by the National Trust, it was opened to tourists, who saw it just as the last occupant had left it, without electricity, indoor plumbing, furnishings, and with only a hint of the original paint.

Those who followed the argument of the nineteenth-century writer and critic John Ruskin would have left Biltmore's Music Room an empty shell rather than speculate, as William Cecil did, on what Richard Morris Hunt and George Vanderbilt had in mind. Or, if plaster fell and the paint peeled in the château's dining room, it would have been left that way. "We have a tendency to clean old buildings too much," Ruskin wrote, "to strip them of their age and character, to make them look too new, and to turn them into spectacles, rather than allow them to look old and merely befriended."[4]

This was nonsense, Cecil countered. His grandfather would never have settled for peeling paint and falling plaster. On a visit to one historic house, Cecil asked his tour guide about loose plaster he noticed on one wall. "I said, 'What about that? Are you going to repair that?'" He said his guide told him, "'Well, it is the original plaster.' I said, 'What are you going to do? Box it?'"

More often than not, Biltmore's critics had never visited the property. Rather, the estate was known by the company it kept. While Cecil considered himself a preservationist, he was best known in the early 1970s as a spokesman for travel and tourism. He made several appearances on Capitol Hill during the 1973 energy crisis pleading the case of Biltmore—as well as Disney World—in the face of restrictive travel policies aimed at reducing gasoline consumption. He was active in the Discover America Travel Organization and the Southern Highlands Attractions, where he was president in 1972. The Biltmore Company did not become a member of the National Trust for Historic Preservation until nearly five years later.

Tourism was Biltmore's lifeline, and Cecil believed that those responsible for the financial health of historic properties who dismissed tourism promotion did so at their peril. "They forget that entertainment along with learning attracts visitors," he told one gathering. "Too often they consider themselves in the museum business and not tourism. However, tourism is the natural partner of preservation and heritage."[5]

Where Biltmore departed most from other historic properties was in management. Those most responsible for the house were young men whom Cecil had brought up through the ranks, rather than managers with academic credentials or experience in the curatorial ranks. Biltmore's general manager, Don Burleson, had started his career as a teenager working on the gardening crew. Richard Bryson, the estate's operations manager, got his first job as a teenager pulling weeds in the garden. House manager Richard King signed on for a summer post at age sixteen selling tickets. He became house manager in 1975, at age twenty-five, after he earned a college degree in business.

Cecil put little stock in academic credentials. Professional curators left him cold. No one had more interest in preservation than the owner, he believed. "We were 'commercial' in that we pushed the tourist and we didn't bow and scrape to curators," he said. "I don't know if that lamp is 1643 or 1677. I couldn't care less. I do know that lamp is here and it will stay here. I do know the reason people want to see the house is because it is like it is and I will keep it that way. And I will do everything I can to make it comfortable."[6]

Cecil's distrust of professional curators was founded on personal experience, beginning with an episode in the 1950s. Over the years, further exposure had done little to change his mind. "I remember one day a curator from the Smithsonian Museum in Washington, D.C., wanted to visit Biltmore because we had an ancient 'spinet piano' and the museum was trying to find all the spinets in America," he recalled. "The great day arrived and the curator came to my office. The day before I had photographed the spinet in question and I showed him the pictures. His comment, which I will remember for the rest of my life, was, 'Oh, a Baltimore spinet. I am a European spinet curator.' With that he got up and left, not even bothering to visit Biltmore, which he had never seen. I suspect that that jaunt cost the taxpayers a thousand or more dollars, which, of course, was of no concern to the curator of European spinets."[7]

"My problem," Cecil said, "is that a curator is a most important cog in the preservation wheel, but he or she is not, nor, because of training, ever will be an effective administrator. These are two totally different fields of expertise. The curator has to fight for every penny in order to conserve the items under his or her care. The administrator has to secure the funds. Both are jobs of the highest importance, and neither is or should be mutually exclusionary."[8]

This emphasis led to divergent points of view. Cecil found that those who rose to their positions from the curatorial ranks did not understand the value of promotion and weren't attuned to the cultivation of tourists. In fact, while they might acknowledge that more visitors could improve the bottom line, they resisted growth because additional foot traffic on the floors of a historic house only increased the challenge of protecting and preserving the property.

Preservation was more than history, Cecil believed. It was a state of mind. Speaking in the late 1970s, he told a conference of managers of historic properties, "If you put in ten paper clips and three paper cups, I'll preserve that just as much as a Pellegrini ceiling or a Rembrandt on the wall or whatever. The last person we put on the payroll is the curator. Not the first, the last, because we believe in paying our bills first, and we preserve."[9]

Cecil continually performed a balancing act between promotion and preservation. While he might admire the success of Colonial Williamsburg, he also paid close attention to Walt Disney World and other tourist venues in the Southeast that were competing for vacationers' dollars. As soon as he could afford to, he had expanded his newspaper advertising into major cities in Florida, and especially Atlanta, all of which had become more accessible to the estate since the opening of interstate highways.

There was no denying his decisions on where to invest in the house were determined by where he could best see a return. For example, Cecil knew in the early 1970s that the library ceiling needed repair. Yet he completed the Music Room first because it promised to increase tourist traffic. "That room was paid for by the increase in visitors who came to see what we were doing," he told a management group from historic properties. "You pick your capital projects very carefully in order to benefit from promotion."[10]

Susanne Brendel claimed she had four strikes against her when she came to work as the Biltmore historian in the summer of 1975. "I was a Yankee, a woman, well-educated, and young."[11] She also was a curator, despite the euphemism of her official title. Brendel had discovered Biltmore quite by accident. She was taking a course at Columbia University under James Marston Fitch, one of the leading scholars in the preservation world, who asked for a volunteer to undertake an archiving project in connection with Alan Burnham's work on the Biltmore Music Room.

"I went to the library and looked [Biltmore] up," she later recalled. "I took one look at it and said 'Wow.' It looks pretty exciting to me." The pay was low, just expenses and a student stipend, but Brendel eventually turned her work archiving Hunt's drawings into her master's thesis and an article in *Antiques* magazine. It also landed her a job at Biltmore as its historian.

Brendel was the first full-time Biltmore employee whose sole responsibility was preservation. Earlier work—the cataloging of the library in the 1950s and an inventory of the house in the 1960s—had been attempts to simply take account of what was at hand. Since then, little had been done to organize—or protect—George Vanderbilt's personal papers, the thousands of documents related to the construction of the house, and the more than fifty thousand items that were part of the Biltmore collection. "Until Mr. Cecil came back," King said, "everybody thought of this as grandpa's old house, not truly as history, or part of our American heritage and, therefore, worth preserving and saving. He feels that this is not only his personal heritage, but the country's. He thinks of himself as a preservationist, but it is still his grandpa's house. He wages that internal battle. Over the years, he is the one who has informed us that this is not just grandpa's house, it is history, it is important."[12]

Brendel put an even finer point on it and brought her professional training to bear on the contents of the house. "Oh my," she said some years later. "It was in some state. It was overwhelming. Things stuffed in closets and drawers and God knows where. In tin and lead boxes." In addition to piles of correspondence from Vanderbilt's chief agent, Charles McNamee, she found letters between George Vanderbilt and his artistic friends, including John Singer Sargent, James McNeill Whistler, and Henry James. There were hundreds of family photos as well as personal diaries. "It was stuff. A lot of stuff. Helter skelter."

"What's wonderful is that it has some fabulous objects," she said. "Not everything is fabulous, but it was a representative collection of the family. The real beauty of important historic houses is when you have the original furnishings. You see the way that the family lived it. It is not a re-creation. It is the real thing."

Once she got her bearings, Brendel started work on the most fragile pieces in the collection—those on paper. "My first concern was to see that things were properly stored," she said. She moved next to the collection of hundreds of rugs and secured the aid of a specialist to identify valuable pieces and assist in preparing them for storage.

Brendel could not have arrived at Biltmore at a better time. The opening of the new rooms on the first and second floors produced a new energy and interest in the estate from visitors who produced additional income for the company. Between 1974 and 1976, visitation increased 38 percent to nearly four hundred thousand. Traffic was such that guests could no longer hope to find a parking space near the front door. Instead, visitors parked their cars in a new lot that Cecil built off the Approach Road a hundred yards outside the entrance gates to the esplanade.

More importantly, the changes gave Cecil bona fides within the preservation community. With the new work, he had demonstrated that his interest in Biltmore went beyond simply opening the doors and letting visitors walk through the house. The company had invested hard cash in the Morning Salon and the Music Room. The completed work was done with professional advice, precision, and care. That a distinguished delegation from Great Britain would include Biltmore on their tour of great homes added an impressive endorsement to his efforts.

By the mid-1970s, Biltmore seemed to be awakening from a long nap. Since his arrival in 1960, Cecil had done more for the care and improvement of the house than anyone had in the past fifty years. There had not been such investment in the château since Edith Gerry was regularly at home in North Carolina. And then, the changes were mainly for modern comforts, such as the installation of an outdoor swimming pool. Some of the earlier handiwork had actually detracted from Hunt's masterpiece. A frightful set of awnings was hung over the front terrace. The sleeping porch added by the Cecils on the north side broke the lines of the Hunt's graceful facade.

Clearly, Cecil's reputation as a capitalist did not preclude investment in proper restoration. "They were receptive to ideas," Brendel said of Cecil and his brother. "Biltmore had to find a balance between being an attraction and being an historic site and museum. Mr. Cecil wanted to keep that balance. When they have ideas, they have money to invest in them. In the nonprofit world, there are good ideas but no money to invest in them."

"Colonial Williamsburg is driven from scholarship. At Biltmore, yes, we tried to have that research base and create something that was real," she said. "Mr. Cecil felt much more that the other voice we had to listen to was the public."

One of the ideas that blossomed early in Brendel's time at Biltmore was extending the open days to include the Christmas holiday. The holiday season had been a feature of Colonial Williamsburg since 1936, where it was immediately popular, even though it stretched the standards of historical accuracy. The houses on Duke of Gloucester Street were decorated with a 1930s notion of the eighteenth-century holidays with luscious wreaths and decorations made from fruit. Even the wealthiest of colonists were loath to spare a precious fresh orange in the dead of winter for the sake of a wreath on the door.

Christmas at Biltmore began almost by accident. Cecil had arranged for the taping of a Christmas holiday television special, and in mid-November, the Winter Garden was filled with the sounds of musicians from the North Carolina School of the Arts and the Piedmont Chamber Orchestra from Winston-Salem, North Carolina, as well as choirs from nearby Warren Wilson College, Mars Hill College, and All Souls Episcopal Church. Evergreen outfitted with golden balls and twinkling lights provided an inviting backdrop to a program that was packaged into a one-hour presentation

The château was dressed in period decorations and opened for the Christmas holiday in 1979. These extended hours proved to be the most popular addition to the Biltmore experience.

of holiday cheer. If the house was going to be all done up in holiday finery for the television production, Cecil reasoned, then it might as well remain open for the Christmas holidays, so the routine of closing for six weeks ended.

The first Christmas decorations were modest. Brendel and King brought in a few average-size fir trees and outfitted them with hand-me-down ornaments from the Cecil family. The response was impressive, even if the decorations were not. More than thirty-eight hundred visitors turned up in December. The previous year, by the time the house closed on December 15, fewer than nine hundred tickets had been sold.

The public enthusiasm inspired Brendel and King, who told Cecil, "You know, if we're really going to do Christmas here, we need to do it first-rate. And he said, 'Okay, go out and do it.'" More trees were added in 1976; this time, the pair decorated the house with greater historical accuracy as well as with considerably more financial support. "I spent $5,000," said King. "I remember it well, because I about fell out of my chair. We spent $5,000 on that Christmas. Just ornaments, that was just the ornaments we bought for that first Christmas."

Brendel scoured the literature and found other decorations appropriate for a Gilded Age mansion. "Poinsettias, we had lots of poinsettias," said King. "We had pomander balls. Real ones. And put them everywhere. Happy hands at home. We personally did a lot of the decorating. We used anyone we could dragoon. We put up a lot of roping."

Visitation doubled in 1976, with more than seven thousand guests in December. The following year, visitors enjoyed not only the house but the seasonal music provided by area musicians, including the Piedmont Brass Quintet from the North Carolina School of the Arts in Winston-Salem, where Mimi Cecil was a member of the school's board of trustees. A mile of pine roping hung from the balconies and mantels and was accented with sprays of holly and balsam. Altogether, sixteen Christmas trees were set out in the house, including one in the Banquet Hall that stood forty feet tall. "We do not contend that this is authentic—this is not George Vanderbilt—but it is inspired by the era." But what visitors saw more closely reflected the era of the Gilded Age than the colonial version of Christmas presented at Williamsburg.

By 1979, Biltmore's December ticket sales had climbed to nearly twelve thousand. Like the opening of the new rooms, the introduction of Christmas to the Biltmore schedule was further confirmation to Cecil that tourism was the engine to support more restoration and eventually secure Biltmore's future. He remained largely alone in that belief within the company, however. Since the dairy business had gone into decline in the late 1960s, his brother and others in the company talked of selling real estate and other assets to make up the losses.

In the midsummer of 1979, the differences over the future of the company were finally put to rest. William and George Cecil reached agreement on a division of their shared inheritance that would profoundly affect their families and the future of the house and gardens. On July 31, 1979, almost fifty years to the day after his mother inherited the estate, William Cecil became the sole owner of his grandfather's château, his gardens, and about eight thousand acres of surrounding land.

The offer to split the company had been made by George, and the negotiations over a settlement arrived at a very challenging time for William. The nation was in the throes of yet another gasoline shortage that curtailed travel in the spring and summer months, the peak of the Biltmore season. Across the country, 250,000 employees in the travel industry had lost their jobs. Summer employment was down by a like amount.[13] At Biltmore, attendance was off by more than twenty-five thousand in July and that much again in August. Loss in ticket revenue for those two months alone amounted to about $350,000.

CHAPTER 12

Voice in the Wilderness

O ne of William Cecil's familiar mantras was that he didn't preserve Biltmore to make a profit—he made a profit to preserve Biltmore. Granted, the margins were thin in the years following his first experience with black ink in 1968, but they were real and had grown steadily in the 1970s. As he set forth on his own without the heft and history of the dairy business behind him, he knew he would need more than symbolic profits. All in all, he enjoyed a terrifying freedom.

Driving the brothers' division of the company was the inevitable accounting that their heirs would have to make in the years to come. Inheritance taxes loomed large over both William and George, especially as the fortunes of the Biltmore Company that they owned jointly and equally began to change in the 1970s. After several years of operating losses, Biltmore Dairy Farms could no longer be depended on as the company's financial engine, and the accumulating losses created an urgency to find new ways to generate cash.

The decline of the dairy had begun in the late 1960s, just as William's tourist business had started to display a hint of promise. Local and regional dairy operations like Biltmore were disappearing in a nationwide consolidation of the industry. In addition, old ways were going by the boards, making it harder to compete. Biltmore had long depended on the work of families who lived on individual farms and tended portions of the Biltmore herd. New wage and hours laws that took effect in the 1960s required employers such as Biltmore to pay any family member who worked, not just the head of the household. Operating expenses began to climb steadily.

The early 1970s caught most dairy companies in a price squeeze as customers' shopping habits changed. Families dropped home delivery—a profitable line of sales—in favor of cheaper house brands that supermarkets, especially the large chain stores, sold from their dairy case as a loss leader. As revenue began to decline, the Biltmore dairy management shelved needed repairs and improvements and trimmed other expenses in an effort to ride out the shifting market. The strategy did not work, and the deferred spending only complicated production. Quality was called into question. At one point, William Cecil pulled Biltmore-brand fruit drinks from the snack bar at the house after visitors complained about the taste.

In 1976, the brothers were considering the future of the company as they awaited an offer on the sale of the dairy operation. The Biltmore brand remained popular, and the company was the largest independent operator in western North Carolina. As they talked about the prospects, William had argued for shifting the company's emphasis to tourism and seeking out more creative uses of the farmland. He believed his experimentation with a small vineyard near the Conservatory offered new opportunities for pastures that would no longer be required to support a herd of milk cows.

Similar discussions explored the possibilities of real estate development. With twelve thousand acres of land, much of it within minutes of downtown Asheville, the options were virtually unlimited. There was talk of housing subdivisions, shopping malls, even a contained, planned community on Biltmore land. Such proposals bothered William. He warned that opening the estate up to commercial or residential development could drive up the tax value of the remaining property. He worried most about the threat to the integrity of the estate. He remembered a lesson from his old mentor at Chase, Al Barth, who told him, "You make money buying, not selling."[1]

The talk about land sales did not include the château and the gardens, but the discussions to put this part of the estate into a nonprofit foundation did not suit William, either. "By the midseventies," Cecil said, "I was quite sure that in my remaining years we would be profitable and, in any event, I was not prepared to see the estate decimated and turned over to a group of well-meaning but nonbelieving trustees."[2]

A further concern for William was his own future role in the company, should his brother's responsibilities change if the dairy business was sold. William made it clear to George that he would resist any attempt to relieve him of his management of the house and gardens. The overarching concern of both men was inheritance taxes and whether their patrimony, be it land, a historic house, a collection of art, or a cow or two, could be passed to another generation without producing a financial upheaval for either brother.

The discussions came to a head just before Christmas 1978 when George informed William of his desire to split the company. William walked out of the meeting with his brother at the Frith to find his wife, Mimi, startled at his ashen face as he relayed word of George's desire for a corporate divorce. She encouraged him to press on. The brothers hired New York City law firms to arrange the division of the assets. Cadwalader, Wickersham and Taft, Mimi's old firm, handled William's interests. The negotiations passed with remarkable smoothness and efficiency. Only close family friends were aware of the historic transfer of property that was being prepared. The first public notice of the separation didn't appear in the newspaper until six months after the deal was struck, and then the report was spare in details.

In the end, the division of the estate met the needs of both men. The brothers agreed at the outset that the house and its contents were of equal value to the holdings of the dairy operations, which left only the outlying real estate to be distributed. George took the dairy business and about four thousand acres, including unsold lots in Biltmore Forest. His land lay on the perimeter of the estate and was considered the most suitable for development. With six children, he would find these assets more liquid and far easier to manage than parts of a larger whole.

William received the château, all that it held, and about eight thousand surrounding acres that made up the heart of his grandfather's great estate. The boundaries lay along the Blue Ridge Parkway where it crossed south of the house, across the river to Interstate 26. William received land north of the Blue Ridge Parkway and east of the interstate; George took the remainder. William's share—which he had made clear he had no plans to sell—was large enough to provide a buffer for the château and gardens, where visitors could enjoy, with a minimum of intrusion from the twentieth century, the countryside and the mountain vistas that had captivated George Vanderbilt nearly eighty years earlier. William's holdings also included more than three thousand acres on the west side of the French Broad River—which would come to be called the West Range—that George would continue to lease for use until the dairy herd was sold.

The settlement relieved William of the competing interests and inconsistent management styles that had characterized the Biltmore Company under the dual management. He would now be able to focus the attention of the entire operation on tourism, rather than the dairy, whose control of the company had gone unchallenged even in the face of declining profits. (It was not until the brothers finally settled accounts that George and William discovered that the profits of tourism in recent years had more than compensated for the years of subsidies that the dairy had made to the operation of the house and gardens. William called the news a "burden lifter.")

Yet, stripped of its dairy subsidiary, the Biltmore Company that Cecil now owned outright was a shadow of its former size. Overnight, the company was reduced to $3 million in annual revenue from $44 million and from over five hundred employees to about sixty. George also took the corporate infrastructure. When William arrived at his office on August 1, 1979, he owned a company with landlocked assets, slim profit margins, a "senior" staff composed of his general manager, who was in his early thirties, and two other associates, Richard Pressley and Steve Miller, who were even younger. Pressley was Cecil's chief financial officer; Miller's forte was marketing. Cecil had little margin for error, and some gave him short odds on making a success of it. The attorney who had handled his negotiations in the settlement told William he was doubtful of his prospects.

"He didn't believe we were making money," Cecil said. "He said, 'No way. I have tried it at Flagler [Museum in Palm Beach].' By 1978, we were making money, not too much, but enough to say we were making money. I gave him the audit. He called me the next day and said he read it on the plane going up, and, he said, 'If the accountants say you are making money, I have got to believe it.'"

Indeed, the new arrangement was sobering. Despite the differences with his brother, the old ownership had allowed William the luxury of experimenting with ideas while performing over a safety net. If something didn't work, he had the cushion of the dairy business to help overcome the losses.

Even the economy seemed to be against him. Gasoline supplies were cut short in the summer of 1979 just at the height of the Biltmore's busiest season. And looming ahead was the question of whether he could solve the inheritance tax problem for his family. The division had only compounded William's problems. Shortly after the split, his attorney told him that inheritance taxes by his estimate far exceeded William's liquid assets. In short, to keep Biltmore intact, his heirs would have to sell a portion of the estate. He advised William that he'd best serve his own interests if he let Biltmore deteriorate and lose value.

William Cecil had been working for years on a solution to the taxation threat that faced property owners like him. He argued that historic properties should be excused from all taxes as long as the property was kept open to the public and owners met a rigorous standard of operation. Given such exceptions, these owners would be held accountable by a presidential commission. When the property passed to the next generation, the heirs would enjoy the same tax-exempt status as long as the property continued to meet standards. If the ownership of the property changed and it was no longer available for public visitation, then the owner would be liable for a portion of the postponed taxes.

The impact on the public treasury would be small, he argued, and would involve no more than a hundred properties per state, some of which were already managed by nonprofit foundations. More important, the public—as well as the property owners— would be served by such an arrangement. "The effect of this program would give tremendous prestige to the designated properties thus enhancing their viability while at the same time reducing the national burden of preservation by the treasury of the United States," he said in a letter to one of President Gerald Ford's advisers in the mid-1970s.[3]

Cecil talked to whoever would listen, including the White House staffs of Presidents Richard Nixon, Gerald Ford, and Jimmy Carter, as well as assorted members of Congress. He lobbied owners of other properties and tried to enlist the aid of the National Trust for Historic Preservation in bringing private owners together to lobby for such changes in the tax code. Most of his efforts came to naught. Tax relief for the descendants of the Vanderbilts didn't sit well in Washington.

At the National Trust, Cecil ran up against broader issues. The era of the historic house had run its course, reaching a pinnacle of popularity in 1976, the year of the nation's bicentennial. Preservation fever was high, but advocates across the land were moving beyond single properties to focus more attention on entire neighborhoods, commercial buildings, and even the nation's maritime history. "We were one house," Cecil said of his lobbying efforts. "And they were interested in the big picture. We also were an oddity because we were doing it differently from everyone else."[4]

And therein lay the rub. Cecil should have been able to find a host of allies among other private owners. A study conducted in the mid-1970s found that about one in five of the twelve hundred National Historic Landmark sites belonged to private individuals.[5] Among them were historically significant properties such as Berkeley Plantation on the James River in Virginia and Liberty Hall in New Jersey. Cecil discovered, however, that ownership was about the only thing he had in common with other owners. On virtually every other measure, Biltmore was different.

No other nongovernmental property compared to Biltmore's 250 rooms and seventy-five acres of well-tended gardens. Some houses were small two-room dwellings that could fit, foundation and all, into Biltmore's Banquet Hall. It was no wonder that smaller house museums were struggling. Owners found it impossible to move a sufficient number of paying visitors through the space available to generate a profit. Biltmore could handle hundreds of visitors each hour without crowding. With so many sizes and styles of structures, the costs of maintenance and restoration varied widely. There also was a wide array of uses; some were still private residences. Moreover, if these properties were open to the public, none was operated with the serious intent of making a profit. For many, the "museum business" was just an aside. Unlike Cecil, who was devoted to increasing the number of visitors to Biltmore, some owners listed "too much visitation" among their problems.

Perhaps most discouraging for Cecil was that most of the other property owners did not face as great a threat from taxation. A survey of privately owned historic landmarks found that individual owners were more concerned about raising money for upkeep and restoration than the threat of estate taxes.[6]

Owners faced with problems similar to Cecil's usually had taken an alternative route rather than seek to change the laws. Charles H. P. Duell's situation in Charleston was a good example. In 1969, he had inherited Middleton Place, an Ashley River plantation that had been in his family for more than three hundred years. Fires set by the invading Union Army during the Civil War had destroyed the main plantation house. Only one of the flanker buildings was left standing, yet it remained a family home. In the 1930s, Duell's grandfather had opened Middleton's remarkable gardens to the public. A stop at Middleton was as much a part of a visit to Charleston as Biltmore was when tourists came to Asheville.

When Duell received his inheritance, many had suggested he turn the estate's 6,545 acres into a residential community. He would have made millions of dollars with the decision. Instead, he transferred ownership of the house, gardens, and land to a foundation, protecting it for the next generation. As he saw it, he wasn't giving away Middleton Place, he was giving it to itself. "I believe in the idea of stewardship—and I am now the steward of Middleton Place."[7]

His sentiments were not that different from Cecil's. "[Middleton] really belongs to the American people," Duell said. "We're just the stewards. It is an 'American story'—one Middleton was in the Continental Congress, another signed the Declaration of Independence, another the Articles of Secession."[8]

Cecil objected to being forced to give up control of Biltmore. He sincerely believed that private management was superior in all respects and that only a private owner could give a historical property the attention it deserved. He didn't like the foundation solution, and turning the house over to the government was out of the question, even if the government would take it. As he struggled to find a solution, the National Park Service was trying to figure out what to do with Mar-a-Lago, the Marjorie Merriweather Post home in Palm Beach, which had become a financial albatross. At the time, it was costing the government $100,000 a year in maintenance alone. The endowment left for care of the estate was insufficient to meet the needs.

It was not until the summer of 1976 that Cecil finally found an audience who was sympathetic to his situation and who had done something about it. They weren't Americans, however. They were the British.

As Cecil entertained the delegation from England traveling in the United States on a bicentennial goodwill tour, he learned about the creation of the Brit's Historic Houses Association (HHA), which recently had won tax concessions in Parliament that encouraged private preservation of historic properties. The government's new Capital Transfer Tax plan was remarkably similar to Cecil's own idea. Under the new British law, owners of historic properties were excused from death taxes and other levies as long as their homes remained open to the public. Some were not even required to be open year-round. In addition, the contents of these houses—such as Woburn Abbey's collection of paintings by Rembrandt, Canaletto,

Reynolds, and Gainsborough—likewise qualified for the exemptions as long as they remained on view and were not sold. Once ownership of a house or any of its contents changed hands, taxes came due.

More encouraging, Cecil found among the British a welcome spirit of enthusiasm for private ownership. In England, Cecil's idea that government was the preserver of last resort was well regarded by Parliament as it became burdened by the upkeep of a host of palaces, castles, and the like. "[The British National Trust] has always recognized that the best solution for the country house is the private owner," said one official of the British National Trust. "Its aim is to act as a safety net should the maintenance of a house prove to be beyond the family's means."[9]

The British had an advantage over their American counterparts: Access to the stately homes of England had long been a favorite of the average Englishman. In the early years, it was generally the butler who opened the door in the owner's absence in exchange for a suitable gratuity. After World War II, when the British became serious about tourism, the owners took a more active interest in their property, especially after some of these old homes fell to the wrecking ball. The HHA was organized first as a committee of the British Travel Authority but became a full-fledged independent body in 1973 under the presidency of Lord Montagu of Beaulieu.

Montagu was a promoter. The family's stately home at Beaulieu had long fallen to ruin, but the Great Gatehouse and Beaulieu Abbey were stunning enough, even before he added another popular attraction—an antique car collection. His National Motor Museum, with a gallery of international favorites, would help Beaulieu surpass Shakespeare's birthplace at Stratford-Upon-Avon in popularity among tourists. His attraction, while successful, was not that well received by some of his peers. When Cecil asked his cousin, David Burleigh, the marquis of Exeter, about publishing a book featuring the great houses of the world—a group in which he included Biltmore along with the marquis's Burghley, Blenheim Palace, and Beaulieu—the marquis asked Cecil if he really wanted to associate with a "garage mechanic."

In the summer of 1977, Cecil visited England at Montagu's invitation to attend a meeting of the International Heritage Conference at Woburn Abbey. Cecil was introduced to the owners of other great houses, as well as homes in Belgium, Italy, France, Germany, Sweden, Austria, and the Netherlands. He returned to the United States with a head full of ideas, including new projects for Biltmore, and riding a new wave of energy that held some promise for results. Later that year after he returned from Australia, where as a guest of the government of New South Wales he had talked about private preservation, he began making plans for a special session at the upcoming meeting of the National Trust for Historic Preservation in Mobile, Alabama.

Biltmore had been a corporate member of the National Trust for only a year when Cecil was asked in the summer of 1977 to present his thoughts on the role of national organizations in the future of the private historic house museum. The invitation was a bit surprising, considering Biltmore's relationship with the organization, but Cecil eagerly accepted National Trust president James Biddle's offer to be part of the thirty-first annual meeting in Mobile in October.

Cecil's platform was to be a special workshop for historic house museums. More than sixty delegates from historic properties settled in for the half-day session upon the opening of the three-day annual meeting. Just before the workshop ended and members headed out for a reception at Mobile's Fort Condé, a reconstructed French battlement, Cecil stepped forward and made the case for a separate organization that would consolidate the interests of the historic house owners. This new group would provide a pool of technical knowledge for owners, encourage visitation among member properties, speak to mutual problems, and work toward changes in the tax laws.

Two days later, fully to his surprise, Cecil had what he asked for when Biddle announced the creation of the Historic House Association. (The name was later changed to the Historic House Association of America [HHAA] to distinguish it from its British counterpart.) At an organizational meeting the following January, Cecil became its chairman.

That following May, Cecil was host for three days to the first HHAA annual meeting in Asheville. The meeting gave Cecil an opportunity to showcase Biltmore to an audience of preservationists. Delegates found more than they expected. When they arrived at the house and stepped into the library, they found scaffolding for workers who were restoring the Pellegrini canvas on the ceiling. They watched furniture craftsmen Werner Katzenberger and Alvord Nelson at their work just outside the carpenter shop in the stables. In the afternoon, they sipped champagne in the Winter Garden and dined on the estate at Deerpark, a restaurant that had just opened in what had once been the maternity barn for the estate's dairy herd.

In the coming years, HHAA would attract nearly twenty-five hundred members, publish *Historic Houses* (a newsletter), provide a forum for all the topics that Cecil had outlined in Mobile, and more. The National Trust supplied an executive director, office space in Washington, D.C., and administrative support. Cecil's position gave him the opportunity to expand his international connections. He made little progress on changing the tax laws, however.

After a few years, membership dwindled and Cecil found himself putting in larger and larger personal contributions to help keep HHAA afloat. One criticism of the organization was that it did not relate to the owners of smaller houses; its board of directors suggested a group of elitists concerned with large estates. In 1984, after a change in administration at the National Trust and a lapse of financial and staffing support for HHAA, the organization was folded into the work of the National Trust and slipped from the scene.

It was an exhausting run. Cecil's perspective as a private owner never meshed with the curatorial disciplines that outnumbered owners and whose opinions largely overshadowed business principles. Cecil's own style—he could be charming but also commanding—irritated some. "He was always a voice in the wilderness," said one of Cecil's advisers, Maury Winger Jr.

"I am not a very good lobbyist," Cecil related some years later. "We had a fair amount of success [during the energy crisis]. I never won my battle on the inheritance tax. There are a half dozen of us who would benefit from it. Probably, only me in the really big scheme of things. Politicians look at it and say, 'Ah, give an individual a tax break.' I haven't learned the art of getting them to focus on the other side of the coin—that we are a national historic landmark. It is not Bill Cecil that owns it that is important."

"The prime objective of preservation is to preserve the best of our ancestors for the benefit of our descendants," Cecil told one international gathering, and inheritance taxes are "devastating to our prime purpose."

CHAPTER 13

"Be Reasonable—
Do It My Way"

One day, William Cecil was winding up a meeting with his department heads when he asked Richard King, the Biltmore house manager, to remain behind. "Do you know what my problem is?" Cecil asked King. Surprised at the question, King stumbled for a response before finally settling on a simple, "No." "I have a hundred ideas a day," Cecil said. "I know they are not all good, but my problem is I think they are."

In his first twenty years in Asheville, Cecil's "yeasty mix of ideas," as one friend called the stream of untested notions that flowed from Cecil's mind, had transformed Biltmore House and Gardens from an expensive drain on the family-owned business into a potential profit center with annual revenues of $3.5 million. In that time, visitation had grown tenfold, to more than four hundred thousand. Most summer travelers came to Asheville for two things: to drive to the heights of the Great Smokies and to visit

Biltmore. His grandfather's romantic vision had produced the remarkable château and gardens, but it was Cecil's profluent creativity that was turning Biltmore into an icon for western North Carolina.

Cecil's imagination had carried Biltmore into varied enterprises. He published books and ran his own advertising agency. The estate's nurseries and fields produced flowers, tomatoes, and other crops that eventually were sold to consumers around the Southeast. For a time, Cecil had hired out the estate's landscaping department to service commercial establishments off the estate. By 1979, the first bottles of Biltmore wine, produced from the grapes in Cecil's modest vineyard, had gone on sale.

He had proved to be a natural promoter. To encourage support for Biltmore among those most familiar with the place, he created a special Ambassador ticket that offered free admission to anyone who brought two paying guests. Nothing seemed too ambitious, or too small. For a time, he carried a supply of nickels in his pocket to plug expired parking meters downtown to help out-of-state visitors. Drivers of the graced vehicles found a note explaining the extra time was courtesy of Biltmore. Cecil also saw to it that parking attendants at the house fixed flats for free and helped visitors refill their tanks when they ran out of gas.

He was always on the hunt for ideas and processed what he gathered from visits abroad. After enjoying a cold buffet that was served to visitors at Woburn Abbey in England in 1977, he arrived home with plans to expand Biltmore's food service from an ice cream cart on the library terrace to the estate's first restaurant, Deerpark. It opened in 1979 in the refurbished barn. Cecil enjoyed his first meal there as the host for the first meeting of the Historic House Association of America.

Oftentimes, Cecil's subordinates caught the first rush from his fertile mind while seated at the rim of his desk in the Biltmore

Company offices. Cecil arrived at his office around nine in the morning, and his door was usually open throughout the day. That made it all the easier for him to snag his two young associates, Steve Miller and Richard Pressley, for impromptu conferences when the synapses were hitting. Secretaries could measure the length of the meetings by the density of the cloud of cigarette smoke that accumulated overhead. All three were heavy smokers, with Cecil favoring filtered Lark cigarettes.

The challenge for Miller and Pressley, green and unseasoned as they could be in the early years, was isolating the rough gems of their boss's ideas that could be polished and turned into real jewels while finessing the rest. That could prove difficult with a boss who prominently displayed the slogan "Be Reasonable—Do It My Way" at the front of his desk.

Cecil had a bullish nature, and his criticism could be withering. At the same time, he would give his people their head, even when he did not totally agree. He enjoyed the give-and-take that came from meetings with Miller, Pressley, and the others he depended on to keep the house in tip-top shape, the gardens trimmed, and the tourists flowing through the Lodge Gate. In the fall of 1979, there was a new sense of urgency to the work that lay ahead. Cecil was now on his own. "He had staked his reputation on making this thing successful," said Pressley. "And I think that's a lot of what gave him the pure determination to make it work. [He was saying] 'I'm going to prove to you that it can work.'"

The conditions were troubling. After an exhilarating rise in visitation and revenues throughout the 1970s, the numbers for 1979 were weak. Attendance for the year was projected to come in at 16 percent below the year before. The reasons: rising gasoline prices, a long string of rainy days during the summer, and a wane in consumer attention. An unnerving number of Asheville residents told a survey team put in the field by Cecil in late summer that they

had seen all that Biltmore had to offer and weren't planning to return anytime soon.

Compounding Cecil's problems was resistance to the steady increase in ticket prices. Adult admission had risen from three dollars
to seven dollars in ten years. In 1979, if mom, dad, and the two
kids wanted to see Biltmore, it cost the family twenty-four dollars.
Customers had voted with their feet. Word-of-mouth was the leading reason visitors gave for choosing a visit to Biltmore, and the
word in Asheville was that Biltmore cost too much.[1] The graphs
charting attendance and revenue looked like ski slopes for downhill
racers.

In addition to everything else, the national economic picture
wasn't pretty. Personal income was not keeping pace with inflation,
which was expected to soar to 15 percent in 1980. Interest rates
were on the rise and would soon climb to near 20 percent. All were
anxious as Cecil and his unseasoned management team headed to
an annual planning retreat at his home in Palm Beach, Florida.

The Cecils' Florida home is an Italian-styled villa designed and
built by Maurice Fatio at the height of Palm Beach's glory in the
1920s. It sits on a large lot on a quiet street between Lake Worth
and the luxurious mansions fronting on the Atlantic Ocean. It has
tall ceilings, tile floors, stucco walls, and airy rooms. French doors
open into a spacious enclosed garden. When the Cecils bought the
house in the early 1960s, the sale included furnishings that had
been in the house when the interior was featured in a 1930 edition
of *Town & Country* magazine. The same pieces were there in 1979.
Cecil called his home "the Frithlet."

William and Mimi avoided the usual social swirl of the Palm
Beach winter season, despite sufficient pedigrees from either side
of the family. During his weeks of retreat to warmer weather that

began shortly after Christmas, William usually reconnected with a group of cronies he had come to know over the years. They entertained one another with a baseball pool, weekly lunches at a popular eatery called Testa's, and outings to preseason games at the nearby spring training camps. Membership in the Palm Beach Baseball Authority was by invitation only; no women were allowed. Mimi was often in and out of town. Her interests were mostly back home, where she was a member of the Buncombe County Board of Education.

Cecil had begun holding annual planning meetings at Palm Beach in the 1960s. They usually took place toward the end of the year as the château was being prepared for the Christmas hiatus. It was an opportunity for Cecil to corral those on whom he depended for the day-to-day management of the house and gardens and talk shop without the distractions of the nontourist side of the business. The group was small but always included his general manager, Don Burleson, and Carl Nicholson, the Biltmore Company's chief financial officer. Others from the Biltmore Company staff were brought in as needed.

Cecil had picked Burleson out of the crowd of Biltmore workers in the early 1960s. He had come to work on the estate when he was sixteen years old and was pulling weeds on a gardener's crew when Cecil returned to Biltmore. Burleson showed some promise, and in 1965 when he was twenty-five, Cecil named him general manager and put him in charge of seventy employees. Nicholson had joined the company in the early 1960s after years with a leading accounting firm.

These meetings were no vacation, despite the luxurious surroundings. Wives remained at home, and the comfortable Florida residence with its fancy address became known as the "Palm Beach Prison" by those called to appear before the management tribunal. Cecil began daily sessions early, and they ran late as he reviewed every line of his budget and pushed department heads to defend their numbers and plans to the penny. Capital projects were picked apart and defended. If the nursery needed a new tractor, Cecil wanted to know the make, model, and delivery date. His questions were direct and pointed. New proposals might be examined in detail one year, postponed, then rehashed again the following year.

The regulars were lucky to get a half day of free time for golf, fishing, or just riding a bicycle during the exhausting two to three weeks of work. They were well cared for, however. Cecil provided a fully staffed kitchen capable of turning out a tantalizing range of dishes from menus that he prepared in exacting detail. He had the taste of a gourmet. The offerings were never common fare and were brand-new to young men who had never traveled far from home. When one diner was told the origin of sweetbreads, a dish he associated with cinnamon and sugar, he left the table after taking his first bite and rushed outside to throw up.

Cecil called for complete honesty from his subordinates. He expected managers to defend their plans. If he pushed, he expected his people to push back. "There was one fixed and inviolable rule," he said. "Whatever was said or discussed at the Palm Beach meeting would forever remain confidential."[2]

"It was a very good planning process," said Miller, "because we knew we had to have things put together and then we'd go down there to debate whether those were the kinds of things to do or not. Now sometimes they were pleasant, sometimes they were contentious. Usually they were some of both."[3] Even though tempers would flare, Miller said "the rule was, 'I want you to say what you think and what you really believe. I want you to argue your case. If we disagree, and have an argument about it, that's okay.'"[4]

"It was part of mine and Steve's training with Mr. C," Pressley said. "He will push you and if you just cave and give in and say yes, yes, you get pushed aside. He will respect your opinion. He may not agree, but he will respect it. He will expect you to voice your opinion and then come up with a decision. It was a good time for us to get to know each other."[5] When the grueling work was over, with all the players worn and weary, Cecil believed plans for the coming year had been rigorously tested.

"Never did we leave the Palm Beach meeting before we had all the next year's ducks in a row," Cecil said.

Advertising executive Charles Price, whose client list included McDonald's, Honda, and other national accounts, told Miller that in his experience of working with major corporations, Cecil's planning process, homegrown as it was, was one of the best he had ever seen. Price's presentations for ad campaigns were thoroughly screened. His clever copywriters were never allowed to go over the line. "Appropriate good taste," Price said. "That was what Mr. C was all about."

Pressley had attended one meeting prior to the 1979 session. This was Miller's first. Though they were recently recruited to Cecil's management team, they had some knowledge of each other's abilities. Together, they had launched the Deerpark restaurant with Pressley overseeing the operation of the kitchen and staff and Miller handling marketing. Burleson was the old hand, but he would leave the company a few months after the 1979 retreat, so virtually all the challenges of the coming years would fall on Miller and Pressley, neither of whom had reached the age of thirty.

Miller was twenty-four and a talented and eager go-getter. He had grown up in Asheville, where his parents ran a small jewelry store. He was looking for summer work after his freshman year at the University of North Carolina in Chapel Hill when he applied at Biltmore for a job on the landscaping crew. That position fell through, but he was recommended to Mimi Cecil as a stable hand. He spent that summer mucking out the stables behind the Frith and handling odd jobs for the boss's wife. Miller and Mimi Cecil, both of them chatty and gregarious, shared opinions about politics, the weather, and whatever happened to be the topic of the day. He had only passing contact with William Cecil. Each morning, Miller brought Cecil's car around to the front door all washed and gassed.

Miller made an impression, however. Before the next summer, Cecil called Miller's parents and asked what career they had planned for their son. The Millers found the inquiry quaint and frightfully British. Miller's mother said whatever her son chose for himself was fine with her. During his second summer with the company, Miller became a management intern, and Cecil told him he would have a job waiting for him when he graduated. Over the next two summers, Miller sold tickets, parked cars, worked in the garden, and assisted at the château. He graduated Phi Beta Kappa with a degree in business in 1977 and was considering law school when a professor told him that with his creative mind he'd find more satisfaction in business than in law. Miller joined Biltmore as an assistant to Cecil and Burleson. Two years later, he was buying the company's entire advertising schedule.

Pressley was three years older than Miller. He was driving a truck after a stint in the navy when he decided to use his GI benefits to get a college education. He chose accounting and got his degree while working nights to support his family. Two job offers arrived on the same day after graduation. One was with a grocery chain and the other was as a clerk in the comptroller's office at the Biltmore Company. "The only thing I knew about Biltmore Estate was what I remembered seeing as a child," he said. He and his wife rode through Biltmore Forest; then he accepted the Biltmore offer.

Pressley replaced Tench Jackson, a forty-two-year veteran at the company who had become the chief clerk in the front office after he lost a leg while working as a farmhand on the estate. When Cecil returned to Asheville, Jackson was the man who called out each man's pay before handing him his pay envelope. Pressley had been at the company for about eighteen months when the Cecil brothers announced they were splitting the company.

Pressley was buried in the accounting department. His introduction to William Cecil was a phone call one day from someone who identified himself as "Mr. C." At the time of the split, Pressley believed his future lay with William Cecil, not the dairy company. His decision was encouraged by Nicholson, who told him, "Those guys down there have a lot of young ideas and they are very energetic." Pressley later said, "I decided this was a golden opportunity."[6]

Tension hung over the 1979 Palm Beach meeting. "Now he was on his own," Pressley recalled. "He didn't have a brother to depend upon. He wanted to make sure things were on track and that his vision for the company was going to be fulfilled.

"I didn't have at stake what he had at stake," said Pressley. "I can imagine him thinking I am going to make this work. I have told my brother all along I would make it work. He was putting everything he had at risk."

Cecil had already taken some steps to counter the impact of the gas shortage by the time he arrived in Florida. With Charles Price's help, he had initiated an advertising campaign paid for by tourist-related businesses—Biltmore, hotels, restaurants, others—called "Cool, Green Asheville." The promotion produced some extra visitors and had taken some of the edge off of what was an otherwise dismal year for all. As a leader in the North Carolina Travel Council, Cecil had even succeeded in generating some extra money from the state to underwrite the television campaign that promoted the entire region. What Biltmore—and Asheville—needed now was something to continue the momentum into 1980.

Midway through the meeting, Richard King back in Asheville got a telephone call from the Florida compound. Could he come to Palm Beach? And could he bring along Susanne Brendel-Pandich, Biltmore's recently married curator, as well as the plans the two of them had been putting together for opening the downstairs of the house? And, by the way, be here tomorrow.

Cecil had learned with the opening of the Music Room that "something new to see" at Biltmore were the four most powerful words he could put in an ad. The opening of new space gave people something to talk about and renewed the interest of those who had not seen the house in recent years. The Music Room had produced some of the company's biggest gains in revenue. Perhaps the debut of additional space would put life back in the numbers.

The downstairs had long been a fascination of visitors, who frequently asked about the kitchens, the pantries, and other workaday corners of the château that had never been on the tour. Except for the early years when the restrooms near the gymnasium were in regular use, the downstairs area was off limits to everyone except the staff. Much of the space was empty or used for storage. Workers in the house—guards, hostesses, housekeepers—used a portion of the kitchens and adjacent rooms as a break area. There was a locker room for those in uniform.

The curiosity of visitors seemed to grow in the 1970s with the popularity of the BBC series *Upstairs, Downstairs*, which focused on the lives of social classes in pre–World War I London. Cecil had heard about interest in the lower level from King as well as from visitors. He had resisted extending the tour to that region, and in 1976 informed a guest that opening the downstairs was problematic. The stairs were narrow, and he worried that visitors might fall and injure themselves.

King continued to compile visitor interest. Not long after Brendel-Pandich arrived, the two began to gather information on what would be required to return the space to what it once had been—the supporting pillar of daily life at Biltmore. On the west side of the north end were the kitchens, the walk-in refrigerators, the pantries, the wash rooms with huge machines, and a heated drying room with racks large enough to hold a full bed sheet.

Another popular addition to the tour of the château was the downstairs in March of 1980. The kitchens and service areas, along with George Vanderbilt's gymnasium, bowling alley, and swimming pool, were opened to visitors.

There was a staff dining room and servants' hall, and midway under the house, sleeping rooms and quarters for Vanderbilt's staff. Some workers spent virtually every minute of their lives downstairs and were always on call. Apparently, it was the only place in the château where time really mattered. Large wall clocks with bold numbers were visible at every turn.

Under the Library and Tapestry Gallery was George Vanderbilt's indoor playground. Here was the fifty-three–by–twenty-seven-foot indoor swimming pool with diving platform and chandeliers. Nearby were the bowling alley, gymnasium, and dressing rooms. One particularly large space designated as a storage area was called the Halloween Room. In the 1920s, Cornelia Cecil and her artistic friends had gaily decorated the walls with images from Pushkin tales as a backdrop for a costume party.

Archival material in the house was of some help to Brendel-Pandich and King as they set out to account for what was on hand and what was missing. Brendel-Pandich consulted the Smithsonian Institution to learn more about the operating details of kitchens of the day, pored over domestic service manuals, and called on the Library of Congress for further information.

By the time King got the call from Palm Beach, he and Brendel-Pandich had tallied the amount of money they needed for restoration, along with a proposed tour route for visitors to see a portion of the house where even Vanderbilt's guests never ventured. With their proposal in hand, they headed to Florida and made a pitch for the $50,000 they estimated was necessary to restore the downstairs to what it was at the beginning of the twentieth century. The addition to the tour would be the most extensive expansion of the public's view of Biltmore since the house first opened in 1930, adding more than two dozen rooms to the Biltmore experience.

When Cecil approved the plans, he issued definitive orders to King: "Don't just do it for show. Make it work."

Most of what King and Brendel-Pandich needed to meet Cecil's expectations was relatively close at hand, although many of the workaday items were dusty, dirty, and in need of repair. With the aid of Warren Moore, who had been a regular hand at the house for thirty years, King found some of the old laundry equipment in a trash heap at the old kennels. The machinery was brought back and refurbished, along with the huge, cast-iron kitchen stoves, fired by wood or coal, which required new fireboxes. After the flues were thoroughly cleaned, King called in another estate veteran, Bruce Maxwell, who was familiar with the mysteries of woodstove cooking and set out to create a meal. "Whatever temperature you needed," King said, "he could nail it."

Walls were painted, curtains were hung, and tables and chairs for the servants' dining room were repaired and brought to a shine. Plumbing that had been rerouted over the years was returned to what Richard Morris Hunt had specified in his plans. Brendel-Pandich found a source for pre–World War I packages of bleach, starch, and laundry soaps and purchased period models of cans, boxes, barrels, jars, and crates. The only piece of equipment that had not survived the years was a turn-of-the-century Troy-model washing machine. Brendel-Pandich finally located one for sale from an ad she placed in *Drycleaners' News*.

Beds and furnishings were repaired and placed in the rooms where some of the household servants had once made their home. The large wall-mounted electric clocks were reconnected to the master timepiece that kept all at the same minute and hour.

Some purchases were required to fill out the supply of fencing equipment in the gymnasium, which also needed a new rowing machine. New cotton duck curtains were hung in the dressing rooms. The seventy-thousand-gallon swimming pool was scrubbed and the ropes replaced. It was left empty of water, and not solely for safety reasons. John Cecil was the last one to attempt to restore the pool for use. Much to his chagrin, he discovered that after sitting empty for years, the grout had separated from the tiles and water leaked out almost as fast as it went in.

The regulation-size bowling alley was directly below the seventy-five-foot-long Tapestry Gallery on the first floor. It had seen only occasional use since the Cecils' day. When George's and William's children were young, they sneaked downstairs to bowl a game or two. King found the original pins and balls that had come from the Brunswick-Balke-Collender Company in 1895.

Biltmore introduced the downstairs tour on March 15, 1980—the fiftieth anniversary of the opening of the house to the public. By the end of the year, attendance had surpassed projections of four hundred thousand visitors by more than 5 percent. Seventy-five percent of the visitors in 1980 chose to pay an extra three dollars—with the regular house and gardens tour at seven dollars—for a tour of the downstairs. King said many guests told him that they could more easily imagine life as a house employee than as a guest or a resident. The $50,000 invested in restoration was recovered within a matter of months.

Years later, Cecil liked to use the addition of the downstairs tour as an example of the superiority of private management and ownership of historic properties. It was unlikely that a government-sponsored property or one run by a part-time board of directors for a nonprofit foundation could move as quickly to add to the visitors' enjoyment and understanding of how a historic house worked. In less than a year, Biltmore had expanded the Biltmore experience—it now took nearly twice as long to tour the house as before—and reversed the downturn in revenue. Moreover, Cecil had given all those who said they knew Biltmore a reason to return.

With a new marketing slogan—"A faraway place that's not far away"—Cecil began working on a strategy to make Biltmore a destination where visitors planned on spending an entire day rather than a few hours on the way to someplace else.

William Cecil routinely invested 25 percent of his operating budget in advertising—a figure well above that spent by most managers of historic properties. Biltmore's first legitimate winemaster, Frenchman Philippe Jourdain, was featured in an early ad for the winery that showed Jourdain standing in Cecil's first vineyard planted below the château.

*　*　*

The downstairs work coincided with a flurry of restoration work elsewhere in the house. Even before the downstairs tour was brought to the Palm Beach planning meeting for approval, Cecil was making plans for John Finnie of Campbell, Smith and Company, Ltd., an English firm specializing in decorative restoration, to restore the Pellegrini canvas on the Library ceiling. Cecil had been concerned for some time about the deteriorating condition of the magnificent Rococo-era painting titled *The Chariot of Aurora*, which Giovanni Antonio Pellegrini had completed in about 1720. Portions of the large central section of the canvas had become detached and were sagging. In addition, the varnish had begun to yellow and the pigment was drying out. Over the years, water from leaks in the roof had softened the plaster on the walls behind the side panels of the magnificent work.

George Vanderbilt had purchased the Pellegrini canvas in Paris, but during his lifetime he had never revealed the source. It was said he promised the seller not to disclose his name to avoid embarrassment at a time when many Europeans were angry over the sale of their art treasures to wealthy Americans. The only documents on the work in the Biltmore files were shipping bills from Paris, but they didn't reveal the name of the seller. During one of William Cecil's trips abroad, he finally determined that the canvas had come from the Pisani Palace in Venice, which, by the time he arrived for a visit, had become a home for retired musicians. The ceiling where the Pellegrini canvas had once commanded attention was still a blank space.

Though the work appears as one continuous piece, it is actually a composite of thirteen sections that cover an expanse that is sixty-four feet long and thirty-two feet wide. The central portion—and the largest—weighs more than five hundred pounds.

Cecil had expressed concern about the condition of the ceiling in the early 1970s when he and his brother held joint responsibility for the care and upkeep of the château. At the time, revenues from tourism were barely keeping pace with expenses, so there was no spare cash for what both believed would be an expensive undertaking. In addition, Cecil had been unable to find anyone qualified to handle the assignment. Faced with these challenges, he had opted to invest in the completion of the Music Room and the improvements to the Morning Salon.

Though the ceiling work was postponed, Cecil had continued to look for restoration experts who were qualified to do the job. Following one of his trips to England in the mid-1970s, he learned of the Campbell, Smith firm in London. Their credits included work in virtually every room of Buckingham Palace, the House of Lords, the faces of Big Ben, and the regilding of the royal carriage. As Biltmore's profit picture improved, Cecil contacted Finnie, who was Campbell, Smith's decorative arts expert, and asked him to come to Biltmore. Finnie arrived in Asheville in May 1979. Before he returned to London, he informed Cecil that the cost for restoring the canvas and making repairs to the peeling plaster would be $65,000.

Six of Finnie's artists began their four months of work in the spring of 1980 after scaffolding was erected to put them within seven feet of the twenty-six-foot-high ceiling. The artists applied a protective covering to the face of the painting, then carefully lowered it onto the scaffolding for restoration. Next, they attached fresh linen to the plaster, then applied a newly developed reversible adhesive. The canvas was carefully smoothed back into place. Finnie's artisans restored the side panels without removing them. The end panels were not part of the original Pellegrini work and had been added when the canvas was installed at Biltmore in order to center Pellegrini's work over the room. Finnie's painters improved on the 1895 work to bring the additions into proper perspective.

The ceiling work went so well that Cecil asked Finnie and his team to apply their talents elsewhere. Painters adjusted Alan

Burnham's decorative trim on the ceiling beams in the Music Room to colors that more accurately reflected the Gothic design. Finnie told Cecil that some of Burnham's colors, such as his brilliant blues, were out of place with the motif. The architect's busy stenciling on the walls was replaced with a more appropriate design. As a final touch, Finnie designed tall, period-correct floor lamps. He sketched out the design for the lamps, and Biltmore craftsman Werner Katzenberger produced them in the Biltmore carpenter shop.

As the retouching was completed on the first floor, Brendel-Pandich completed a reworking of the so-called Victorian Suite on the second floor, which had been opened in 1974 before her arrival. These three bedrooms were refurbished to more accurately reflect Hunt's original plan as the Sheraton, Chippendale, and Old English rooms.

There was a new attitude taking hold within the company that combined Cecil's appreciation for the family history with the greater significance of Biltmore. Long regarded as grandpa's old house, Biltmore was becoming more of a historic house where accuracy and faithful presentation were paramount. "[Mr. Cecil] feels that this is not only his heritage," said King, "but the country's. Over the years, he is the one who has informed us that this is not just grandpa's house, it is history, it is important."

Cecil and Finnie meshed like old friends, although they were an unlikely pair. Finnie was a devoted socialist; Cecil was a conservative Democrat who often voted Republican. Finnie was working class, a slight man with a thick Scottish accent and heavy tortoise-shell glasses. Cecil was tall and imperious, equally English when he wanted to be, and decidedly upper crust. Cecil was struck by Finnie's creative mind, his energy, and his enthusiasm. Finnie found in Biltmore an unending canvas upon which to apply his creative talents. By the time Finnie's team had finished its initial round of work on the estate in Asheville, he and Cecil were partners in a new enterprise, Biltmore, Campbell, Smith Restorations Inc. (BCSR).

What Cecil had discovered on his way to repairing the library ceiling was a need in the United States for a firm that could provide quality restoration work. If there was such a shortage of qualified restorers in the United States, then why shouldn't Biltmore, with its own experience, its superior standards for craftsmanship, and its reputation for fine art, offer its services to owners of other historic properties? The idea came as naturally as his grandfather's decision to sell surplus milk from the estate's dairy or Cecil's own conversion of the landscaping crew to a for-profit service to customers off the property.

The new company got off to a rousing start with large contracts for work similar to the assignment that had brought Cecil and Finnie together in the first place. The state of Pennsylvania was looking for specialists to restore the work of the American muralist and Pennsylvania native Edwin Austin Abbey that filled the lunettes behind four great arches high in the dome of the State Capitol in Harrisburg. Previous restoration efforts had been done poorly. As a result, the mistakes obscured much of Abbey's images, and water leaking into the dome posed a serious threat. A preservation committee awarded BCSR a $2.2 million contract to return the paintings to their former glory.

BCSR imported a team of six British conservators and began work in March 1985 on an assignment that would require more than two years to complete. The work proved to be a difficult challenge, especially after it was discovered that the paintings could only be treated by complete removal from the plaster. A complex system was designed to handle the canvases that weighed between eight hundred and a thousand pounds each.

Other clients expressed interest. Working from an office on the estate, BCSR's portfolio of work included clients from across the eastern United States. A parquet floor in the office of the vice president in the Old Executive Office building in Washington, D.C., was one project. The company worked on the Tennessee State Capitol and researched the decorative finishes of the twenty-four-room Hay House mansion in Macon, Georgia. Projects were completed at the Breakers Hotel in Palm Beach, which was undergoing a major renovation, and at Flagler College in St. Augustine, Florida. The college building had once been a grand hotel and was built by Henry Flagler in the era of Biltmore's opening.

Work on smaller pieces of art was carried out in a section of the château where a heat vacuum table was built to assist in the restoration of paintings that could be dismounted from their frames, cleaned, and carefully restored. Some of these jobs included work for the estate, such as fine cabinetry work on a range of pieces from sixteenth-century Spanish to nineteenth-century French.

Finnie helped Cecil create the Biltmore Guest Cottage, with BCSR's artisans completing the decoration of a farmhouse that had once been the truck farm manager's residence. The one-and-a-half-story home was built in 1896 and featured Hunt's distinctive pebbledash exterior, brick trim, and tile roof. It anchored a small complex of buildings located along banks of the Swannanoa River near the old Victoria Bridge. The house had been empty for several years, and the adjoining brick courtyard, where vegetables had once been sorted and prepared for market, was falling into disrepair. Cecil resurrected the house and converted it into a comfortable four-bedroom, private bed-and-breakfast where the company could put up special guests. (The Guest Cottage was flooded in September 2004 when the swollen Swannanoa once again devastated areas of Asheville, including Biltmore Village.)

During the heady, early days of BCSR's life, Cecil considered the restoration company to be one of the brightest jewels in the Biltmore crown. The opportunities looked endless. In addition, the restoration business added cache to the Biltmore portfolio and extended the company's reputation for quality and perfection. Cecil also found it useful to have in-house talent upon which he could call for special projects such as the estate's new winery, where construction began in 1983.

Unfortunately, BCSR's fortunes fell nearly as quickly as they rose. Cecil found too much of the business was wrapped up in Finnie after his friend and colleague fell ill with cancer and died in 1987. The company struggled to maintain its balance for two more years before the books were finally closed on BCSR and an English subsidiary.

Cecil was philosophical about the end. Some ideas work; others don't. If one fails, you close the books and move on. The BCSR experience had a lasting impact at Biltmore, nonetheless. Two English artisans were brought over before BCSR's decline to begin the restoration of the tapestries in the house. This work continued beyond the existence of the company.

BCSR was instrumental in creating a decorative restoration program at Asheville-Buncombe Technical College. Cecil had helped launch the program to train local talent in an effort to overcome the expense of importing workers and craftsmen from England. With many contracts going to the lowest bidder, BCSR found its low expenses for travel put it well above competitors.

Cecil helped arrange the endorsement of the technical college training program by the British guilds. The program included classroom instruction and an apprenticeship. After completing written and craft examinations, graduates became eligible for an internationally recognized craftsman certificate. Before he retired in 2004, Derrick Tickle, who took over the program after its first year in 1988, produced more than two hundred graduates who secured jobs in the decorative arts and restoration world.

One of Finnie's last projects at Biltmore was in the tasting room at the new winery, where he designed the decorative stenciling incorporating the family crests and supervised the restoration and installation of the John La Farge stained-glass windows. They had once been part of William Henry Vanderbilt's New York City residence.

While Cecil had great ambitions for BCSR, nothing matched his enthusiasm for the future of the Biltmore winery that he had been anticipating for more than a decade. Cecil had long believed that the one thing missing from Biltmore was a winery. He was not going to be persuaded otherwise.

CHAPTER 14

Biltmore by the Bottle

W illiam Cecil had enjoyed other celebrations at Biltmore, including sumptuous dinners in the Banquet Hall, but nothing was comparable to the three days of dining, touring, and visiting that accompanied the introduction of the Biltmore Estate winery in May 1985. It was, in Cecil's words, the most historic event since his grandfather had opened his estate to his family on Christmas Day ninety years earlier.

The winery had been more than fifteen years in the making, but Cecil had started looking for ways to develop the estate's agricultural potential well before he settled on establishing a vineyard. In the 1960s, he had expanded the sale of flowers and bedding plants from the greenhouses, which had been an off-and-on business for some years. Next, he experimented with the commercial-size crops of salad tomatoes and mushrooms. All had met with mixed success. One year, a greenhouse full of lilies failed to come into bloom at Easter and he was left with a host of unusable plants; no one wanted to buy green pods yet to burst into glorious white blossoms.

The tomatoes had offered the greatest promise. In 1964, Cecil had put in fifty acres of plants that produced small, red, gumball-size "tommytoes," as he called the tomatoes that were becoming popular toppings for salads. The following year, he increased the plantings and recruited area farmers to grow the tomatoes on their own land and market them through Biltmore. After a couple of years, however, he had abandoned his venture into the produce business due to problems with distribution.

Cecil began investigating the potential of a winery in the early 1970s. The idea of a vineyard had intrigued him ever since he had traveled in France's Loire River valley, where he had seen the châteaux that had been the models for Biltmore. They all sat high on a hill with a river curled around the flat bottomland, much like the location of Biltmore from its spot overlooking the French Broad River. "We said we have a river, we have a château, we have the land, we have no vineyard. Every French château has a vineyard," he said.[1] After he saw a visitor pulling grapes from an arbor in the Walled Garden—a treat not included in the price of admission—he decided he'd make those vines pay.

When he first broached the idea of a winery at one of his Palm Beach meetings, everyone told him he was nuts. Soon afterward, at a June 1971 meeting of the Biltmore Company board of directors, William told his brother and the other directors that grapes were the agricultural alternative that could return Biltmore to profitability. Just like the dairy in its heyday, a vineyard and commercial winery would generate additional income as well as enhance the house and gardens as a tourist attraction.[2] Again, his idea was dismissed.

Nonetheless, a year later, Cecil began preparing a site on a southern slope below the Conservatory where he installed an experimental vineyard. His vision of a winery on Biltmore Estate remained as clear as ever, regardless of the naysayers. That made the morning of May 15, 1985, all the more glorious when the sun finally broke through a heavy gray sky just before he escorted a host of friends from the United States and abroad through the estate's new $12 million winery.

In the early days, Cecil's proposition for a winery was as problematic as his notion in 1960 that tourism could be profitable. When Cecil planted his first vines, there wasn't a single North Carolina vineyard producing juice for fine table wines even though the state had once been home to more than two dozen wineries. Most had disappeared prior to World War I when local prohibition campaigns swept across North Carolina closing saloons and outlawing alcohol.

Caught in the sweep were many of North Carolina winemakers who had found some success with wine made from the Scuppernong grape, a bronze variety of Muscadines and the country's first cultivated wine grapes. Scuppernongs were native to eastern North Carolina and were growing with abandon on Roanoke Island when Sir Walter Raleigh stepped ashore in the sixteenth century. The island's so-called mother vine was said to have a trunk two feet thick and was still producing in the 1950s when the Mother Vineyard Winery, the last of the North Carolina wineries, closed.

During the 1930s, popular North Carolina wines had been red and white varieties of the Virginia Dare label. They were the products of an ambitious vintner named Paul Garrett who produced the first singing wine commercial ever broadcast. The radio jingle ended with the refrain, "Say it again . . . Virginia Dare."[3] Garrett's wine was produced from a combination of grape juice from California and New York that was mixed with the juice of Scuppernongs, which gave the wine its distinctive sweet flavor. A North Carolina Scuppernong had enjoyed a short revival in the 1960s when the state's laws were being relaxed. Onslow Wine Cellars in eastern North Carolina produced a Scuppernong wine before it closed its winery in 1968.

Creating a vineyard and producing fine table wines at Biltmore was the sort of challenge that most motivated Cecil since everyone said it couldn't be done. He wasn't foolhardy or purely stubborn. Cecil believed that the naysayers had never paid close attention to Biltmore's location in the mountains of western North Carolina. Asheville was at about the same latitude as Gibraltar in the Mediterranean, and with an altitude of between 2,100 and 2,500 feet, the fields on the estate would enjoy warm days and cool nights in the summer. Such conditions were considered to be just right for growing grapes elsewhere in the world. Moreover, Asheville's winters were no colder than those experienced in grape-growing regions of France.

The opening of the interstates spanning the North Carolina mountains to the west and to the south only reinforced his enthusiasm. The new superhighways put Biltmore within a day's drive of the major eastern markets where wine sales—especially imports from France, Spain, Italy, and Germany—were growing at double-digit rates. Biltmore could capitalize on the growing market that California winemakers such as the Gallo brothers of California had created for domestic wines. If it was "Gallo by the gallon," Cecil said he would be satisfied with "Biltmore by the bottle."

A winery remained an audacious idea. Cecil was starting cold with nothing more on his side than a lot of ambition. "We didn't have anyone on the payroll who knew anything about grapes," Cecil said. "It was the blind leading the blind. I said, 'Well, let's grow some.'"[4]

The experience of the Onslow winery in the 1960s had spawned some interest in wine and grape research on the campus of North Carolina State University (NCSU). This work was in its fifth year when Cecil called NCSU and the State Department of Agriculture in Raleigh. Cecil was told that the only varieties that could thrive in the humidity of the eastern United States were French-American hybrids that came with decidedly technical names such as S-5279 and GW-8. It was understood that only California growers, whose vineyards enjoyed drier summers, could cultivate the vinifera vines that bore the familiar names of Chardonnay, Merlot, Gamay, and Riesling.

Following that advice, Cecil planted French-American hybrids on the small plots that he had prepared. It was a picturesque location with a southern exposure that lay just above the Azalea Garden and, farther on, the Bass Pond. As the vines grew larger and leafed out over the trellises, the château in the background provided the proper attitude for promotional pictures. It may not have been the best land, but it was accessible and, more importantly, available.

These early plantings flourished. Within a few years, Cecil was harvesting grapes and preparing to bottle some wine in a makeshift production line on the lower level of the Conservatory. The location was less than ideal. Lighting was bad and water dripped from above when plants were being watered in the Conservatory. Cecil's erstwhile "winemaster" was Ted G. Defosses. He was a handyman on the estate staff with an indeterminate past and varied career honed from an earlier life in northern Vermont, where the locals were never sure whether they were in the United States or Canada. Defosses volunteered to make Cecil's wine. He said he had learned something about spirits and native wines in his early days.

"He squished the grapes with his feet," Cecil recalled. "We got an old cider press and squished some more, put some rice hulls in. The wine was as thick as maple syrup. We threw more grapes in. Then we threw more sugar in and let it ferment for a while." Cecil called it the "crush of horror." Looking back years later, he said, "It was a wonder it didn't blow up."

While Defosses experimented with his winemaking, Cecil's advertising man, William Guillet, designed a label for the bottles and printed some samples in the company's print shop. One version was a simple line drawing of the house framed by bunches of grapes with "Château Biltmore—Asheville N.C." across the bottom. The final design was simple and elegant. The label was topped by an image of the house and carried either a gold or red lion to indicate whether the contents were Biltmore red or Biltmore white. "It made for a pretty good-looking bottle of wine," Cecil said. "Just don't drink it."

Not only were Defosses's wines perfectly awful, they were also decidedly illegal. In his rush to get started, Cecil had not bothered to secure the necessary licenses for the production of wine in North Carolina. The company's attorney was sent scurrying for the proper documentation as required for even bad home brew.

The following year, Cecil tried another pressing and put it to the test of a visiting Frenchman, a Russian émigré named Pierre Troubetzkoy, who was a cousin of Dolly Morgan, whose husband's family had taken refuge in the Gardener's Cottage on the estate during the Depression. Troubetzkoy gave Cecil some faint hope that perhaps his years of work and investment of a substantial sum of money were not in vain.

"Pierre would stand there and say with a lot of work, this would be very good," Cecil said mimicking the Russian's accent. "He didn't knock it. If he had, we would have quit." On another visit to Biltmore a year later, Troubetzkoy declared Cecil's wine better than before and offered to use his contacts in France, where he was familiar with the French agricultural ministry, to help Cecil find a proper winemaster. In the fall of 1977, Cecil stopped in Paris on his return from Australia and interviewed several candidates summoned by Troubetzkoy. Cecil's pick was Philippe Jourdain. That following February, Jourdain visited Biltmore to survey the possibilities.

A tall man with broad shoulders and a thick shock of graying hair, Jourdain was forty-nine years old, about Cecil's age, and at a flexible junction in his life. He had grown up in French Algeria, the son of an admiral in the French Navy. Rather than follow his father into the military, he had responded to his mother's persuasion to become a winemaker, adding to the six generations on her side of the family. He took a degree in agricultural engineering from the Ecole Nationale d'Agriculture d'Alger and spent two years studying enology, the science of winemaking. He was teaching and managing a small vineyard in France with other members of his family when he met Cecil. Although Cecil had asked Troubetzkoy to find someone who spoke English, Jourdain spoke only French. Nevertheless, the two understood each other perfectly. Cecil's French was impeccable; Jourdain accepted Cecil's offer. "He gave me carte blanche," the Frenchman later said. "That was my dream."[5]

Cecil saw in Jourdain the experience and desire that he was looking for and made him an offer similar to one he had heard the Mars candy company people had used to build their expertise in chocolates. Overshadowed by the Hershey empire, the Mars company had raided the Nestlé establishment in Switzerland and persuaded accomplished chocolatiers to bring their experience to the States. Like the Mars company had reportedly done before, Cecil offered Jourdain good wages, money for travel to and from France, and a retirement income once he had trained his successor.

By the time Cecil and Jourdain met, the Biltmore vineyard had switched to include vinifera grapes. Specialists from the University of California at Davis, the recognized center of winemaking research in the United States, had persuaded Cecil that some viniferas might work in the East if they were grafted onto hybrid root stock. It was believed that the two in combination could produce a plant resistant to the diseases and pests that had bedeviled eastern growers in the past. Jourdain urged Cecil to continue experimentation with the grafted vines and suggested other viniferas to accompany those already in the ground. Jourdain said that until these new vines were ready to produce, Biltmore was not ready for him, and he returned to France.

Throughout the following year, Jourdain made other visits and offered further advice in pages of correspondence that Cecil had translated by a member of the faculty at the University of North Carolina at Asheville to ensure accuracy. Just as Cecil was settling affairs with his brother in 1979, Jourdain returned to Asheville to supervise the harvest and oversee the first wines actually offered to consumers under the Biltmore label. With some fanfare, Cecil announced that the new Biltmore vintages would go on sale in December. About five thousand bottles of red and white were available to buyers.

This early Biltmore wine would prove to have little more than novelty value, however. The vineyard had produced generous yields from the hybrid stock, but Jourdain could not eliminate the distinctive and unpleasant aftertaste that came with the wines. Some years later, Cecil laughed about a bottle of his 1979 offering that he had taken to his English cousin, David Exeter at Burghley House. Cecil had delivered it with instructions that it not be drunk "until the day after I had joined our ancestors either above, or below, since the wine would never amount to anything we would wish our friends to partake."

In recounting the episode to Exeter's daughter, Cecil recalled that her father ignored his advice, opened the bottle immediately, and served it all around "either out of a sense of humor or mischief." He then "delivered one of the greater lines in the English language when, after having realized the contents were undrinkable, he turned to his butler who was offering him some more, and said without cracking a smile, 'Oh, no thank you. I want my guests to enjoy it.'"

It was a humbling beginning, but Cecil was confident that the future looked promising with Jourdain installed at Biltmore. As those first bottles disappeared into the hands of customers, he had on his desk a report from Jourdain that read, "I believe that a truly superior quality of wine may be possible. . . . This is only a dream and we must wait to make our first vinifera wines to determine if this is realistic or not. We must not claim victory before it is actually realized."[6]

When Cecil set about on his own in 1979, without the drag of dissent from others in the company, he did not see the wine business as a novelty or just another attraction for the estate. He believed the wine business was the financial engine that would carry the company forward. If he was successful, the winery would secure Biltmore for the next generation.

In short, the winery was not an option; it was a necessity. Cecil was perhaps the only person who believed that the house—which had known days when not a single visitor appeared at the gates—would eventually reach its capacity for visitors and be unable to produce the revenue necessary to maintain and preserve the estate. "Sooner or later," he said, "the house would be full, which was an unheard of thought. We would need something else."[7]

There was more to it than that, according to Cecil's friend and counselor Maury Winger Jr. "Bill had a dream that he inherited from his British ancestry," Winger said. "When you live on a big estate, the first obligation is to preserve it. The second is to improve it. The third is to leave it in better shape than you found it."[8]

As the president of American Enka, Winger was one of Asheville's leading corporate executives when he became acquainted with Cecil in the 1970s. At its peak, Winger's company had employed about fifteen thousand workers in its plant near Asheville and at two other locations, one in Tennessee and the other in South Carolina. Nearly half of the company's employees worked in North Carolina, and many lived in a model town that Enka had created west of Asheville in the 1930s. The neat streets and trim houses accompanied the huge plant that sat in a valley just over a ridge from Biltmore's west side. Forty years later, Enka and the international textile markets were changing, and Winger was the man responsible for reducing the company's operations in the South.

The favorite watering hole for businessmen such as Winger and Cecil was the Mountain City Club in downtown Asheville. Usually over lunch, businessmen would talk and challenge one another over politics and business. "We'd just lie like hell," Cecil said, "and talk about freight rates after the Civil War. It took your mind off the horrors you had to deal with that particular day."[9]

Winger also happened to be a neighbor in Biltmore Forest, but the two men didn't get to know each other well until Cecil called and invited Winger to attend the Super Bowl. "I didn't even know he cared about football," said Winger. "I was amazed and said, 'Sure, let's do it.'" They flew to the game, spent a delightful weekend together, and repeated the excursion on a couple of other occasions. In time, Cecil invited Winger to become one of his advisers. Winger said yes.

Over the years, Cecil had turned to close friends outside of the company for advice and counsel. An early confidant was his Biltmore Forest neighbor, Charles D. Owen Jr., a textile executive who had known William and George since the brothers had arrived in Asheville. Plainspoken and honest, Owen was free with his advice. After sampling some of the early Biltmore wine, he told Cecil he should forget the winery and build a golf course instead. Cecil was equally at ease with Charles Cummings, a medical doctor whom Cecil had met while Cummings was barbecuing slabs of bear meat at a neighborhood get-together. Cummings was the object of one of Cecil's practical jokes. On that Easter Sunday when the Biltmore lily crop failed to bloom, Cummings awoke to find all the unsold plants ringing the perimeter of the large front porch of his Biltmore Forest home.

An early ally in the tourist business was Hugh Morton, the owner of Grandfather Mountain and, like Cecil, an accomplished amateur photographer. In the late 1960s, Morton convinced Cecil to become active in the Southern Highlands Attractions (SHA), a group Cecil had once viewed as ineffective and pedestrian. Their relationship had an auspicious beginning; Cecil had barred Morton from entering the château with his camera despite Morton's protests that he was there at the request of North Carolina governor Dan Moore, who was hosting a special dinner for southern governors in the Banquet Hall. Morton encouraged Cecil to become more active in the SHA, and he ended up serving as the president of the organization. They appreciated each other's respect for honesty and frankness. "We were probably the only ones who told the truth about attendance at the Southern Highlands meetings," Morton said.

Morton, Owen, and Cummings were friends with whom Cecil could share some of his private concerns in the tentative early years when he was running Biltmore in tandem with his brother. Now that he was on his own, Cecil was looking for the kind of advice that most chief executives of multimillion-dollar companies found in an experienced top echelon of management or on a board of directors. The "new" Biltmore Company had neither. Cecil's top managers were young and untested, and the company's directors were mostly family members.

Cecil's answer was an outside board of advisers. It was a small, solid group of men who expected nothing more from Cecil than his friendship and in whom he confided his concerns, even fears. They were his "shoulder to cry on," as he once called the group. "It would be sympathetic, but it would not be family."

Winger was the only one who was immediately at hand. The others lived up and down the East Coast. Cecil kept them informed through correspondence, and the group met with some regularity in Asheville or Palm Beach. One early member was Henry Hoffstot, a distinguished Pittsburgh, Pennsylvania, attorney with an affinity for old cars and bow ties. The Hoffstots were Palm Beach neighbors. Henry's wife, Barbara, was a member of the board of directors of the National Trust for Historic Preservation. She was also the author of a book on Palm Beach architecture. Hoffstot succeeded Cecil as the chairman of the Historic House Association of America (HHAA) and negotiated its merger with the National Trust. His firm also brought talent to bear on Cecil's concerns about inheritance taxes. For a time, Cecil called on another Palm Beach neighbor, the former NASA engineer Dr. Robert Terry, who was a regular in the Palm Beach Baseball Authority.

None knew Cecil better than E. McGregor Strauss, a Rhode Island investment banker. Strauss was one of the first Americans whom a young, lean, strapping William Cecil had met in 1949 when he arrived in the United States. Edith Gerry asked Strauss to help her grandson get settled at Harvard, where Strauss was also a student. After Harvard, Strauss did a tour in the army, joined a New York brokerage, then moved his business to Newport, Rhode Island. Over the years, he had helped Cecil work through his entrepreneurial exercises. On occasion, he had provided Cecil with an inside look at how Newport preservationists were handling the mansions in their care. When the HHAA was organized, Cecil recruited Strauss for the board of directors. He was probably the only one who fully understood Cecil's drive to secure a future for Biltmore.

Winger's early participation was part-time, but when he retired from Akzona, Enka's parent company, he became the Biltmore Company's vice president and general counsel. Winger brought not only experience as a corporate executive but his training as an attorney.

"When they split," Winger said, "George took all the corporate structure. We had no outside accounting firm, no internal operations. He needed everything. He had to start from scratch."[10]

"My senior staff were all without expertise," Cecil said. "[Maury Winger] was particularly well suited to this task since he had helped and nurtured a division of American Enka through its growing pains."

Even before his formal retirement, Winger had worked with Steve Miller and Richard Pressley to develop a financial plan for the winery. Winger brought his experience in running production lines to finding some answers for Cecil. As the computer made pass after pass on various financial projections, the three men adjusted the numbers on vineyard production, winery capacity, and sales projections in an attempt to find a scenario that would show a profit. In the end, the success of the venture boiled down to how many bottles of Biltmore wine could be sold. Cecil's market seemed endless, whereas Miller, Pressley, and Winger were more cautious. Even when they agreed on something in between, with the sales projections on the high side, the final financial pro forma was not that impressive.

Strauss had always believed in Cecil's plans for Biltmore, especially after the interstate highways opened in the late 1960s. Yet he had never been keen on Cecil's ambitions for a vineyard and a winery. "I said, 'Bill, please don't do it. It just can't go. It is the wrong climate. It is the wrong soil. Alluvial soil in a bottom. It is too hot in the summer. I thought of every reason I knew.'"[11]

On one level, Winger agreed with Strauss. The numbers were weak. "But," Winger argued, "you have to take into account the built-in market we have. We have X thousand visitors every year and they are going to be interested in buying wine made at Biltmore."

Cecil gathered the opinions of each of his advisers, but he never called for a show of hands. "Bill didn't want a vote," Winger said. "He was going to make his own decision anyway."

Indeed, by the time Winger began running his calculations, Cecil was expanding the vineyard onto 150 acres on the west side that had once been used to pasture the Biltmore dairy herd. It was second-rate soil for a vineyard, poor in nutrients, with a top level of established grass that fought easy cultivation. Cecil had little choice, however. It was the best land available under the terms of the agreement with his brother, who retained use of the former cow pastures for a limited time. Cecil began planting there in 1981. As plans progressed for the winery, Jourdain suggested that the west side might be the best location because of the favorable connections to the interstate highways.

Cecil never gave the west side much consideration as the site of his winery. He would put the vineyard there, but he wanted the winery to be part of the Biltmore experience. Instead, he had his eye on the old dairy barn and a complex of buildings that had long been in need of attention.

In its day, the Biltmore dairy barn had been a distinctive focal point of the estate's farming operation. Finished at the turn of the twentieth century, it was the largest in a complex of working buildings that stood at the edge of a broad plain beside the banks of the French Broad. The barn was an impressive structure large enough to handle hundreds of cows that, twice daily, moved in and out of three milking parlors as long as bowling alleys. This was a milk factory. Underneath the building were vaulted tunnels with walls reinforced with stone. A narrow rail system in the tunnel floor carried carts filled with manure out to be recycled onto the estate's pastures. An overhead conveyor carried cans of raw milk across the road to the creamery, where it was processed into milk and ice cream.

The complex had seen little use since the late 1950s when the new processing plant had opened on Hendersonville Road just south of the Lodge Gate. Over the years, the barn and its accompany-ing buildings had become dilapidated. Loose boards hung from the fences. Vines covered the walls, and weeds choked the walkways. Windowpanes were broken or missing. Cecil heard about the rough condition of the bold barn from visitors, whose exit from the château carried them beside the huge eyesore. They told him that he ought to clean up the place. "It was just sitting there like a lump, deteriorating," he said.

This was where Cecil wanted his winery. He called in a Cali-fornia engineering firm to determine if the buildings were sound enough to be used for the production of up to seven hundred thousand bottles of wine a year. Richard Keith, whose clients were a Who's Who of Napa Valley winemakers, told him that despite the shabby exterior, the basic structure could be adapted to a new purpose. The tunnels were foul, but they could be sanitized and used for aging wine and champagne at a constant temperature of fifty-four degrees. The clock in the tall, multistage gabled tower that had once set the pace of the farmworkers' day could be re-turned to service as well. All in all, the necessary additions for pro-duction designed by the Asheville architect James Padgett would blend nicely with the original pebbledash walls that testified to the architectural style of Richard Morris Hunt, whose son had super-vised the completion of the barn in 1902.

In September 1983, Cecil announced that work would soon commence on the Biltmore Estate winery. This first portion to be built was thirty thousand square feet of production and office space that would be housed in a largely nondescript building located to the side of the main dairy barn, thus leaving the old structure as the tourists' first image. The new building, with its huge stainless steel vats and bottling machinery, was due to be ready in time to produce the next pressing of Biltmore wines.

* * *

The public got its first look at the winery on May 15, 1985. A few days earlier, the Cecils welcomed family and friends from around the world for a dedication ceremony with special meaning. Cecil was not only opening the winery that he had been planning for many years but was also introducing a new Biltmore Company and a new era for the estate. Biltmore was no longer a unique house with extraordinary gardens. Now, Cecil believed, the estate was on its way to returning to what it had been once before—a self-sustaining entity that thrived on the bounty of the land through innovation and creativity.

The occasion gave William and Mimi Cecil great personal satisfaction. Both of the Cecil children now had a stake in the family business. When the Biltmore Estate Wine Company was created in 1983, ownership was given to the Cecils' children. "I made them negative millionaires," Cecil said.

Their daughter, Diana, or Dini as she was called, had finished college and worked for a short time outside of the company before she joined the Biltmore marketing department. She was recently married to George W. Pickering II, and the couple lived in a log home that Dini had built in the woods not far from the château. The floor plan was modeled on her great-grandfather's Buck Spring Lodge. "I had an opportunity to look around [at other jobs]," Pickering said. "This place is very magnetic. Once you start heading in this direction, it is hard to think about anything else."[12]

The Cecils' son, William Jr., was called Bill. He left Asheville after high school convinced he would never return to North Carolina. He studied geography and Chinese philosophy at the University of Colorado. After graduation, Bill joined the professional ski circuit, where he placed in the top rank. He kept his hair in a ponytail, didn't own a suit, and worked on a housing crew to help make ends meet. "I spent $30,000 [traveling on the tour] and I made nothing," Bill Cecil said. "If I had won, I would have won a lease on a car. I had a car. I needed a job."[13] In the spring of 1982, he took his father up on an offer to be part of the Biltmore Company. Lean and trim, Bill gave up his ponytail but kept a neat mustache. In his new profile, he favored his great-grandfather. He and his wife, the former Ginger Rott of Asheville, had celebrated their marriage at his sister's home. They lived on the estate in a house on Cedarcliff Road.

Unlike their father, Bill and Dini had literally grown up on the estate. As children, they lost and found their friends in games of hide-and-seek in the upper stories of the château. Dini and her friends pulled her great-grandmother's dresses and feather boas out of the closets and played dress-up. Her favorite rooms were the Winter Garden and the Louis XV bedroom on the second floor where her father was born. Their mother arranged an overnight stay in the house. Dini and her companions camped out in one of the tower rooms and endured the spooky sounds of the night. Bill favored the outdoors and was an early competitor in the 100-mile ride, the annual event his mother had organized in the 1960s that tests the endurance of both horse and rider. One of the rangers on the estate taught him how to shoot a pistol and a rifle. He would later place in competitive shooting.

William Cecil had allowed his children to choose their own careers, but he had long hoped they would finally succeed him at Biltmore. Even before they joined the company as employees, he asked them to attend annual meetings of the corporation where the plans for the coming year were open for discussion. This early exposure increased their understanding of their own future responsibilities.

For years, William Cecil had tried to interest other fathers in the preservation community in creating a training program for the next generation of owner-operators. With a limited pool of similarly situated families, nothing much came of it. His connections at the great houses abroad proved more useful. Before Bill Cecil settled into a regular assignment at Biltmore, he worked for several months in a rotation with the families and companies running historic houses in England. Upon his arrival in London, Bill said it was the first time a stranger had correctly pronounced his name (Sess-syl instead of Cee-cyl).

When Bill returned from England, his father assigned him to Maury Winger, who made him "clerk of the works" at the winery. Bill monitored the progress of construction and came to know the cost of every nail and two-by-four and where they were installed in the building. His reports were thorough and exhausting in detail. "He knew everything going on down there," Winger said. Bill augmented his training in Winger's business boot camp with enrollment in courses in statistics, accounting, and business at the University of North Carolina at Asheville.

Dini Pickering's first major assignment was planning the celebration for the opening of the winery. Working closely with her father, the two developed a program that included most of William Cecil's favorites in life: good food, classical music, and high-profile guests. The event was both an occasion to enjoy and an opportunity to make a statement.

The National Trust's new president, J. Jackson Walter of Washington, D.C., agreed to speak. (It was the first visit by a National Trust president to the property.) Hans Wanders, the president of the Wachovia Corporation, the parent of Biltmore's primary lender, Wachovia Bank and Trust Company, also took part. Two years earlier, Ernest Ferguson from Wachovia's Asheville office had submitted the first Biltmore proposal to borrow nearly $10 million to the bank's headquarters in Winston-Salem. Nobody there knew anything about vineyards and wineries, but they did know William Cecil. "There was a leap of faith," Ferguson said. "No doubt about it."[14] Cecil knew that doubt of his plans abounded. "Nobody believed we could do any good with it, but that didn't matter that day. The sky didn't fall in. All was well."

The day had begun overcast and rainy. Then, just as the ceremonies opened, the sky cleared, and William Cecil hailed the winery as a tribute to his grandfather's vision for the estate. Mostly, Cecil said, the winery was a testament to private preservation. "We have shown here today that it can be done even when others say it can't," Cecil told a crowd of several hundred.

"Biltmore has a tradition of excellence in architecture and design," the Trust's Jackson Walter said. "This adaptive use of the dairy barn preserves that tradition. This is another example of the creativity that owners can exhibit."

Banker Hans Wanders complimented Biltmore's contribution to the local economy. "Grapes can grow into a cash crop for farmers dependent on burley tobacco," he said. "The future grape farmers should say thanks today."[15]

Indeed, the opening of the winery coincided with new life that was emerging in the state's wine industry. Biltmore Wine Company was now one of five wineries in the state. None was as large as Biltmore, with fifty employees, an annual payroll of $500,000, and an initial capacity at the winery of more than thirty-two thousand cases a year.

Cecil's new building was impressive. The old clock in the barn tower was restored, and a new face visible from the pasture had been added. A large brass weathervane found in the old barn had been returned to its rightful spot atop the tower. What was once a milking parlor was now the tasting room decorated with John Finnie's restorative touches, a stencil pattern that incorporated the Vanderbilt and the Cecil crests. Later, stained-glass windows by John La Farge that had come from William Henry Vanderbilt's New York City residence would be installed.

Architect James Padgett had incorporated all the character and style of the old barn into the new building. The conversion changes had been more severe than anticipated and cost Cecil money-saving preservation tax credits. He was pleased with the result, nonetheless.

(top) The conversion of the dairy barn for the Biltmore Estate winery began in the early 1980s. (bottom) William Cecil saved as much of the original structure as possible to create space for wine production and a (facing page) tasting room.

At the opening celebration, guests enjoyed dinner in the Banquet Hall, a ball accompanied by a chamber group from the Asheville Symphony Orchestra, and bottles of Château Biltmore Riesling '84 and Château Biltmore Sparkling Champagne '83.

William Cecil had bound himself to never bet the farm. Whatever he did, he was determined to keep the estate safe from risk. He came mighty close to crossing that line when he gave his personal guaranty for the company's loan from Wachovia Bank. It was a huge liability, and for the next decade, the top priority of the wine company was to reduce debt.

Thanks to his early years at Chase Manhattan Bank, Cecil was comfortable with bankers and financing. Unlike some businessmen who closely guarded their company's financial details, Cecil believed he was best served if his banker, as well as his lawyer, his accountant, and others who advised the company, knew what the company was capable of doing. It was not uncommon for outside professionals such as Wachovia's Ferguson or attorney John S. Stevens to spend a few days at the annual Palm Beach meetings.

The partnership paid off during the construction of the winery when midway through the project Cecil determined that the company would need more money to build everything he wanted. When it became obvious during one session that the original loan of nearly $10 million was insufficient, he told Richard Pressley to get Ferguson on the telephone and explain their needs. Ferguson approved the additional amount requested.

The winery was indeed a test of Cecil's tolerance for risk. In late January 1985, an arctic cold front swept through western North Carolina. Temperatures dropped to twenty-three degrees below zero, and the hard freeze devastated the vineyard. Nearly 70 percent of the plantings on the west side were lost. The cold had humbled all the defenses that Cecil had installed, including the warming influence of a thirty-two-acre lake built in 1983. "All I could say after it was over," Cecil later wrote, "was, 'Well, now we know which varieties are hardy.'"[16]

When the dedication ceremonies were taking place in May, nothing was said about the loss. If asked whether the harsh winter had affected the vineyards, Cecil replied that they were assessing the damage. Cecil was particularly concerned about morale among his management team, who had seen much of what they had worked for shrivel and die in the passing of one cold night.

"I insisted that in the summer, the senior staff—Steve, Richard, Philippe—book rooms overlooking the vineyards that were dead in France," Cecil recalled. "Philippe said, 'Why do you want to do that?' I wanted to show the staff that it happens to others just like it happened to us. It is part of the business of growing grapes. You have bad years, but you pick up your socks and go back to business. It is not isolated. It is not due to the climate of North Carolina. It is not picking on us. It is just the way grapes are. [That summer] we saw more damn dead grapes than I have ever seen in my life. But the point was made."[17]

The losses in the vineyard were compounded by higher startup costs than expected. "I don't recall it was a crisis," said Winger. "It was no bonanza. It was a little disappointing."

Wine sales also failed to meet projections. Cecil had counted on selling, on average, at least one bottle for every visitor to the estate. Those taking home two and three bottles of Biltmore's best would make up for those who bought none. Actual sales showed that the winery was selling only one bottle for every three visitors.

Cecil discovered that the early calculations had not fully accounted for the drinking habits and moral convictions of visitors from the estate's traditional visitor base. The taste for wine and spirits among residents of the Carolinas and elsewhere in the South was well behind the preference in California and New York. When the winery opened in 1985, North Carolinians were just getting used to restaurants in urban areas that had only recently been allowed to sell mixed drinks. The old brown-bagging laws—where customers brought their own bottles and purchased ice and mixer—had stood until the late 1970s. The only way Cecil and others in the travel industry could overcome the opposition to mixed drinks was to push through legislation that allowed local communities to decide whether alcohol would be sold at all. In the early 1980s, only the state's most populated counties had approved mixed drinks. Many counties, especially in western North Carolina, prohibited the sale of any kind of alcoholic beverages.

Perhaps more discouraging were market studies that revealed first-time Biltmore wine customers weren't coming back for more. Jourdain learned from visitors' comments compiled in the tasting room that his wines were probably suited for a more sophisticated palate. To recover, he turned the tasting room into the "testing room" and experimented with varieties that were more pleasing to the Biltmore clientele. Meanwhile, unsold wine filled the storage areas to capacity, and the company had to relieve its inventory with hastily organized wholesale deals.

At first, the parent company covered some of the wine company's losses by allocating a portion of the admission price to the estate. That worked for a time, but then visitation to the estate began to slow. Attendance was flat in 1987 and actually declined in 1988. The company needed more cash flowing into the wine operation. To Steve Miller and others who had been watching Biltmore's competitors in the travel industry, the answer was an expansion of retail sales, which had never been part of the Biltmore revenue stream.

While Biltmore had long labored under the complaint that its operation was too commercial, the only items that had ever been offered for sale at the estate were sleeves of photographic slides, postcards, and a book or two. Numerous opportunities had been presented over the years, but all had been rejected. One reason was local competition. In the early days, Junius Adams did not want to upset area merchants, many of whom made good money on the sale of souvenirs. Adams mentioned that reason and one other more important consideration in 1956 when one of the businessmen connected with the Grace Kelly movie proposed installing a gift shop in the unfinished Music Room.

"The suggestion," Adams responded, "cannot receive very serious consideration in view of our fixed policy, adopted when the House was opened, that we would minimize what might be called the commercial aspect of the operation as we felt that anything of the kind would not be in keeping with the atmosphere that we hope to preserve for the place."[18]

Income from retail shops had long been important to many historic sites in the United States, yet Cecil continued the tradition honored by Adams. He was not unaware of the possibilities. When he was traveling in England with his son in 1982, he had learned from the management of the stately Blenheim Palace that the duke of Marlborough depended on receipts from his gift shop to make ends meet.

Cecil had never told his subordinates all his reasons for opposing a gift shop. Those who had argued the case for a gift shop figured that his objections were a holdover from the days when tourist haunts in western North Carolina were loaded with trinkets and gimcrackery. What those favoring retail finally came to realize, however, was that Cecil's objections had nothing to do with the quality of the merchandise they might offer for sale but everything to do with the objections first posed by Adams, as well as the way Cecil had been raised. Admonitions from his father held as firm in the 1980s as they had in the 1940s when Cecil learned there were simply certain things that the British upper class did not do.

"I was brought up around late-nineteenth-century values," Cecil said. "Some of them are silly. My father would tell me, we couldn't play tennis on Sunday and that jobs open to us were very few. You could be a banker. Possibly a stock broker. But not a green-grocer. Not in trade."[19]

Cecil's appreciation of social class finally bent under the weight of his obligations to the bank. In order to generate more cash to pay off the debt, Cecil agreed to a retail shop at the winery that offered what Steve Miller called "ancillary merchandise."

"It had to be related to wine experience," explained young Bill Cecil. "Wineglasses, cork screws, that sort of thing. We expanded wine into 'food and wine.' Wine as pure alcoholic beverage is a negative thing. You don't want wine as a bag under the bridge. You want to elevate quality wine as part of a meal experience, as part of a healthy lifestyle." The shelves were soon filled with cooking utensils, cookbooks, and quality items for a well-stocked kitchen, as well as a wine cellar.

Eventually, the folks at the château began asking why Biltmore-related merchandise couldn't be sold there. Miller told Cecil that the visitors were paying ten dollars and more for the baseball caps bearing the Biltmore logo that the company issued to employees. When he suggested high-quality T-shirts, Miller found he had gone too far. "I'll be damned if I'll sell underwear," Cecil responded with a firm tone of finality.[20] He finally agreed to "crew shirts" that had a collar, a suggestion from his son-in-law, George Pickering. A retail shop was opened in the Halloween Room.

In time, the financial pressure was relieved, thanks in part to Cecil's continued investment in the marketing of Biltmore Estate as an authentic national treasure. In 1998, the final note with Wachovia was retired, on schedule. It had taken Cecil twenty years to build and pay for his winery. In 2004, the wine company sold

1.4 million bottles of Biltmore wines. It was the first year that more wine was sold off the estate than on the property.

"The rule in the [wine] business is you grow the vineyard for your grandchildren," Cecil said. "It has been a lot of fun. We needed something. We needed something to do with that big mess [at the dairy barn]. We are in restoration, so you fix it up. What's missing now? Nothing's missing."[21]

CHAPTER 15

Putting It Right

On most days, Four Mile Branch is an all-season mountain stream wide enough to stretch the legs of an athletic youngster and easily waded when the days are hot and refreshment is in order. Fed by springs in a draw that drains a corner of Biltmore's eastern boundary, the creek is a relatively insignificant flow until its fall to the French Broad River is interrupted by a dam that Frederick Law Olmsted built to form George Vanderbilt's Bass Pond.

Olmsted created the five-acre impoundment to serve as a distinctive boundary between the woodlands downstream and the cultivated gardens that rise to the Conservatory and Walled Garden on the château's south side. Chauncey Beadle's Azalea Garden fills a glen immediately above the pond. Nearby is the tall cucumber magnolia that was planted in honor of Cornelia Vanderbilt's birth in 1900. A graceful, arched brick bridge once carried her father's carriage over Four Mile Branch along what later became the main exit road from the château.

The Bass Pond completed Olmsted's landscaped transition from cultivated gardens to rambling forest. The landscaper left nothing to chance, however. He designed the plantings in the "wild" ravine below the pond dam just as he did in the orderly gardens above. In the pond, he created two low "islets," as he called them, to confuse the eye and suggest a wider body of water than what was actually between the steep banks. They rose no more than three inches above the water line in order to encourage the nesting of swans and wildfowl. Paths of rock were placed underwater between the islands and the pond's edge to prevent the rooting of water plants that might interfere with the daily habits of the birds.

Most intriguing was another feature that was entirely out of sight along the pond floor. Olmsted built a tapered brick flume that reached from the base of the pond's twenty-foot-high stone dam up the channel of Four Mile Branch to a smaller dam, where a gate opened and closed automatically when the creek was in flood. A combination of gears and levers opened the mouth of the flume to divert the muddy runoff to the flume, where it was carried to the dam and released back into the stream.

Olmsted hoped his ingenius bypass would inhibit the silting of the pond, which was a particular hazard in the early years when most of the surrounding landscape was rough and easily eroded. Thus, Olmsted saw to it that the waters in the pond remained clear for the comfort of the nesting wildlife and the pleasure of George Vanderbilt and his guests.

Sometime in the first half of the twentieth century, the system failed. By the early 1950s, the flume was clogged and silt had filled the pond, leaving it something akin to a large mud puddle. Junius Adams had the pond drained and the silt dredged and carried away, but the flume was not repaired. A generation later, the pond was once again nearly full of silt. It was shallow enough in some places for William Cecil to walk from one side to the other without wetting his belt.

As Cecil fixed his attention on the restoration of Bass Pond, he considered it no less important than any of the rooms under the roof of the château that had felt the restorer's touch. The pond had been a favorite outdoor space and a quiet retreat where Vanderbilt and his guests floated about in light skiffs and dipped a line into the water. As the sun fell lower in the sky, a butler would deliver refreshments to the boathouse that stood on the bank near the Carriage Road. If Cecil did not intervene, this "room" would be reduced to a soggy marsh suitable for frogs but certainly not bass.

In 1990, Cecil had the pond drained, and a contractor removed fifty thousand cubic yards of muck, which was deposited on a field beside the banks of the French Broad River where the nutrients could be put to use. Once the bottom was cleaned, William Alexander, Biltmore's landscape manager, and an engineer began repairs on the bypass system. They were working blind, however. Olmsted's plans for the mechanics of his bypass system were nowhere to be found in the Biltmore archives.

Alexander discovered that the flume gradually decreased in diameter along its thousand-foot length from an opening of seven feet across upstream to roughly half that size when it reached the lower dam. The taper increased the force of the water and was supposed to keep it clear. Over the years, large pieces of debris had broken through a screen upstream and become lodged in the flume, closing it to the regular flow of water. During the repairs in the 1950s, Adams had holes punched in the flume to reach the debris and remove it. For reasons not explained, however, the flume was not restored to its original condition, and the muddy flow from the flooding stream once again was allowed to settle in the bottom of the pond.

George Vanderbilt and his guests enjoyed the Boat House beside a pond created by Frederick Law Olmsted. Olmsted also designed a flume system to reduce silting of the pond, which diverted water when the creek feeding the Bass Pond was flooding.

In the early 1990s, William Cecil restored the flume to operation after it had been neglected for nearly fifty years.

The mechanism that Olmsted devised to divert the water into the flume was driven by simple physics. When the stream was flooding, the excess water overflowed into a brick chamber with a metal pan. As the pan filled and became heavier under the weight of the water, it lowered, tripping a lever that closed a valve and diverted the floodwaters into the flume. When stream flow returned to normal and no longer entered the chamber, the water in the pan emptied through small holes in the bottom, and as it rose, the action of the valves was reversed and the stream resumed its normal course.

Repairs of the flume were simple enough. The holes were patched and the huge brick pipe was made sound. Restoring the mechanical gate was more problematic. With no detailed specifications at hand, the decision was made to use a simpler float system. Several years later, a manually operated system was installed as a substitute, and a duty officer was detailed to open and close the drain when needed.

The pond restoration was a major undertaking that occupied Cecil's attention for months. It was also expensive; the final bill came to $423,000. Like the restoration of the library ceiling, it was an expense that went largely unnoticed by visitors once the pond was refilled. Yet it was a measure of Cecil's commitment to his ambition to return the estate to its original condition and, when possible, pass it to the next generation even better than when he found it. "It was one of many chores that had to be done," he said. "My whole point was to get the estate in one hundred percent condition. Everything I did was geared to that."

"A public manager wouldn't have done a lot of the things we did," Cecil said, confessing that some in his own organization had disagreed with his decision to push ahead. "They would have said we can't afford it." Inertia, committees, and expense all get in the way of mounting such expensive projects at many other historic sites. But, he said, "If you have a Bass Pond, you have to clean it up. If we didn't repair it, in five years or so, it would have silted up. The cheaper thing was to clean it up and put that pipe back in."[1]

Cecil was in his early sixties when he took on the restoration of the Bass Pond. He had devoted more than half his life to the care of his grandfather's house and gardens, as well as attending to its unappreciated dimensions, such as Olmsted's flood control. Over the years, he had come to appreciate that Biltmore "was not an idle toy of the rich. This property was a working place that had to be productive and by being productive could also be beautiful."[2]

In that he had clearly succeeded. The Biltmore Company had prospered nicely since the division of the property with his brother in 1979. The estate was no longer an architectural oddity or an attraction that lured visitors off the highways by billboards. By 1990, the estate had become a major tourist destination, as much as Walt Disney World in Florida and the Mall in Washington, D.C. With more and more of the house open to visitors, what had once been a two-hour stay now required a six-hour tour of the property. Guests saw rooms that George Vanderbilt had seldom entered. They wandered paths of a maturing landscape that Olmsted had envisioned on paper and, if they chose, could enjoy a leisurely lunch at Deerpark. Within the company, there was talk of expanding the offerings. Steve Miller and Richard Pressley, along with Cecil's children, Bill and Dini, were working on plans for a hotel—something Vanderbilt himself had considered. Cecil was not enthusiastic about providing overnight accommodations; he said he wasn't ready to be called out at night to unclog a toilet.

The Biltmore Company's revenues had grown more than ninefold to a profitable $28 million a year, with half of that contributed by a growing retail business. Most of the profits were pumped back into the restoration and maintenance. The average annual investment in restoration was $400,000. Bringing a single room back to life could cost as much as $25,000 to $35,000, not including the expense of in-house labor. Restoring Mrs. Vanderbilt's bedroom had cost close to $200,000. The cost of replacing worn-out equipment and maintaining the estate boosted overall reinvestment to an average of $1.5 million per year.[3]

With more than five hundred employees, the company was among the top ten employers in the county and one of western North Carolina's most important economic engines. Biltmore visitors accounted for about $100 million in business annually for area hotels, restaurants, shops, and other vendors.[4] The company was one of Buncombe County's largest taxpayers. Annual taxes, fees, and licenses amounted to nearly a half-million dollars. Cecil's New York lawyer, William Moss, had been right when he advised him at the time of the division of the estate that continued support of Biltmore would only cost Cecil money. The assessed value of the estate in 1991 was $16 million—double what was put on the books a decade earlier.[5]

This exhilarating spiral of growth had begun with the introduction of the downstairs tour and had continued as new areas of the house were added every few years. In the early 1990s, visitors could take in the world of the fabulously wealthy in the 1890s on three levels, from life downstairs to unimaginable luxury in the master's quarters on the second floor. There was nothing else like it in the United States. If Williamsburg owned Colonial America, Biltmore owned the Gilded Age.

More than 40 percent of all of Asheville's visitors said Biltmore was their reason for coming to the city. As a result, paid attendance had nearly doubled in the previous ten years to more than seven hundred thousand visitors a year. On peak days, such as Thanksgiving weekend, as many as six hundred visitors an hour went through the house. Some historic properties didn't see that many paying guests in a month.

When Mrs. Vanderbilt's bedroom was redecorated, William Cecil located the French firm that had produced the original fabric, whose weavers were able to use the same looms and jacquard cards to produce exact replicas of textiles that had become worn with age.

Biltmore kept people coming back. The spring season had received a boost in 1986 with the introduction of the Festival of Flowers that featured croquet on the lawn and tea in the Stable Courtyard. Even an unexpected freeze just days before the gardens went on display did not dampen enthusiasm. Nothing added to the bottom line like the candlelight Christmas tours that began in 1984.

The public response to the expanded Christmas offering was almost overwhelming, as Cecil, Miller, and Pressley discovered when they were returning from their planning session in Palm Beach on the company airplane in 1984. As the pilot made his final approach in a turn that took them over the house, they looked out the window and saw below that the esplanade was ringed with travel buses. Once on the ground, they hurried to the house to find tour leaders carrying a copy of the American Bus Association's guide to the 100 top attractions in the United States. On the cover of the current edition was a picture of Biltmore at Christmas. Sixty thousand enjoyed the new candlelight tour that December, nearly twice the number as the year before. In 1991, more visitors stepped through Biltmore's front door in December—once the time when the staff was on vacation—than they did the previous July.

Portions of the house that had long been open to the public were now even more stunning than before. The textiles in Mrs. Vanderbilt's bedroom—draperies, upholstery, wall coverings, and bedcovers of silk velvet—had been replaced in the 1960s with near-enough reproductions. As these materials began to show their age, Cecil discovered that the manufacturer of the original cut silk brocades, Tassinari and Chatel in France, could make identical fabric using the same jacquard cards on the same looms that had produced the material for his grandfather in the 1890s. An Italian weaver offered to replicate the fabrics in one-fourth the time and at two-thirds the money, but the French looms were chosen for accuracy and correct reproduction. The investment for replacing textiles in the bedroom and the Breakfast Room (earlier called the family dining room) and other renovations cost $600,000.

The tapestries in the château were in better condition than they had been in years, even centuries. Their conservation had begun in 1987 after one of the trophy heads fell from its mount in the Banquet Hall. On its way to the floor, the horn of a stuffed caribou tore the fabric. The tear was repaired, but the accident prompted Cecil to take a closer look at all the tapestries, including the three sixteenth-century Flemish silk and wool hangings in the gallery.

One by one, they were taken down, carefully cleaned, and repaired. To his surprise, house manager Richard King discovered that at some time, probably before the tapestries arrived at Biltmore, one of them had been judiciously sanitized. He found that a scene depicting Venus and Mars in a compromising position had been painted over, but the images were still faint under paint that had been partially removed.

Farming on the estate also had undergone a revival. Cecil gained full use of the fields and pastures after the Biltmore dairy herd was sold in 1982, and he began developing his own herd of beef cattle. Under a new farm manager, Ted Katsigianis, the estate began producing cattle feed and harvesting other crops that were shipped to market. Fields of carrots went into Campbell's soups while Anheuser-Busch bought Biltmore potatoes to make into its own brand of potato chips. The purebred black Angus that grazed the pastures became part of a "field-to-table" program that supplied Deerpark.

In the late 1980s, Cecil became intrigued with raising fish and took a fancy to a domestic version of caviar from American Paddlefish, a creature shaped like a shark but with a long, narrow snout. Its tasty roe was said to compare favorably to that harvested from sevruga sturgeon from the Caspian Sea. He dispatched his son, Bill, and Richard Pressley to investigate paddlefish farms in Arkansas. They attended aquaculture conventions and corresponded for several years with a German firm that sold a large contained system for raising this strange fish. After some study, the project was discarded as too expensive. The estate did begin raising trout in the lake beside the vineyards at Long Valley, and ponds were built in the flats below the horse barn for an experiment in raising freshwater prawns.

The company had established a presence in the heart of Asheville after years of being the city's nearest neighbor. In 1987, Cecil bought a distinctive seven-story building on Pack Square that the renowned architect I. M. Pei had designed for the Akzona Corporation. The building's stark, flat exterior featured alternating layers of tinted glass that was in contrast to the Gothic styling of structures built in the 1920s, especially the slender thirteen-story Jackson Building with its gargoyles and spires. The reflections of the vintage facades shimmered in the windows of Pei's new building.

The Pei building was finished in 1981 and cost nearly $15 million to build. Yet the Dutch company occupied it for less than two years before putting it up for sale in the wake of a downsizing of its business. Asheville's new downtown showpiece sat empty for four years before Maury Winger Jr. negotiated a sale for Cecil from his former employer at about one-fifth of the original cost.

"We were in the original office my grandfather used," Cecil said. "It was a lovely old building, more or less modernized, but now bulging at the seams. After lunch one day, I idly inquired as to the availability of the I. M. Pei building. Richard Pressley had a budget of about $2 million [for a new building on the estate property]. Everyone sort of snickered, but Maury wondered if this might not be a good idea. After all, it was a building designed by a world-famous architect. It had more room than we needed but we could rent out the rest of the space."

Cecil moved his office to the building's fifth floor in a large space that offered a commanding view to the east. The company occupied the upper two floors, and Winger went looking for tenants for the other space.

Relocation of the company's offices to downtown Asheville put Cecil farther away from the château than he had been since he left Washington, D.C., in 1959. For thirty years, he had seldom been beyond earshot of the estate's property lines, either at his home in Biltmore Forest or his office on Biltmore Plaza just beyond the Lodge Gate. Nonetheless, he continued his daily rounds of the estate with a critical eye for details. With the introduction of two-way radios, employees broadcast his movements, so those working the front of the house were on their best behavior when Cecil arrived.

To visitors, the tall, portly gentleman in his sport coat—often a burgundy worsted blazer—and tie was just another guest. One day, Cecil was standing in front of the house talking with one of the staff when two ladies approached with a question. After they had their answer, Cecil had moved on when one of the ladies said, "I wish I could meet the person who owns this place." "You just did," she was told.

Managing the house was more complicated than ever before. As the number of visitors increased, so did the challenges. Cars finally were banned from the Esplanade after new parking lots were built off the side of the Approach Road out of sight of the entrance gates. Eventually, shuttle buses would carry visitors from additional parking lots built ever father from the house. All this cost money, as did other basic improvements, such as restrooms. Over about ten years, Cecil spent almost $400,000 on lavatories for guests and employees.

At one point, he considered air-conditioning the house, not so much to control the temperature—the thick walls and vents installed by Hunt took care of that—but to reduce humidity that built up in the summertime. Climate control had long been a concern, both for visitor comfort and for the condition of the contents of the house, some of which were quite delicate. The difficulty, Cecil discovered, was not the installation of interior ductwork but finding a suitable location outside the château for the large and noisy air-handling equipment. "The cost, as I remember," Cecil said, "was to be about $2 million. While not an insignificant sum, it was not out of reach. The project was dropped until the noise problem could be solved."

Some adjustments had been made to provide more interpretation to the house and its collection. Cecil finally overcame his objection to personal audiotape players that carried a narrative of the house and individual rooms. Writing in the 1970s, Cecil had said, "They are fine in an art gallery," but "they tend to bunch people [creating] a security risk. Apart from this, they are very expensive to install."[6] In the early 1990s, the company began renting tape cassette players near the Entrance Hall that featured a script produced in-house. The new income added to the bottom line.

Parking lots and restrooms had been major concessions to the demands that crowds of visitors placed on the property. By and large, the integrity of the house and grounds remained intact aside from alterations to accommodate the flow of traffic. When the Louis XVI room was opened on the second floor, visitors could only view it from the one doorway that opened at the top of the grand staircase. The limited viewing created a bottleneck on the stairs, which was perhaps the worst place in the house for a traffic jam. To relieve the congestion, Cecil created another doorway into the room by opening one wall of what had once been a bath. Restoration carpenters replicated the original door, and hinges were designed to match.

The alteration had deeply troubled Susanne Brendel-Pandich, the Biltmore curator. "Mr. C said we knock through a closet and come out the other side. At first he and I got into it. You shouldn't destroy the original floor plan," she said. "I have to say, looking back on it, we were going through a doorway. It was the only thing that made the floor plan work. In the long run, it was the right decision. I just didn't want to see them knocking through the walls."[7]

Nearing the centennial of the opening of the house in 1995, work remained to be done. For example, the rows of fifty-two tulip poplars that flanked the Esplanade were beginning to show their age. A few of the exposed trees on the south side had already been removed due to damage from lightning strikes and disease. Some had suffered from compaction of the soil due to heavy traffic. The paving of the drive restricted water and oxygen for the roots.

Cecil was also concerned about the swimming pool on the South Terrace that had been installed in the 1920s by his grandmother. It required frequent cleaning and was a potential hazard. He worried that children might mount the fence and fall in. He had it removed in 1994 and the terrace returned to its original grassy state.

And, of course, there was the usual repair and maintenance that came with any aging structure. The problems were just a bit more unusual at Biltmore, however. State regulators wanted safety features installed on the caged Otis elevators, among the first ever installed in the Southeast. Repointing the mortar on the limestone exterior and replacing copper gutters had cost more than a half-million dollars. Security was a continuing concern, even though a modern security system had been installed after a stunning theft from Vanderbilt's library in 1980.

The book theft was discovered in the spring during a social event for the cast and crew of the movie *Private Eyes*, who were just finishing production. When a copy of Samuel Johnson's *A Dictionary of the English Language* was pulled from the shelf to show to the actor Tim Conway, Cecil discovered that the book's case was empty. Upon investigation, he found that 234 books were missing. Many were relatively inexpensive volumes, but also missing were quite valuable items such as Muybridge's 1887 *Animal Locomotion*, which was said to be worth $100,000.

The thief turned out to be an employee who was working part-time as a guard and helping with the conservation of damaged volumes. "We checked on [the thief] at libraries around the country and they said, 'He did that to you, too,'" Cecil said. "There was a code amongst some universities that they will not tell you about book theft. They are afraid that it will be known that their security is not what it should be.

"We found books all over the country. Bank of America bought one of our books from a dealer in Texas. So did someone in London. Sotheby's and Christie's said we can't check the provenance of every book. I said, 'Someone comes in from some little town called Asheville, which you have never heard of except it has a big old house named Biltmore, which you have heard of. And this kid comes in and says he runs a little bookstore and brings in twenty or thirty very valuable books with [a label reading] Ex Libris Biltmoris in there, and you don't check.' And that is what they all did because they bought them really cheap."[8] It took Cecil more than two years to recover the missing books, most of which had been sold to dealers around the country.

The filming of *Private Eyes* marked a renewal of interest in Biltmore for location work. North Carolina's reputation among filmmakers was growing, and the state had begun actively wooing producers in the late 1970s. Biltmore was popular because it offered a secure, closed set as well as fabulous backdrops, both architectural and natural. *Being There*, a Peter Sellers film, was shot at the house and in the gardens in 1979. Shortly after Cecil completed work on the Bass Pond, location filming for *The Last of the Mohicans* featured the bridge over Four Mile Branch. Later movies included *Forrest Gump* (a portion of Tom Hanks's marathon run included a stretch of road near the winery) and *My Fellow Americans* with Jack Lemmon and James Garner.

For Cecil, the moviemakers were a mixed blessing. He was happy to see them arrive with their pockets full of cash to pay his location fees, for which he charged handsomely without apology. He was just as happy to see them leave. The director of one production demanded Cecil close the gates to visitors to accommodate

Beginning in the years following World War II, the estate became a popular spot for moviemakers producing full-length features, such as The Swan, *staring Grace Kelly and Alec Guinness, as well as television commercials. In 1987, George Plimpton, seated third from left, was on the set for the promotion of Asheville tourism. William Cecil is standing behind him.*

his shooting schedule, much as Adams had done in the 1950s when the estate became a set for the Grace Kelly movie. This time the request came at the height of the Christmas season, and Cecil flatly refused. With that, the director called North Carolina governor Jim Hunt, who appealed to Cecil. Again he refused. When the director told Cecil he could go to Blenheim Palace in England just as easily, Cecil answered, "Do you want me to call my cousin, the duke of Marlborough, and tell him you are coming?" Cecil said, "That was the end of that."[9]

Biltmore's growing success compared favorably with that of other historic properties, many of which were struggling financially. Colonial Williamsburg had reached a peak attendance of 1.3 million paid visitors in 1976, the year of the nation's bicentennial. By 1993, attendance had slipped to 949,000. Mount Vernon, another popular spot, was also losing its place among the well-attended sites in Washington, D.C.

The challenges facing managers at Biltmore and elsewhere were much the same. Changing American lifestyles and expanding choices for vacationing families were cutting into the revenues of once-popular sites. Colonial Williamsburg had opened at a time when parents alone determined the destination of family vacations. Now the kids had a voice in how the family would spend its time. When offered the choice of two days immersed in history—the length of stay that Williamsburg counted on to make its financial model work—the youngsters objected. As a result, a typical family spent a half day at Colonial Williamsburg and two days or more at nearby Busch Gardens, the expansive theme park that had opened in the mid-1970s on land once owned by Colonial Williamsburg.

"We had positioned ourselves as an organization and a museum that people would always come to, regardless, like *Field of Dreams*," said Timothy Andrews in Colonial Williamsburg's public relations department. "We woke up and that was not the case."[10]

Cecil pushed to make Biltmore fresh and inviting. Continued investment in promotion brought visitors to the gates. Whenever advertising budgets were reduced, Steve Miller saw the results quickly. Plus, Cecil had never taken his visitors for granted; he could remember the "blank days" of the 1960s. The comfort and satisfaction of those who paid to see his grandfather's house was the primary responsibility of everyone in the company, from the bus drivers in the parking lots to the senior staff downtown. Visitors remembered the courtesies of the staff, as well as the grandeur of the château and the peacefulness of the estate. Follow-up opinion surveys showed visitor satisfaction ratings at the top of the charts, equal to five-star resorts. Success flowed from the presentation of the estate as an experience and an escape from the frantic pace of modern life, not a history lesson.

"Biltmore is a treat, it is unique, and so well done," said Don Logan, the chairman of Time Warner's Media & Communications Group. Logan had come to know Biltmore in the early years when he was with *Southern Living*, the popular regional lifestyle magazine. "When you go, you always have lingering memories. So many destinations are fleeting. Biltmore is not like that."[11]

In December 1993, members of the staff and board members from the National Trust arrived in Asheville to meet with Cecil and see Biltmore. Included in the group were the organization's new president, Richard Moe, and board vice chair Nancy Campbell. For some in the group, it was their first visit to the estate. Cecil gave them a tour of the château from top to bottom while Miller, Pressley, and others delivered detailed presentations of the company's entire operation, from its aggressive marketing program to the painstaking conservation of the sixteenth-century tapestries. Pressley reviewed the company's finances, dispelling any lingering notions that a trust fund left by the Vanderbilt family lay behind the company's financial success. After dinner at the Frith, Cecil led them on an after-hours walk through the candlelit château, which was dressed in its Christmas finery.

Cecil's overview of Biltmore was heavily laden with the particulars of his philosophy of private preservation: disciplined management, accountability, measurable goals, and attention to the bottom

The calf maternity barn was renovated for use as Deerpark, the estate's first restaurant. Later, a portion of the stables was converted into the Stable Café.

line. Campbell, whose husband, Colin, would become the president of Colonial Williamsburg, later joked about the Cecil "school" she attended. But she took pages of notes that she could still retrieve ten years later. She appreciated her host's willingness to share and his honesty. Cecil also gave his guests an account of missteps along the way.

Marketing did not compromise quality, she found, and details matter. She scribbled a reminder about Cecil's advice that area hotel clerks share in the discounts as an incentive to promote the sale of admission tickets at the front desk. The work of the Biltmore conservators surpassed what many had seen anywhere. At the end of the two-day visit, Campbell told Roderick Heller, another vice chair, "If we had our druthers, we ought to send our site managers to business school."[12] Moe subsequently asked Cecil to repeat his presentation at an upcoming annual meeting of the Trust.

The meeting led to further sessions including an exchange with Colonial Williamsburg that was worked out after Lawrence Henry, a Colonial Williamsburg executive, happened onto a visit to the estate. Henry was trained as a historian and was as steeped in the discipline as any of his peers in Virginia. When he found himself in Asheville for a bicycle race, he called and asked to see the estate. Steve Miller met him at the Lodge Gate and devoted an entire afternoon as his escort. Henry left impressed, not only with what he saw in the house and elsewhere on the estate but with Miller's enthusiasm and his genuine "awe" for the house and its collection, despite his many years with the company.

Upon his return, Henry produced a three-page memo, which he circulated among his colleagues telling them about what he had seen and learned in Asheville. The response was lukewarm, in spite of the lessons he suggested could be applied to Colonial Williams-burg. When he suggested that Miller, Pressley, and Cecil meet to share ideas with their peers at Colonial Williamsburg—an idea endorsed at Biltmore—it was like saying "pigs can fly."[13] The estate was considered even more of a theme park now that the winery was open. Old-liners were especially suspicious. "How could they do it and how could they do it with legitimacy?" they asked Henry, who later became the chief executive at South Carolina's Brookgreen Gardens.[14]

After some months of work, Henry finally organized a visit to Virginia for Cecil, Miller, and Pressley. While the Biltmore vice presidents met with their counterparts on the Colonial Williams-burg staff, Henry escorted Cecil around the reconstructed colonial capital. The two had never met, and based on what he had heard about Cecil's irascible nature, Henry believed he was in for a dread-ful afternoon. He was delightfully surprised; Cecil was disarmingly charming, genuinely interested in his host, and intensely keen on adding to his library of cookbooks. Sometime later, the Colonial Williamsburg team made a visit to Biltmore.

Cecil initiated periodic meetings with the National Trust's Moe and Robert Wilburn, who was then the chief executive officer at Colonial Williamsburg. The topic was often the federal tax code and its impact on private owners of historic properties. "I always liked and admired Bill," said Wilburn. "I could see where some people would be turned off. But if you have worked with CEOs of large corporations, you find that same sense of focus. It is that same determination to win. That kind of personality makes an organization go to a higher level and achieve things it hasn't achieved before."

Moe took advantage of Cecil's experience and recruited him to provide an appraisal of some troubled National Trust properties. At the time, the organization was at a crossroads with Montpelier, President James Madison's home in Virginia, which had been left in its care. Cecil had answered similar requests in the past. In the 1970s, he had surveyed Graylyn, the impressive country home in Winston-Salem, North Carolina, that belonged to Gordon Gray, who was a former chair of the National Trust. Gray had given the home to Wake Forest University in the 1960s, but the school was at a loss over how to use it. Gray retrieved the property and asked Cecil for ideas. Cecil told him to convert the impressive country house into a conference center, an idea that his heirs finally subscribed to some years later.

The U.S. Park Service had called on Cecil in 1975 when it was seeking an alternative use for Mar-A-Lago, the Palm Beach estate Marjorie Merriweather Post had left to the government for use as a presidential retreat. The property had never proved suitable as such, and an endowment she left to pay for upkeep failed to generate income sufficient to cover expenses. Cecil applied what he had learned at moving people through Biltmore and reported that opening the house for public tours was feasible only with a pricey entrance fee, a condition incompatible with the government's method of operation. Cecil also produced an appraisal at Kykuit, the Rockefeller estate on the Hudson, and Lyndhurst, another National Trust property. The challenges were never the same, Cecil said. Not all houses are suited for streams of tourists. For example, Cecil forecast serious bottlenecks in traffic flow at Kykuit because of the narrow hallways.

Over the years, the inquiries had been frequent enough for Cecil to consider establishing a property management division in his own company. Perhaps he and his staff could export what they had learned over decades of moving hundreds of thousands of people annually through confined spaces, among valued objects, in a delicate environment. For Cecil, the challenge was not whether Biltmore talent could be useful elsewhere but whether the owners of the other properties would provide sufficient freedom for his managers to do their jobs. Federal agencies and nonprofit owners had never been exposed to "optimizing the profitability of their operation," as Maury Winger Jr. stated in his study of the prospects.[15]

Overcoming years of a different way of thinking was a considerable feat. Cecil's visit to Montpelier was a good example. Miller was traveling with his boss on the site visit, and he saw Cecil's blood rising as they listened to the hand-wringing of the professionals who worked in well-appointed air-conditioned offices while simple repairs and maintenance went unattended in the public area. The staff wanted to talk about how to return the mansion to what it had been in Madison's day. Cecil believed that Montpelier's problems were more basic than that. He was confounded by a lack of attention to rudimentary upkeep and repair. Finally, he stopped his host in her tracks and told her that what she really needed at Montpelier was someone who knew how to use a hammer.

"Well," Cecil was told by a pedigreed curator, "we didn't need outsiders to come in and tell us the place was filthy. We know that. We wanted people to tell us what to do about it."

"I said, 'Clean it up.'"[16]

Biltmore probably would remain the exception, Cecil said. The gulf in attitude was probably too great to use his style of management in other properties. Cecil looked beyond the obvious to figure out how visitors could enjoy a historic property, whereas curatorial managers were limited in their perspective. "If the curatorial world is there, they are going to say, 'You can't walk on the carpet.' I can understand why you can't walk on the carpet, but the solution is not to leave the carpet and keep the tourists off. Move it to where it is safe and you can see it, and enjoy it, but let the tourists walk where they can see it and enjoy it as well."[17]

At the same time, Cecil's solutions were not always appropriate for other locations. "My feelings are that the least change necessary to accomplish the desired result, preservation, is the best," Cecil said. "Too many horror stories abound where upon seeing how Biltmore is seen to be a wonderful example of success, it becomes the model for a property, which can, at best, handle twenty visitors an hour. Further disciplined research and thought must be given. This is a slow and often painful process."[18]

In February 1994, Cecil announced the opening of a new visitor center. It was built about a half mile inside the Lodge Gate on a hill overlooking the broad cornfield that highway engineers had once wanted to fill with a concrete overpass for Interstate 40. The building reflected the estate's architecture with a Hunt-inspired red-tile roof and pebbledash walls. The new building relieved congestion at the Lodge Gate and was twelve times the size of the thousand-square-foot ticket office that Cecil had erected on a tight budget in 1962.

Work was also under way at the château, where the commercial options of the stable area were being expanded. The carpenters had been moved out of the west end to make way for an enlarged gift

*A new welcome center was opened just before the 1995 centennial to replace a
modest building put up more than three decades earlier just outside the Lodge Gate.
By that time, attendance had grown from about thirty-six thousand annual visitors
to more than eight hundred thousand.*

shop in 1987. New retail stores—a confectionery, a bookstore, a
turn-of-the-century Christmas shop, and a toy shop—were now
added along the central corridor. In 1995, the Stable Café was renovated and expanded.

Food service had become an important ingredient in Biltmore's
financial pie. What had begun as soft drinks sold from a cooler
on the Library Terrace had expanded into Deerpark, which Cecil
had first envisioned as an elaborate picnic area selling prime-grade
frankfurters and hamburgers. Seated dining was added later. In
time, the interior had been reconfigured to accommodate lunch
with a new menu. The new Stable Café met a growing demand for
food service from visitors who weren't in and off the estate in a few
hours, as was once the case.

"I never thought that we would have to add to Biltmore," Cecil said. But he did. The kitchens for the cafe could not be accommodated within the footprint of the original stable building. An addition was built behind the stables and connected to the limestone exterior as gently as possible. The lines of the new building closely follow those of the stable. Cecil would later joke that only six bolts held the structure in place and thus it could be easily removed. More would be required than that, but his description conveyed the attention he was paying to his own rule to keep the house within six months of returning it to its original state.

The Stable Café and ice cream shop on the stable courtyard underscored Biltmore's attention to Cecil's rule of tourists: "Every twenty minutes, they eat, buy something, or go to the bathroom."[19] A third restaurant, the Bistro, was under construction at the winery and would open just in time to entertain out-of-town guests for the centennial celebration.

In a sense, the preparations for the centennial celebration had been thirty-five years in the making. They began in the 1960s when Cecil first set out to save Biltmore from an uncertain future. At the time, his attention was not focused on 1995, of course. He had more pressing challenges, such as how to increase the number of visitors next month. Each step that he had taken over the following three decades—the creative promotions, the restorations, and the construction of the winery—had moved him closer to a firmly fixed goal. By the time he handed the estate to the next generation, he wanted Biltmore returned to what it had been in his grandfather's day.

Diana Pickering pulled together all the particulars for the celebration of the centennial, under the close attention of her father. Since joining the company in the early 1980s, she had become immersed in the operations of the business, first in the marketing operation and later as the head of the company's move into reproductions. Along with her brother, she was a member of the company's board of directors. "Dad is very easy to work for. He knows exactly what he wants," she said. "We wanted to celebrate we were a hundred years old, we were privately owned, and we were making a go of it. We were being very successful."[20]

Most of the focus of a year's worth of events on the estate turned on the legacy of George Vanderbilt. Rooms on the third floor, the so-called Tower Rooms, were opened to visitors in April. They had last been used on the occasion of Cornelia's wedding when the house was full of guests. Objects long tucked away for safekeeping were brought out for display. An interpretive exhibit of a hundred pieces made up a new display called "George Washington Vanderbilt: The Man and His Treasures" and went on the road to museums around the country. Included in the presentation were elaborate silver pieces by DeLamerie and Crespin, paintings by Monet and Whistler, as well as rare books and prints.

A new book, *Biltmore Estate: The Most Distinguished Private Place*, was published by Rizzoli, adding more national attention to the upcoming centennial. John Bryan's architectural history of the château, as well as Olmstead's landscapes, was produced in cooperation with the American Architectural Foundation. It was a dazzling display of old and new photography, renditions of Hunt's drawings, and a thorough examination of the inspiration, planning, and years of work behind the creation of the estate.

Cecil was clear about one other thing in his planning for the events: the centennial would be a tribute to the thousands of people—past and present—who had helped preserve Biltmore for the future. Most often, Cecil had appeared larger than life in the Biltmore story, but he was well aware of the contributions of others who had helped preserve the estate since his grandfather's day.

Talking about this sometime later, he recalled the story he had heard about the town of Luten, an industrial city outside of London. On a visit there, he was shown the charred remnants of the town charter. The rest had burned in 1918 when the mayor and his council had thrown a party to celebrate the end of World War I, inviting only the notables and military officers, and not the soldiers who had endured the misery of the trenches, many of whom were then unemployed and hungry. In retribution, they burned down city hall, and the remains included a shred of the charter titled "How to Replace an Alderman."

His grandfather had showed no less consideration when he brought in the estate families to celebrate his first Christmas. The tradition of presents all around had continued for generations; modern-day workers participated in a share of the profits. Some continued to make their home on the property. "People don't give their employees enough recognition," Cecil said. "We had over two thousand people for dinner on the lawn. They all behaved extraordinarily well. There was never any question about it. They say, 'Oh, they will put their foot in the jam.' But they don't. They know how to behave just as well as you and I do."

"So," Cecil said, "when we had the centennial, the big thing is it is not just us. We were going to have a party, yes. A nice party and high quality." But there would be parties for all. Accordingly, there were fireworks, barbecue, and a symphony concert in the moonlight for everyone from the front office to the parking lot. For Pickering, it was the most memorable night of the entire affair.

Cecil himself provided the finishing touches for the September celebration. An inventory of the original silver service showed that over the years it had become so depleted by breakage and losses that there were insufficient pieces to accommodate a full seating for dinner. Cecil purchased a new service for 128 engraved with the Cecil crest from Tessier's on Bond Street in London. "I think the generational changes must reflect the change in family control," he told a friend.[21] In addition, a full set of Baccarat glassware and a new china service were added to the collection.

On Saturday evening, September 30, 1995, William and Mimi Cecil welcomed sixty-four guests for dinner in the Banquet Hall. Among those on hand were family members, including his brother, George, and George's wife, Nancy, who appeared in the gown worn by Edith Vanderbilt Gerry for her wedding portrait. Mimi wore a pants suit; William was in a green velvet smoking jacket. Those who dined with the Cecils were old friends, the Biltmore management team he had cultivated over the years, and family. The heavy baroque chairs were pulled to a table arranged in a large U that all but filled the Banquet Hall. A chamber orchestra of players from the Asheville Symphony accompanied the meal with selections from Strauss, Haydn, Mozart, Lehar, and Boccherini.

More than three hundred other guests invited for the event had dined at private homes off the estate. Before they arrived for an evening of dancing and music in the château, Cecil rose and introduced his dinner guests. He had earlier circulated some suggested toasts to his daughter, but if one was chosen from the list, it was later forgotten in the wake of a surprising announcement. As he finished his brief remarks, he nodded to his son, Bill, and said, "Come tomorrow morning, this young man will be in charge."

With that, the dinner was done. The Cecils welcomed their other guests to the house as a dance band performed in the Tapestry Gallery. "Biltmore champagne and white wine flowed as fast as the French Broad in full flood," Cecil later reported to a friend. After a midnight breakfast buffet, guests were once again escorted off the estate to the sound of Scottish pipers well after midnight.

Then the party was over. A new era, a new century for Biltmore, had begun.

CHAPTER 16

Lady on the Hill

William Cecil's announcement transferring the management of Biltmore to his son caught everyone by surprise. Cecil had talked of retirement "someday," but no one—including his wife—knew he had a timetable or would use the centennial banquet to disclose his plans. Most of his friends and close associates had decided that he couldn't really leave Biltmore in the care of others. It had been a part of his life for far too long. "He had been talking about it," said his daughter, "but he had never said this is the deadline, this is the day." The Asheville newspaper missed the news entirely. Ten days passed after Cecil's announcement before a small notice appeared in print that Biltmore had a new president.

"He had been talking about it for six months," Mimi Cecil said. "Steve [Miller] and Richard [Pressley] didn't believe him. Maury [Winger Jr.] didn't believe him. I didn't believe. Nobody believed him. He wasn't a retiring type. And, by golly, he did it. We had a big party, a whole bunch of friends at the house, and he retired.

William Cecil with (standing, left to right) his daughter, Diana; wife, Mimi; and son, William Jr.

He didn't go to work for three or four weeks. Then he went down to the office, *with no tie on*. Then they realized he meant it."

Cecil's exit was accompanied by an honor from the National Trust for Historic Preservation. Two weeks after the centennial celebration, he received the National Trust Preservation Award for his "unique vision and achievement in the restoration and economically viable administration of the Biltmore Estate." Recognized along with him that same evening was the Pennsylvania Capitol Preservation Committee, for work that included the restoration of the ceiling by Biltmore Campbell Smith Restorations. Cecil's cousins, the Derick Vanderbilt Webb family, were also recognized for the preservation of another Vanderbilt property, Shelburne Farms in Vermont.

Cecil had barely returned to Asheville before he received a copy of the latest issue of the Trust's *Historic Preservation* magazine. Biltmore was the lead story; the cover photo was taken in the vineyard. "America's largest house is a regional destination for tourists, a self-supporting museum, the employer of hundreds of workers, and a model of private enterprise,"[1] declared a subhead on the article. Cecil couldn't have written a more flattering summation of Biltmore and his own career.

Cecil's departure was not as precipitate as it appeared. He could be impulsive and for years had frustrated his subordinates with last-minute changes that often ran projects over budget. "He was always adding things," said his son, Bill. "'While we are at it' are dangerously expensive words." This, however, was different. He had been quietly planning the transition for some time. In the mid-1980s, after his son had joined the company, Cecil circulated a memo to Winger, Miller, and Pressley asking them to focus on the future, including the state of the company following his own retirement. Long-range plans reaching to the centennial in 1995 followed with detailed reports from all segments of the company.

In the early 1990s, he had tested his son by naming him president of the wine company. Meanwhile, Bill had enrolled in a management training program at the University of North Carolina's Kenan-Flagler Business School, where he had performed with high honors. "It took me five years to get the ducks in a row," Cecil said later.

"It was obviously time for me to retire," he said some years later. "I had been working up to that, to get Richard, Steve, and Bill and everyone happy, one with the other. It was my ambition to replace all the things that had been stolen, or disappeared, or were just used and broken, because I knew darn well no one else would because that era had gone by. I knew the next generation would not do that. They would spend their money elsewhere."

He had kept his announcement to himself, he said, because "I didn't see any point in getting people upset beforehand. We were working right to the end. I wanted to make sure everybody was on board and was happy. What is it Shakespeare said, 'when the stars are in the proper order.'

"I didn't warn Bill. He had been looking for it. He knew it was going to happen." The announcement at the centennial banquet still came as a shock to the young Cecil.

In the years following his retirement, Cecil remained close at hand as the chairman of the company's board of directors and its largest shareholder. The parking space reserved for him beneath the Biltmore Building in downtown Asheville was usually empty, however. In time, e-mail became a familiar and regular form of communication. He dabbled with the idea of finding a seaside cottage in England to use as a retreat, but he discarded that in favor of remaining closer to home. Instead, he had a retreat built on nearby Busbee Mountain.

His daily visits to the house and gardens came to an end. However, he was on hand in the summer of 1996 to welcome Charles, the prince of Wales, to Biltmore. The prince's visit was on behalf of

In 1996, William Cecil welcomed Charles, prince of Wales, to Biltmore when the estate was one of the sites for his American summer school on architecture and building arts.

his first American summer school on architecture and the building arts. The château was the first stop for students who later spent from a week to two weeks at Monticello in Charlottesville, Virginia; the National Trust's Decatur House in Washington, D.C.; and a location in Richmond, Virginia.

The prince's visit caused quite a stir among excited tourists who got more than they paid for on July 17 when the royal entourage arrived. Prince Charles shook hands all around with those who were waiting for him at the front door to the château. Cecil gave him a tour, and the prince delivered a short address to students and about a hundred others gathered around. Lunch followed under a tent in the gardens of the Frith. The main course of Biltmore trout was accompanied by an estate-bottled Chardonnay.

In 1999, when an antique Skinner organ was finally installed in the Banquet Hall, Cecil came over to try out the keyboard and play a few tunes. The instrument filled the blank space that had been left by his grandfather. The period instrument was just right for the château. It was a gift to the estate, but the company had to spend $200,000 to see that it was properly restored and installed.

Biltmore's winery was under the care of a new winemaster, Bernard De Lille. Philippe Jourdain's retirement coincided with Cecil's own departure from daily involvement with the company. The wine business had improved, and Biltmore wines had won recognition in competitions around the country. Late in 1998, the company made the final payment on the money that Cecil had borrowed fifteen years earlier to begin construction of the winery. Within the year, the Biltmore Company would announce plans for a hotel called the Inn on Biltmore Estate at a cost of $32 million. Following years of studying and planning, it was the first major undertaking of the management team now led by Cecil's son.

William Cecil had always had a hard time explaining to strangers exactly what he did for a living. His interests rebounded across a broad spectrum like a pinball. He was involved in preservation, advertising and promotion, real estate management, horticulture, architecture, the arts, restoration, winemaking, and business. "Indeed," he said, "when I would return from a trip abroad, the immigration officer would ask me what I did for a living and I always had difficulty replying. I preserved an old house, I managed some land holdings, we were in the travel business, and we were in the business of preserving national landmarks."

He brought all those talents to bear to preserve, restore, and pass on what had been left to him by his family. In the end, he went well beyond the work of those who had preceded him. Edith Vanderbilt Gerry had protected the estate from subdivision and even destruction in the years following her husband's death. It really never was hers, but she honored her husband's memory by ensuring that it remained as he had left it before it was passed on to his daughter. It would not have survived without the enterprising rigor of Junius G. Adams, who had built up the estate through the renewal of the dairy operations or the careful attention of Chauncey Beadle. But it was William Cecil who worked to rebuild the unity of the estate. In the end, he was the only one to fully invest himself and his fortune in the vision of his grandfather. When Cecil was through, Biltmore was not only as brilliant as it had been during George Vanderbilt's day but far more financially viable.

One goal that Cecil had stubbornly pursued for three decades eluded him still. At the time of his retirement, he was no closer to a solution to the inheritance tax problems than he was twenty years earlier when he and his brother had gone their separate ways. "This is one hurdle I have never been able to conquer with the state government or the federal government. The fact that you own [a historic property] temporarily and guard it during your lifetime has nothing to do with the price of eggs," Cecil said. "They say, 'Well, you own it and can do anything you want with it.' I say, 'Yes, but if I sold a painting, I would be sure and pay taxes on it, just like everyone else.'"

He was distressed that after a lifetime of work, all he had achieved could be dismantled with the stroke of the taxman's pen.

He had made one final run at congressional action in tandem with the owners of Berkeley Plantation, one of the historic properties along Virginia's James River. The effort showed some promise but not much. With the British solution as a model, the proposed federal legislation went from "zero to a Hail Mary," as Cecil's attorney, John S. Stevens of Asheville, put it. The broad concept of tax concessions for owners of private property just didn't fit into the U.S. tax code. Nonetheless, Stevens and others trimmed and tuned a bill equipped with tight restrictions to fit the political landscape—eligible properties must be national landmarks open to the public, plus other qualifications. It was something Cecil could live with. Legislators backed off after President Bill Clinton's Treasury Department forecast serious tax consequences.

Said Cecil, "If you ask the Congress to give a little inheritance tax relief to the private owner struggling to maintain, without government support, a National Landmark visited by a million or more people a year, the senator or representative, the governor or legislator, just looks at you and says, 'We do not, and cannot, use taxpayer monies to support the Vanderbilts.'

"It does not matter that the owner in most cases has worked hard and, in most cases, is not rich, having reinvested all the funds the property has earned back into the property. Nor does it seem to matter that the private preservationist is the only preservationist who has paid income taxes over the years. All that the officials want is to be left in peace and not to be reminded that the [public] properties under their care are deteriorating to such a degree that soon they will be declared unsafe and then will have to be torn down, thus saving the taxpayer from further maintenance."

The nut of the problem for Cecil was that Biltmore—as it was in his grandfather's day—was an exception that no one could quite explain. Successful private preservation was as misunderstood in the late twentieth century as had been a rich man's French château nestled in the mountains of southern Appalachia.

Over the years, Cecil did what he could to mitigate the impact of inheritance taxes. The wine company belonged to his children, and in the 1990s, Bill and Dini purchased several thousand acres on the estate's west side, which accounted for nearly half of the company's land holdings. The hotel was organized in similar measure with ownership-vested trusts for Cecil's grandchildren.

Cecil's achievement at Biltmore remained unmatched in historic preservation. And the continued success following his retirement was a testimony to the sound business he had organized. Under the management of his children, the estate continued on the same course that he had set years before. Each new venture—such as the hotel—was related directly to Vanderbilt's own plans for the estate. Ticket sales climbed in the late 1990s, and paid admission to the estate eventually surpassed sales at Colonial Williamsburg by more than two hundred thousand visitors.

By contrast, other historic house museums scrambled to make ends meet. Some became ludicrously promotional. The Eastman House in Rochester, New York, offered speed dating in an effort to attract a younger clientele. The management of some properties borrowed directly from the lessons learned at Biltmore. For example, Mount Vernon, the nation's first historic house museum, became Mount Vernon House and Gardens, rather than solely the homeplace of the nation's first president. The opening of a gristmill was in the works, as was the restoration of Washington's distillery. "This is more than just a house," said Mount Vernon's director, James Rees. "We want to be looked upon like Biltmore."

For many visitors, the expanse of Biltmore became an oasis from the rush and pressures of modern life. It was a combination of nature preserve, historic house, and leisure retreat. Visitors came for the day, or for several days, overnighting in the 213-room Inn on Biltmore Estate after it opened in 2001. It sits on a hill overlooking the winery and the river valley with service and accommodations designed to satisfy a Vanderbilt.

In 2004, the old horse barn, once the center of social life for the families on the estate, was given new life. The building, which William Cecil had once earmarked for demolition to make way for a larger winery building, offered an introduction to the agricultural dimension of Biltmore. One of Cecil's grandsons—Dini's son, Chase Pickering—helped tend the sheep, chickens, horses, and other animals in the farmyard, where visitors could feed the animals.

Explore Biltmore Estate offered outdoor activities such as horseback riding, bike rides, carriage rides, and float trips on the French Broad.

Some additions to the Biltmore offering would not have occurred on William Cecil's watch. He never had much use for a farmyard, but then the only animals he knew close up were his two large black poodles. And he was impatient with the introduction of garden theater after animated plants and insects were made part of the annual Festival of Flowers. At the same time, he accepted change, as long as it was "appropriate."

"We are probably past the golden era of the house," he said. "Now the house has to be kept up impeccably. That is the success of Biltmore." The grandeur of the house and the artistry of its contents has become the "icon" against which any future changes will be measured. "The lady on the hill is a pretty good disciplinarian for you. She sets a very high standard."

Perhaps the most dramatic change to the château came in January 2004, nearly ten years after Cecil's retirement, when Bill Cecil ordered the removal of the rows of tulip poplars on the esplanade. Over the years, the trees had become even more of a problem due to weak and diseased limbs dropping on passersby. The work was quickly accomplished during January and February when traffic was light and the conditions most appropriate for the planting of replacements. Shuttle-bus drivers carrying visitors from the parking lots prepared their riders for the new perspective of Biltmore that they would see when the bus turned in the gates. The explanations were usually inadequate. The strapping young poplars that stood about eighteen feet tall all but disappeared against the image of the huge château.

Some reacted with shock and dismay, not realizing that the esplanade, as they saw it in 2004, looked much the same as it did in 1904, when Olmsted's newly planted trees were no taller than those growing there a century later. The château was now framed

(top) The view of the mountains to the west of Biltmore Estate remains much the same as it did in George Vanderbilt's day, with the château surrounded by eight thousand acres of fields and forests. (bottom) The diseased and aging tulip poplars on the esplanade were replanted in 2004. Once again, visitors see the château with young landscaping as it was at the turn of the twentieth century.

by the broad shoulders of the distant mountain range. Although in maturity Olmsted's allée had focused visitors' eyes on the château, this restored vision of Biltmore was equally dramatic and broadly romantic for those who were about to be transported back to the era of the Gilded Age.

Afterword

by William A. V. Cecil

Biltmore has always been about family. My grandfather and grandmother would be pleased that families come to Biltmore Estate from around the world to enjoy its architecture and art, its serenity and natural beauty, and the ongoing fruits of its agricultural and viticultural endeavors. I believe they would also be happy that their direct descendants continue to be stewards of their home, grounds, farms, and forests. I like to think they would approve of our commitment to a for-profit self-sufficiency, which has allowed us to achieve our mission of preservation.

My grandfather had the right idea when he conceived of Biltmore as a working estate. His original model is what we strive to attain every day. All that we do is measured by a yardstick of authenticity and with an adherence to his early principles of productivity. As in George Vanderbilt's day, we work to stay on the cutting edge of land management, conservation, creative invention, innovation, hospitality, and stewardship. Some things have changed over the years—our herds are Angus now, instead of Jersey—but our allegiance to preserving the essence of the land and the spirit of the people who respect it holds firm.

It has been quite the ride, and we're not through yet. There is still work to be done to focus attention on our nation's heritage and the preservation of our patrimony. As such, at this writing, the future of Biltmore Estate remains uncertain. The irony is that because we have preserved the property, as the laws currently stand, estate taxes may preclude our being able to remain privately owned and self-sufficient. While we have no crystal ball to predict the future of Biltmore, it is my hope that my descendants will continue to care for the property and that their efforts will continue to enable them to extend this successful and important example of private preservation.

In my own family, I must first give credit to my wife, Mary Ryan Cecil. Mimi has been an integral part of Biltmore Estate's modern-day success story, having supported my efforts for more than forty-five years. She has been a wonderful wife and mother and has offered her considerable gifts, skills, and abilities to our community, our mountains, and our country. I am profoundly in her debt.

I am also proud of and grateful to my children, Bill and Dini, for their interest in and commitment to the continuation of our family's business. Both of them grew up at Biltmore and fully understand the whys and wherefores of its preservation. Each has a family, and each will be challenged to build a strong foundation for generations to come.

I am most appreciative of the intelligent leadership provided by my senior management over the years, particularly that of Steve Miller and Richard Pressley. I have watched these two men move from youthful enthusiasm to wise strategic thinking on behalf of our company. They have been instrumental in Biltmore Estate's success and deserve and have my utmost gratitude.

Finally, I am grateful to my brother, George, and to the dairy operation he managed, enabling me to build on the sound financial foundation of that business. During our minority, the estate was held together by Judge Junius G. Adams and, of course, by the devotion and loyalty of my father, John F. A. Cecil, and my grandmother, George Vanderbilt's widow, Edith Stuyvesant Gerry. None of what we have achieved would have succeeded had we not had the loyal and devoted service of all our employees. They have been an integral part of Biltmore Estate, and its survival in tumultuous times is largely due to their unstinted service.

I hope Biltmore Estate will continue to give its guests one of America's most gratifying cultural and aesthetic experiences for years to come. I also hope that the commitment to preserving the great natural beauty that graces Biltmore is held sacred. The estate has given my family great personal and professional satisfaction over the years, and it has been my pleasure and my honor to share her. Long may the Lady on the Hill stand as a symbol of vision, inspiration, and imagination.

Notes

Chapter 1. A Centennial Celebration

1. William A. V. Cecil, centennial remarks, September 29, 1995, Biltmore Archives.

2. Ibid.

3. William A. V. Cecil to Terry Empson, October 17, 1995, Biltmore Archives.

4. Lawrence Henry, interview with author, May 10, 2004, Biltmore Archives.

Chapter 2. George Vanderbilt's Dream

1. M. V. Moore, paid advertisement, undated newspaper clipping, *Asheville Citizen*, Biltmore Archives.

2. John M. Bryan, *Biltmore Estate: The Most Distinguished Private Place* (New York: Rizzoli, 1994).

3. "G. W. Vanderbilt Is Dead in Washington," *Baltimore Sun*, March 7, 1914.

4. John Foreman and Robbe Pierce Stimson, *The Vanderbilts and the Gilded Age* (St. Martin's Press, 1991), p. 275.

5. Bryan, ibid.

6. *Baltimore Sun*, ibid.

7. John Gilmer Speed, "Vanderbilt Will Take His Charming Bride Next Month," *New York Herald*, May 29, 1898.

8. Bryan, ibid., p. 107.

9. Davyd Foard Hood, National Historic Landmark Nomination, Revised, September 30, 2003.

10. William A. V. Cecil, interview with author, April 15, 2004, Biltmore Archives.

11. Jerry E. Patterson, *The Vanderbilts* (New York: Henry N. Abrams Inc., 1989).

12. "Will Run 'Biltmore' Himself," *New York Times*, October 15, 1905.

13. "Selling Biltmore Horses," *New York Times*, July 2, 1908.

14. "Vanderbilt Taxes Due," *New York Times*, January 5, 1909.

15. John Parris, "Progress Erases a Landmark," *Asheville Citizen*, August 27, 1962.

16. Bob Terrell, "Fond Memories of the Vanderbilts," *Asheville Citizen*, August 29, 1978.

17. Isaac N. Northup, *The Story of a Church, All Souls in Biltmore* (All Souls Church, Biltmore, N.C., 1979).

18. "Threat for G. W. Vanderbilt," *New York Times*, June 28, 1908.

19. "Vanderbilt Choir Strike," *New York Times*, September 21, 1913.

20. "To Stop Forest Fires," *New York Times*, March 16, 1907.

21. Report to National Forest Reservation Commission, Pisgah Forest, May 1913, Department of the Interior, National Archives, Washington, D.C.

22. Ibid.

23. "Government Representatives Inspecting Pisgah Forests," *Asheville Citizen*, May 31, 1913.

24. Ibid.

25. "G. W. Vanderbilt Is Dead in Washington," *Baltimore Sun*, March 7, 1914.

26. "G. W. Vanderbilt Dies Suddenly," *New York Times*, March 7, 1914.

27. "Plans Making Biltmore Home," *Washington Gazette-News*, March 10, 1914.

28. Edith Vanderbilt to the Secretary of Agriculture, May 1, 1914, Biltmore Archives.

Chapter 3. Edith Vanderbilt

1. "Mrs. Vanderbilt Appears Before State Assembly," *News & Observer*, February 2, 1921.

2. Ibid.

3. Ibid.

4. "Mrs. George W. Vanderbilt," recollections by Mrs. Wheeler, Biltmore Archives.

5. "Starts Homespun Fad," *New York Times*, May 18, 2004.

6. "Biltmore Christmas Tree," *New York Times*, December 4, 1906.

7. "Mrs. Wheeler," ibid.

8. Ibid.

9. Lyn Leslie, *Flood of 1916 Changed Biltmore Village and Family Lives Forever*, MainStreet Online, Asheville.com, 2003.

10. "Must Cut Bequests of G. W. Vanderbilt," *New York Times*, June 20, 1918.

11. "Biltmore Estate Land Is Sold for Residence Park," *Asheville Citizen,* June 20, 1920.

12. Douglas Swaim, ed., *Cabins & Castles: The History & Architecture of Buncombe County, North Carolina* (North Carolina Department of Cultural Resources, Division of Archives and History, 1981).

13. Elizabeth B. Ashby to Susanne Brendel-Pandich, August 10, 1984, Biltmore Archives.

14. "Mrs. Vanderbilt Re-elected Amid Great Applause," *Asheville Citizen,* November 20, 1922.

15. Mrs. W. T. Bost, "Mrs. Edith Vanderbilt Is the Central Figure at State Fair," *Greensboro Daily News,* October 18, 1922.

16. "Innovations at N.C. State Fair," news clipping dated September 27, 1922, Biltmore Archives.

17. William A. V. Cecil, interview with author, December 9, 2003, Biltmore Archives.

18. "Prophesies of the Class of '19," Miss Madeira's School 1919 class yearbook.

19. Robert Bunn, interview, Biltmore Oral History, November 21, 1989, Biltmore Archives.

20. Elizabeth B. Ashby to Susanne Brendel-Pandich, August 10, 1984, Biltmore Archives.

21. "Faithful Retainer Overcome by Joy at Happy Occasion," *Asheville Citizen,* April 30, 1924.

22. "Mrs. G. Vanderbilt Happy at Farming," *New York Times,* August 24, 1924.

23. Anne Virginia Mitchell, Parkway Politics: Class, Culture and Tourism in the Blue Ridge (Ph.D. diss., University of Carolina at Chapel Hill, 1997), p. 102.

24. "$250 Cash Prize," *Asheville Citizen,* July 29, 1924.

25. *Asheville Citizen,* July 27, 1924.

26. Frank Coxe, interview, June 6, 1979, Silveri Oral History Collection, Ramsey Library, University of North Carolina at Asheville.

27. Associated Press, "Asheville Stages Comeback on More Substantial Basis," *Greensboro Daily News,* April 25, 1937.

Chapter 4. Judge Adams

1. Joel B. Adams to Joseph Trachtman, April 14, 1961, Biltmore Archives; Biltmore Company corporate minutes, March 31, 1932.

2. William A. V. Cecil, interview with author, December 2, 2004, Biltmore Archives.

3. Francis Heazel, eulogy for Junius G. Adams, Buncombe County Bar, October 1, 1962.

4. Arthur Taylor, interview with Julie Betts, August 29, 1989, Biltmore Archives.

5. Laurence Vail Coleman, Historic House Museums (Washington, D.C.: American Association of Museums, 1933), p. 46.

6. Ibid.

7. Young Horton to *Greenville* (S.C.) *News*, March 1930, Biltmore Archives.

8. "Rules for Lodge Gate Keepers," undated, Biltmore Archives.

9. "Biltmore House & Gardens and Biltmore Estate," undated, Biltmore Archives.

10. Louis Graves, "A Visit to Biltmore House and Gardens," *Chapel Hill Newspaper*, undated, Biltmore Archives.

11. Jane Raoul Bingham, interview with Julie Betts, September 1, 1989, Biltmore Archives.

12. Butler's Log, Herbert Noble, 1930–1936, Biltmore Archives.

13. Ibid.

14. Ibid.

15. Louis Graves, "A Visit to Biltmore House and Gardens," undated manuscript, Biltmore Archives.

16. Ibid.

17. Bingham.

18. Minutes of Biltmore Company Board of Directors, December 14, 1946, Biltmore Archives.

19. Howard E. Covington Jr., *Favored by Fortune: George W. Watts and the Hills of Durham* (Chapel Hill: University of North Carolina Press, 2004).

Chapter 5. The National Gallery's Wartime Vault

1. David E. Finley, *A Standard of Excellence* (Washington, D.C.: Smithsonian Institution Press, 1973).

2. William A. V. Cecil, "Random Thoughts," unpublished manuscript, 1999, Biltmore Archives.

3. William A. V. Cecil, interview with author, August 27, 2004, Biltmore Archives.

4. "Army Returnees Visit Biltmore Estate, House," *Asheville Citizen*, September 14, 1944.

5. Junius G. Adams to Mrs. Peter G. Gerry, September 26, 1947, Biltmore Archives.

6. William A. V. Cecil, "Random Thoughts," unpublished manuscript, 1999, Biltmore Archives.

Chapter 6. A Curiosity or a Treasure

1. Minutes of the Biltmore Company Board of Directors, December 14, 1946, Biltmore Archives.

2. National Historic Landmark Nomination, Biltmore Estate, p. 139.

3. Charles B. Hosmer Jr., *Preservation Comes of Age: From Williamsburg to the National Trust, 1926–1949* (Charlottesville: University of Virginia Press, 1981), p. 44.

4. William J. Murtagh, *Keeping Time, The History and Theory of Preservation in America* (New York: Preservation Press, John Wiley & Sons, 1988).

5. Ibid., p. 80.

6. Laurence Vail Coleman, *Historic House Museums* (Washington, D.C.: The American Association of Museums, 1933), p. 18.

7. James Marston Fitch, *Historic Preservation: Cultural Management of the Built World* (New York: McGraw-Hill Book Co., 1982).

8. Ibid., p. 147.

9. Hosmer, p. 358.

10. Hosmer, p. 359.

11. "Future Development Program Expected to Establish Blue Ridge Parkway as Most Heavily Traveled in U.S.," *Winston-Salem Journal*, July 26, 1946.

12. Bruce E. Johnston, *Built for the Ages, A History of the Grove Park Inn* (Asheville, N.C.: The Grove Park Inn and Country Club, 1991), p. 63.

13. Lynn and Marjorie Mighell, "The Blue Ridge and Smoky Mountains," *Better Homes and Gardens*, April 1954, p. 68.

14. John Parris, "Mountain Region Enjoys Best Tourist Season in Its History," *Asheville Citizen*, September 5, 1954.

Chapter 7. The Airport Fight

1. "Community's Future Is at Stake in Airport Election," *Asheville Times*, April 21, 1955.

2. William A. V. Cecil, interview with author, August 27, 2004, Biltmore Archives.

3. "Rickenbacker Eyes City as Stop for EAL," *Asheville Citizen*, May 8, 1955.

4. "Goodbye Captain Rickenbacker," *Asheville Citizen*, May 8, 1955.

5. "Crocodile Tears!" *Asheville Citizen*, May 8, 1955.

6. William A. V. Cecil, "Random Thoughts," unpublished manuscript, 1999, Biltmore Archives.

7. Junius G. Adams to George Cecil, May 12, 1955, Biltmore Archives.

8. Junius G. Adams Jr. to William A. V. Cecil, March 3, 1958, Biltmore Archives.

9. Howard E. Covington Jr. and Marion A. Ellis, eds., *The North Carolina Century: Tar Heels Who Made a Difference* (Charlotte, N.C.: Levine Museum of the New South, 2002), p. 132.

10. William A. V. Cecil, "Random Thoughts," unpublished manuscript, 1999, Biltmore Archives.

Chapter 8. Homecoming

1. Lou Harshaw, interview with author, August 26, 2004, Biltmore Archives.

2. William A. V. Cecil, interview with author, December 2, 2003, Biltmore Archives.

3. William A. V. Cecil, interview with author, January 20, 2004, Biltmore Archives.

4. William A. V. Cecil, interview with author, December 2, 2003, Biltmore Archives.

5. William A. V. Cecil, "Random Thoughts," unpublished manuscript, 1999, Biltmore Archives.

6. William A. V. Cecil, interview with author, December 3, 2003, Biltmore Archives.

7. William A. V. Cecil, interview with author, December 2, 2003, Biltmore Archives.

8. Junius G. Adams to Everett Mitchell, August 28, 1947, Biltmore Archives.

9. Joel B. Adams to George Geisel, April 14, 1961, Biltmore Archives.

10. Allen Freeman, "Backstage at Biltmore," *Historic Preservation*, November/December 1995.

11. William A. V. Cecil, interview with author, December 2, 2003, Biltmore Archives.

Chapter 9. Mr. C

1. William A. V. Cecil, interview with author, December 2, 2003, Biltmore Archives.

2. Richard King, interview with author, January 8, 2004, Biltmore Archives.

3. William A. V. Cecil, interview with author, December 2, 2003, Biltmore Archives.

4. William A. V. Cecil to George F. Ladd, September 12, 1966, Biltmore Archives.

5. "One-Millionth Visitor," photo caption, *Asheville Times*, June 14, 1960.

6. William A. V. Cecil, interview with author, December 2, 2003, Biltmore Archives.

7. William A. V. Cecil, "Preserve for Profit," speech to Georgia Preservation Society, Savannah, April 1972.

8. Nat Osborne, "Estate Co-owner Calls Ad Campaign the Hard Soft Sell," *Asheville Citizen-Times*, January 21, 1969.

9. "Mansion Is Strictly Business," *Charlotte Observer*, February 14, 1965.

10. William A. V. Cecil to David Ogilvy, October 19, 1967, Biltmore Archives.

11. Mimi Cecil, interview with author, April 14, 2004, Biltmore Archives.

12. Eugene Warner, unpublished manuscript, April 10, 1967, Biltmore Archives.

Chapter 10. The Music Room

1. William A. V. Cecil, "Destination Asheville," October 3, 1974, Biltmore Archives.

2. William A. V. Cecil, testimony before the U.S. Senate Subcommittee on Tourism and International Commerce, March 29, 1974, Biltmore Archives.

3. William A. V. Cecil, interview with author, April 15, 2004, Biltmore Archives.

4. William A. V. Cecil, "Random Thoughts," unpublished manuscript, 1999, Biltmore Archives.

5. William A. V. Cecil, presentation, Meadow Brook Conference, October 14–16, 1979, Oakland University, Rochester, Mich., Biltmore Archives.

6. Ibid.

7. Ernie Wood, "After 81 Years, Biltmore Is Nearing Completion," (Raleigh) *News & Observer*, June 6, 1976.

Chapter 11. Presentation versus Preservation

1. William A. V. Cecil, "Random Thoughts," unpublished manuscript, 1999, Biltmore Archives.

2. William A. V. Cecil, interview with author, January 20, 2004, Biltmore Archives.

3. Mrs. Warren Seybold to William A. V. Cecil, August 24, 1966, Biltmore Archives.

4. John Ruskin, *The Seven Lamps of Architecture* (New York: E. P. Dutton, 1956).

5. William A. V. Cecil, "The Role of National Organizations in the Future of the Private Historic House Museum," Historic House Museum Workshop, October 13, 1977, National Trust for Historic Preservation and the American Association for State and Local History.

6. William A. V. Cecil, interview with author, January 20, 2004, Biltmore Archives.

7. William A. V. Cecil, "Random Thoughts," unpublished manuscript, 1999, Biltmore Archives.

8. Ibid.

9. William A. V. Cecil, presentation, Meadow Brook Conference, October 14–16, 1979, Oakland University, Rochester, Mich., Biltmore Archives.

10. Ibid.

11. Susanne Brendel-Pandich, interview with author, March 22, 2004, Biltmore Archives.

12. Richard King, interview with author, March 23, 2004, Biltmore Archives.

13. "The 1979 Gasoline Shortage: Lessons for the Travel Industry" (Washington, D.C.: Travel Industry Association of America, 1980).

Chapter 12. Voice in the Wilderness

1. William A. V. Cecil, "Random Thoughts," unpublished manuscript, 1999, Biltmore Archives.

2. Ibid.

3. William A. V. Cecil to Wayne H. Valis, February 17, 1975, Biltmore Archives.

4. William A. V. Cecil, interview with author, January 21, 2004, Biltmore Archives.

5. Constance M. Greiff, *Statistical Report of National Historic Properties in Private Ownership*, October 3, 1975, Biltmore Archives.

6. Ibid.

7. Charles Fenyvesi, "The Enduring Mystery of Middleton Place," *Preservation*, April 1986.

8. Charles H. P. Duell, interview with author, May 11, 2004, Biltmore Archives.

9. Stephen Webbe, "What Is Happening to the Stately Homes of Britain," *Christian Science Monitor*, November 25, 1983.

Chapter 13. "Be Reasonable—Do It My Way"

1. Biltmore House Market Study, 1979, Biltmore Archives.

2. William A. V. Cecil, "Random Thoughts," unpublished manuscript, 1999, Biltmore Archives.

3. Steve Miller, interview with author, January 6, 2004, Biltmore Archives.

4. Steve Miller, interview with author, January 18, 2004, Biltmore Archives.

5. Richard Pressley, interview with author, December 8, 2004, Biltmore Archives.

6. Richard Pressley, interview with author, January 7, 2004, Biltmore Archives.

Chapter 14. Biltmore by the Bottle

1. William A. V. Cecil, interview with author, December 9, 2003, Biltmore Archives.

2. Minutes of Biltmore Company Board of Directors, June 2, 1971, Biltmore Archives.

3. "N.C. Winery History," www.ncwine.org, North Carolina Department of Agriculture and Consumer Services, accessed October 2004.

4. William A. V. Cecil, interview with author, April 15, 2004, Biltmore Archives.

5. Philippe Jourdain, interview with author, April 20, 2004, Biltmore Archives.

6. Untitled report, March 1980, Biltmore Archives.

7. William A. V. Cecil, interview with author, April 15, 2004, Biltmore Archives.

8. Maury Winger Jr., interview with author, April 4, 2004, Biltmore Archives.

9. William A. V. Cecil, interview with author, January 21, 2004, Biltmore Archives.

10. Maury Winger Jr., interview with author, April 4, 2004, Biltmore Archives.

11. E. McGregor Strauss, interview with author, March 9, 2004, Biltmore Archives.

12. Diana Cecil Pickering, interview with author, January 28, 2004, Biltmore Archives.

13. William A. V. Cecil Jr., interview with author, January 29, 2004, Biltmore Archives.

14. Ernest Ferguson, interview with author, April 14, 2004, Biltmore Archives.

15. Daniel Nivens, "Biltmore Winery Opening: An International Affair," *Asheville Citizen-Times*, May 12, 1985.

16. William A. V. Cecil, "Random Thoughts," unpublished manuscript, 1999, Biltmore Archives.

17. William A. V. Cecil, interview with author, April 15, 2004, Biltmore Archives.

18. Junius G. Adams to Jay C. Marchant, April 9, 1956, Biltmore Archives.

19. William A. V. Cecil, interview with author, April 20, 2004, Biltmore Archives.

20. William A. V. Cecil Jr., interview with author, January 29, 2004, Biltmore Archives.

21. William A. V. Cecil, interview with author, December 9, 2003, Biltmore Archives.

Chapter 15. Putting It Right

1. William A. V. Cecil, interview with author, April 21, 2004, Biltmore Archives.

2. *Carolina History*, Vertical Files, Pack Library, Asheville, N.C., 1984.

3. Rick King to W. A. V. Cecil, memorandum in file, January 26, 1989, Biltmore Archives.

4. Jeanne M. Desrosiers, Kathryn B. Lawrence, Tonya L. Lynn, and Alfredo R. Valdes, "The Impact of the Biltmore Company on Asheville/Buncombe County," Department of Planning Studies, College of Agriculture, Clemson University, Clemson, S.C., April 1992.

5. Bruce Henderson, "Now, That's an Assessment," *Charlotte Observer*, July 24, 1990.

6. William A. V. Cecil to Ambassador Benjamin Oehlert, July 19, 1976, Biltmore Archives.

7. Susanne Brendel-Pandich, interview with author, March 22, 2004, Biltmore Archives.

8. William A. V. Cecil, interview with author, January 21, 2004, Biltmore Archives.

9. William A. V. Cecil, interview with author, December 10, 2003, Biltmore Archives.

10. Timothy W. Andrews, interview with author, May 19, 2004, Biltmore Archives.

11. Don Logan, interview with author, December 23, 2004, Biltmore Archives.

12. Nancy Campbell, interview with author, May 19, 2004, Biltmore Archives.

13. Lawrence Henry, interview with author, May 10, 2004, Biltmore Archives.

14. Ibid.

15. Memorandum: Preliminary Thoughts on the Feasibility of a Consulting and/or Management Service for Historic Houses Open to the Public in the United States, January 8, 1986, Biltmore Archives.

16. William A. V. Cecil, interview with author, December 3, 2003, Biltmore Archives.

17. William A. V. Cecil, interview with author, April 15, 2004, Biltmore Archives.

18. William A. V. Cecil, "Random Thoughts," unpublished manuscript, 1999, Biltmore Archives.

19. Minutes of Biltmore Company Board of Directors and Advisers, January 24, 1995, Biltmore Archives.

20. Diana Cecil Pickering, interview with author, January 28, 2004, Biltmore Archives.

21. William A. V. Cecil to Sir Nigel Cecil, October 2, 1995, Biltmore Archives.

Chapter 16. Lady on the Hill

1. Allen Freeman, "Backstage at Biltmore," *Historic Preservation*, November/December 1995.

Index